MUSIC
THAT SHOOK THE
WORLD

MUSIC
THAT SHOOK THE
WORLD

120 Unforgettable Moments in Music History

Michael Heatley

Foreword by **Bill Wyman**

COLLINS & BROWN

First published in the United Kingdom in 2008 by
Collins & Brown
10 Southcombe Street
London
W14 0RA

An imprint of Anova Books Company Ltd

Produced by Salamander Books

ISBN 978-1-843404-934

A CIP catalogue for this book is available from the British Library.

10 9 8 7 6 5 4 3 2 1

Reproduction by Dot Gradations Ltd., U.K.
Printed and bound by Times Offset, Malaysia

This book can be ordered direct from the publisher.
Contact the marketing department, but try your bookshop first.

www.anovabooks.com

Right: Bruce Springsteen at a pre-concert soundcheck in Kyoto, Japan, 1985 © Corbis/Neal Preston

"This music is forever for me. It's the stage thing, that rush moment that you live for. It never lasts, but that's what you live for."
—Bruce Springsteen

Contents

Foreword by Bill Wyman 8

Foreword

Music has always been a big part of my adult life. Besides playing it and making my living from it, when I hear a song it often reminds me of where I was when I first heard it or of some other significant event. For me, and I suspect many others, music is life changing, it's powerful, it's sometimes therapeutic, but most of all music is magical.

In 1955 I joined the Royal Air Force and was shipped off to Germany to do National Service, and musically it was the making of me. I would wake each morning to *The Stick Buddy Jamboree,* and I heard the beginnings of Rock 'n' Roll. I was listening to Elvis, Bill Haley, Fats Domino and Little Richard for the first time, all thanks to the American Forces Network. The kind of music they were broadcasting you couldn't hear in Britain, and you couldn't buy the records either.

Two years later, in 1957, I was home on leave and went to a cinema to see the Rock, Rock, Rock revue; first up was the Johnny Burnette Trio and then on came Chuck Berry. I had never seen him before; I'd only heard him on radio. He was wearing a white suit, doing his pigeon toe thing as he duck-walked across the stage, while playing his little Gibson Les Paul and singing "You Can't Catch Me." The hairs went up on the back of my neck for the first time ever, I was in shock—this was it! Later I found out this is how Brian Jones felt the first time he heard Elmore James. He said the earth moved.

I wrote to America to buy Chuck's records, which took an age to arrive. On my return to Germany I formed a skiffle group with some of the other guys at the camp. In Britain skiffle was all the rage thanks to the success of Lonnie Donegan. It was how many British bands got their start— The Who, Led Zeppelin, The Beatles and The Stones—we all started off playing skiffle.

When I finished my military service, I formed a group called the Cliftons in southeast London. In 1962 I joined the Rolling Stones and of course the rest is history. Playing clubs turned into cinemas, then to bigger halls, then to stadiums and outdoor festivals. Our little blues band became what some have even called the greatest rock and roll band in the world… whatever that means!

In 1964 we became part of what has been dubbed "the British invasion," when bands from the U.K. flooded the American charts. Today, most people assume the Stones were in the vanguard of that musical assault, whereas actually we were one of the less successful British bands in America during the year. Of course the Beatles were well ahead of everyone else with five No. 1 records. Closely followed by The Dave Clark Five, Gerry and The Pacemakers, Manfred Mann, the Zombies and even Billy J. Kramer. The Searchers, The Kinks and The Animals, who topped the American charts with "The House of the Rising Sun" in late summer, did at least as well as we did. However, we quickly got into our stride and from then on there was no looking back.

Throughout this time there was ongoing press talk about the feud between the Beatles and the Stones; like many such things, it was a myth. Through our respective managers, Brian Epstein and Andrew Loog Oldham, we were presented in very different ways. Someone once described us, "the Beatles were the living room and the Stones the bedroom." I think that just about nails it. Nevertheless we were always the best of friends and really appreciated each other's music—how else would you explain *Rock and Roll Circus?*

Throughout my career with the Stones we got to meet and perform with a huge number of artists. Some I became friends

The original Rolling Stones line-up posing for a press call in Green Park, London, December, 1967. From left to right, back row: Charlie Watts and Bill Wyman. Front row: Mick Jagger, Brian Jones, Keith Richards.

with and others I enjoyed spending time with. The list of those we appeared with is like a *Who's Who* of rock and pop—the Beach Boys to B. B. King, the Beatles of course, and Ike and Tina Turner to Prince. From all of them you learn something, and you realize just how important music is to people. Whether it's as a marker that anchors peoples' lives—their first date, a wedding, their first child, or some tiny detail of a person's life, it's music that puts us all in a particular time and place. Music brings a great deal of fun and pleasure into all of our lives, no matter whether it's Motown or soul, blues or punk (not my favourite!), psychedelia or country. One thing's for sure, rock and pop music is the most appreciated art form in the world today.

During my musical career I have been lucky enough to play with some great musicians. There's Muddy Waters, Howlin' Wolf, Nicky Hopkins, Billy Preston, Jimmy Page,

Dr. John, Buddy Guy, Junior Wells, Eric Clapton, and of course, not forgetting Brian, Charlie, Keith, Mick, Mick Taylor, and Woody. I have learned from all of them and each one of them has added to my continuing love of music—I'm still a fan. Today with my own band, the Rhythm Kings, I continue to explore my musical heritage and love of what I've been lucky to do for a living for five decades… here's to the next one… or two.

Bill Wyman

1955-1959

1955

Rock Around the Clock

Bill Haley's breakthrough hit was originally a B-side, but when it was used for the title credits to the film *Blackboard Jungle,* it sparked teenage riots.

William John Clifton Haley, chubby-faced and balding, was an unlikely teen hero, especially since he had just celebrated his thirtieth birthday in 1955. Yet the Detroit-born ex–country singer found himself in the right place at the right time to help give birth to rock 'n' roll. His take on Louis Jordan's jump blues music, had youths jiving in the aisles and slashing cinema seats when it was used to capture the mood of disaffected youth in the film *Blackboard Jungle.* When the movie came out in 1955, the featured track shot up on the charts and spent eight weeks at No. 1. Haley, who'd scored his first (No. 7) hit the previous year with a raucous version of Big Joe Turner's "Shake Rattle and Roll," was hardly the rebellious role model, with his kiss curl, unthreatening manner, and conservative dress. But his music, masterminded by producer Milt Gabler at Decca, was popular for two crucial years, from mid 1954 to mid 1956, before a new generation of younger stars swept him away.

His other hits included "Rock-A-Beatin' Boogie" (1955), "Burn That Candle," and "See You Later, Alligator" (both Top 10 singles in 1956). "Rock Around the Clock" charted three times in different decades in Britain, where it became the first record to sell a million copies. Haley and his band also appeared in films, *Rock Around the Clock* and *Don't Knock the Rock,* hoping to repeat their *Blackboard Jungle* success, which, perhaps significantly, had previously featured them only in audio.

Haley had identified the correct musical blueprint for black music meeting white music, but lacked the raw sex appeal to engage the rapidly growing teen audience. In Britain 4,000 young

BILLBOARD TOP 100 MAKES ITS DEBUT

On the week ending November 12, 1955, music trade magazine *Billboard* published its Top 100 for the first time. During the 1940s and 1950s, popular singles were ranked in three significant charts: Best Sellers In Stores, Most Played By Jockeys and Most Played In Jukeboxes. This was the first time all three charts had been combined, giving sales more weight than radio airplay. Tennessee Ernie Ford's "Sixteen Tons" was the first chart-topper. On August 4, 1958, *Billboard* re-branded their singles chart the Hot 100, and it remains the industry standard under that name today.

▲ Singer Tennessee Ernie Ford's coal miner's lament, "Sixteen Tons," was *Billboard*'s first combined chart topper. Ford's nickname was "The Ol' Pea Picker" thanks to his catch-phrase, "Bless your pea-pickin' heart."

Where were you when?

"Looking back at the footage of Haley and the band now, I'm shocked by how old he appears. Yet as a teenager growing up in Columbus, Ohio, he seemed fresh, vibrant, new, a real shake-up to the system."

—Lawrence Bute, Chicago

"The birth of rock 'n' roll for me? Seeing Bill Haley and The Comets in Rock Around the Clock *with my best friend at the time. God, that band SWUNG! We were eleven years old."*

—Pete Townshend, guitarist with The Who

fans met his train when it pulled into London, but few were there to see him leave. The likes of Elvis would soon make him seem passé. As his success faded, Bill Haley became an early star of Richard Nader's Rock 'n' roll Revival Shows and he continued playing until 1979, two years before his death. "Rock Around the Clock," is his epitaph.

Bill Haley and the Comets whip up a storm on their first European tour. ▼

REBEL WITHOUT A CAUSE

With rock 'n' roll deepening the generation gap to a chasm, this year saw movie star James Dean become an instant icon by dying in a car crash aged just 24. A trio of films *East Of Eden*, *Rebel Without A Cause*, and *Giant*, the last released after his death, established him as a moody, misunderstood role model for teens the world over. Several singers, including the Eagles, REM, and David Essex, have since referenced him in song, suggesting he was a rock 'n' roll hero by proxy, while he's remembered as the first in a line including Buddy Holly and Marilyn Monroe to "live fast, die young and leave a good looking corpse."

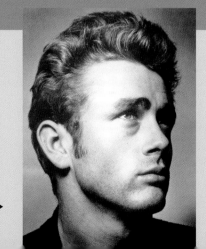

James Dean died at the wheel of his Porsche 550. ▶

1955

THE 45 ARRIVES

Billboard reported in June that the popular 78rpm single format, which replaced the gramophone cylinder in the early part of the century, was finally on the way out. It was being replaced by the 45rpm vinyl disc, pioneered by RCA, which had been available since 1949 but had yet to be adopted as standard by the industry. The change was driven by major record labels supplying disc jockeys and was described in the press as a "money-saving move." The formats would run in parallel for a short while, singles being available as both 45s and 78s, before the former won out. The last 78s were issued around 1960, but record players retained the speed setting for another two decades.

▲ Elvis Presley with the man who would mastermind his 23-year career, Colonel Tom Parker.

Elvis Meets the Colonel

Elvis Presley was already kicking up a storm on the country music scene, but when he signed with Colonel Tom Parker, royalty beckoned.

The birth of Elvis Aaron Presley in his family's shotgun shack in Tupelo, Mississippi, on January 8, 1935, marked the beginning of a musical and cultural revolution. Discovered by Sam Phillips at Sun Records, he released his first single, "That's All Right/Blue Moon of Kentucky," in 1954 to an enthusiastic reception.

Elvis was a dynamic performer, and the band's weekly slot on the Louisiana Hayride radio show helped him and his band—guitarist Scotty Moore, bassist Bill Black, and drummer D. J. Fontana—gain notoriety in the local area. Phillips had long sought the white boy who could sing black, and his discovery would change the face of popular music. An early review in music trade magazine *Billboard* described Elvis as "a potent new chanter who can clearly sock over a tune for either the country or rhythm and blues markets."

Presley's second 1954 release, "Good Rockin' Tonight/I Don't Care If the Sun Don't Shine," was followed by three more Sun singles in 1955. "Milkcow Blues Boogie/You're a Heartbreaker" appeared in January, "Baby Let's Play House/I'm Left, You're Right, She's Gone" in April, and "Mystery Train/I Forgot to Remember to Forget" in August. By that time, Elvis had already traded his truck-driving job for the road to stardom.

Colonel Tom Parker, a wily old pro, was next on the scene. He already looked after country stars Hank Snow (with whom Elvis would tour) and Eddy Arnold, and things moved fast once he became Presley's manager. Parker's title was honorary and helped disguise the fact that he was an illegal immigrant from Holland whose real name was Andreas van Kuijk. Nevertheless, he was soon plotting the Presley career with military precision. (Not too long later he was able to say: "I always knew he had a million dollars' worth of talent. Now he has a million dollars.") Parker's horizons for his young charge were limitless, and it was no surprise when Elvis's contract was sold to RCA in late 1955 for $35,000. The next stop was Hollywood.

July 31, 1955, Elvis sends a Tampa crowd into a frenzy. The image would be used on his debut album for RCA the following year. ▸

Where were you when?

"If I could find a white man who had the Negro sound and the Negro feel, I could make a billion."

—Sam Phillips

◂ Elvis, Scotty, and Bill were big noises in their hometown of Memphis, but a month after the gig at Ellis Auditorium, they failed an audition to get on the Arthur Godfrey talent show in New York.

ALAN FREED'S ROCK 'N' ROLL PARTY

Alan Freed, the Cleveland DJ credited with applying the term rock 'n' roll to popular music, this year branched out into concert promotion in New York. His first Rock And Roll Ball, held over two nights in Harlem's 6,000-seat Saint Nicholas Arena, featured the Drifters, Coasters, Moonglows, Harptones, and Big Joe Turner. The events sold out, grossing $24,000 and underlining the fact that popular music was big business. A Christmas show headlined by Count Basie grossed over $100,000. Freed would fall from grace after being implicated in the Payola scandals of 1959-60.

The self-styled "King of the Moondoggers," Freed took his show from WJW in Cleveland to WINS in New York. ▶

1956

MOVIE TRIVIA

- Elvis only got third billing on the movie behind Richard Egan and Debra Paget.

- James Dean kept Elvis from the *Variety* No. 1 spot when the film was released, as *Giant* was the top-grossing film at the time.

- The song "Love Me Tender" started life as a Civil War ballad originally called "Aura Lee."

- The footage of Elvis singing "Love Me Tender" features him with black hair, which he dyed after filming wrapped and before his extra scene was shot in New York.

▲ October 28, 1956, a 40-foot Elvis Presley figure stands atop the marquee of the Paramount Theater for his movie debut *Love Me Tender* opening on November 15.

Love Me Tender

Love Me Tender gave Elvis the first of 31 movie-acting roles and the only one where he didn't get top billing.

Elvis's move to RCA records late in 1955 set him on the road to superstardom, and 1956 would be the year when he was crowned "The King." The country singer released "Heartbreak Hotel" on January 27, 1956, and in the first three weeks it sold 300,000 copies on its steady rise to the *Billboard* No. 1 in March. In fact it would end up as the top-selling single of 1956. On April 1 the singer screen tested for Hal Wallis at Paramount Studios where he performed a scene from the unmade film *The Rainmaker*. Executives liked what they saw and just five days later Presley signed a three-movie deal.

THE RENO BROTHERS

Elvis's first film would be *The Reno Brothers*, a post–Civil War drama where Elvis played Clint Reno who falls in love with his older brother's sweetheart when he fails to return from the War. When brother Vance shows up though, there are tragic consequences. Preview audiences reacted so badly to the original ending of the film that an extra scene was tacked on that showed a ghostly Elvis singing "Love Me Tender" as the other characters walk off into the sunset.

In the wake of increasing chart success and hysterical reactions to his pelvis-gyrating "Hound Dog" performances on network television, the film was renamed *Love Me Tender* and released nationally on November 21. Such was the enormous interest in the film that crowds gathered simply to stare at Paramount's giant promotional cut-out figure.

Elvis remains the only rock singer to combine a credible movie career with enormous chart success.

Elvis gets a grip on co-star Debra Paget in his debut movie *Love Me Tender*. ▶

MOVIE REVIEWS

"Thick-lipped, droopy-eyed, and indefatigably sullen, Mr. Presley, whose talents are meager but whose earnings are gross, excites a big section of the young female population as nobody has ever done."

—*New Yorker*

"Elvis can act so help me the boy's real good, even when he isn't singing."

—*LA Times*

"The burgeoning teen idol actually handles the straight acting better than could be expected. In fact, Elvis Presley is the only member of the cast with a realistic Southern accent."

—*Variety*

BLUE NOTE

In 1956, Blue Note hired Reid Miles, an artist who previously worked for *Esquire* magazine. The cover art produced by Miles, often featuring Francis Wolff's photographs of musicians in the studio, was as influential in the world of graphic design as the music within would be in the world of jazz. Under Miles, Blue Note would be known for their striking and unusual album cover designs. Miles's graphical design was distinguished by its tinted black and white photographs, creative use of sans-serif typefaces, and restricted color palate (often black and white with a third color), and frequent use of solid rectangular bands of color or white. John Coltrane's *Blue Train* was a classic Blue Note album cover.

1956

CALYPSO CRAZY

Born in Harlem of West Indian parents, Harry Belafonte was pushing 30 when he single-handedly launched the calypso boom. A meeting with Irving Burgie, an American citizen of Barbadian extraction, who performed as Lord Burgess and his Serenaders, opened his eyes to the possibilities of West Indian songs and calypsos in particular, and the resulting album, simply called *Calypso* was a prodigious success, becoming the first long-player to be certified a million-seller. *Calypso* registered 31 non-consecutive weeks at No. 1 in the United States, a record that would endure until beaten in 1962 by the film soundtrack to *West Side Story*.

A youthful Belafonte full of the joys of calypso. Later he would become a leading campaigner and champion of African American rights. ▼

Johnny Cash was selling appliances in Memphis when he finally worked up the courage to audition for Sun Records boss Sam Phillips. He sang mostly gospel songs. Phillips told him to, "go home and sin, then come back with a song I can sell." His first Sun releases were "Hey Porter" and "Cry! Cry! Cry!" but in 1956 Cash and his Tennessee Two hit the big time with a No. 1 on the Country Music chart, "I Walk the Line." ▶

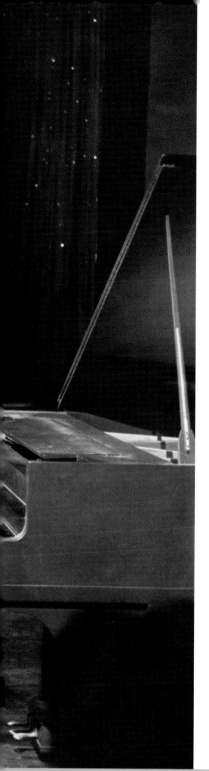

Little Richard

His performance style influenced a generation of musicians and his debut single placed a new word in the lexicon of rock 'n' roll.

Richard Wayne Penniman, otherwise known as Little Richard, burst onto the charts in 1956 with the single "Tutti Frutti" and, in so doing, created a blueprint for starstruck piano players everywhere. Elton John was determined to follow his example after seeing Little Richard play live on a U.K. package tour. And not just piano players: James Brown credited him as an early idol who "put the funk in the rock and roll beat," while Bob Dylan declared in his high school yearbook that his ambition was "to follow Little Richard."

Born one of 13 children in Macon, Georgia, in 1932, Penniman grew up an attention seeker. His flamboyant looks and style—colorful suits, pompadour coif, and camp manner—won him parts in rock exploitation movies like *Don't Knock the Rock*, *The Girl Can't Help It*, and *Mister Rock 'n' Roll* and, through those, a worldwide audience. It spread the visual image of the man, foot up on his keyboard, hammering the ivories, which was as much his trademark as the music itself.

"AWOPBOPALOOBOP ALOP BAM BOOM!"

The hyperactive follow-up hits to his breakthrough—"Long Tall Sally;" "Lucille;" "Rip It Up;" "The Girl Can't Help It;" "Slippin' and Slidin';" "Jenny, Jenny;" "Good Golly, Miss Molly," and "Keep a Knockin'"— provided raw material for many 1960s beat bands, the Beatles among them. More recent artists to have duetted with him in order to acknowledge their inspiration include Jon Bon Jovi, Hank Williams Jr., Elton John, and Tanya Tucker.

Little Richard retired and returned several times over the years, experiencing high spots that included a lifetime achievement Grammy in 1993, an appearance in the 1986 film *Down and Out in Beverly Hills*, and ranking eighth in *Rolling Stone* magazine's 100 Greatest Artists of All Time. (He pointed out that six of the seven artists who preceded him on the list were heavily influenced by him.)

He has also raised funds for AIDS charities, acknowledging his homosexuality. Yet the joyous release of "Tutti Frutti's" payoff line, "Awopbopaloobop alop bam boom!" remains unparalleled in both his career and rock history.

◄ No piano stool required, Little Richard sings live on national television.

THE MILLION DOLLAR QUARTET

Having left Sun Records for RCA the previous year, Elvis Presley returned home to celebrate Christmas. While in Memphis, at the family home, he joined former label mates Johnny Cash, Jerry Lee Lewis, and Carl Perkins at the Sun studios in an impromptu jam session. The so-called "Million Dollar Quartet" sang unrehearsed versions of gospel songs and recent hits, interspersed with jokey conversation. It was all taped but would not be released until after Presley's death. Their name was coined by *Memphis Press Scimitar* entertainment editor Robert Johnson, who broke the story.

From left to right: Lewis, Perkins, Presley, and Cash. ►

1956

NO. 1 SINGLES

"Sixteen Tons"
 —**Tennessee Ernie Ford**

"Memories Are Made of This"
 —**Dean Martin**

"Great Pretender"—**The Platters**

"Rock and Roll Waltz"—**Kay Starr**

"Poor People of Paris"—**Les Baxter**

"Heartbreak Hotel"—**Elvis Presley**

"Wayward Wind"—**Gogi Grant**

"I Almost Lost My Mind"
 —**Pat Boone**

"My Prayer"—**The Platters**

"Don't Be Cruel/Hound Dog"
 —**Elvis Presley**

"Green Door"—**Jim Lowe**

"Love Me Tender"—**Elvis Presley**

"Singing the Blues"—**Guy Mitchell**

▲ Former child star Guy Mitchell started out in life as Albert Cernik. The son of Croatian immigrants would also have a short career singing as "Al Grant." He was signed by Columbia's Mitch Miller who gave him the stage name Guy Mitchell. "Singing the Blues" would be his biggest hit.

Songs for Swingin' Lovers

Frank Sinatra's career looked under threat from the Elvis-inspired generation of rock stars, until the release of a classic album re-established his reputation.

Italian-American singer Frank Sinatra made his name as a solo star after graduating from the big band scene, notching up an impressive 86 hits between 1943 and 1952. But, like his contemporaries, he found the going tough as 1950s youth got their kicks from the rough-hewn appeal of rock 'n' roll. Even so, he overcame a tumultuous private life—split from first wife Nancy and then her successor, Ava Gardner—to get his career back on track. He addressed his depressed romantic situation in 1955's *In the Wee Small Hours*, one of popular music's first "themed" albums, but the following year's *Songs for Swingin' Lovers* took a very different tack and confirmed his recovery.

Swingin' Lovers was an infinitely more upbeat affair than its predecessor and won its creator even greater acclaim. The sessions took place a month after Sinatra's fortieth birthday and were celebratory. Legend has it that orchestra leader Nelson Riddle's arrangement for "I've Got You Under My Skin" elicited applause from the seen-it-all musicians who played it the day after it had been written, in January 1956.

Sinatra would continue the pattern of releasing slow, sad albums and then up-tempo swingers throughout the decade, augmenting them with Christmas celebrations, compilations, and soundtracks. But *Songs for Swingin' Lovers* would remain his best in the eyes of many fans and critics; one critic joyfully proclaimed, "The art of the three-minute pop song begins and ends here," while another claimed it to be "the closest an artist has come to defining the Great American Songbook." Seemingly oblivious to fad or fashion—"Rock 'n' roll is the most brutal, ugly, desperate, vicious form of expression it has been my misfortune to hear"—Sinatra retained his position as an all-around showbiz icon until his death in 1998. His last recording was an album of duets that had singers from Luther Vandross to U2's Bono lining up to share the spotlight with a legend.

◄ Come Fly With Me: Frank Sinatra arrives at Heathrow Airport outside London, April 13, 1956.

JOHNNY CASH CROSSES THE LINE

Sun Records star Johnny Cash and his Tennessee Two—guitarist Luther Perkins and bassist Marshall Grant—played the Grand Ole Opry for the first time in July. Four months later, Cash's "I Walk The Line" reached the U.S. pop Top 20, having been No. 2 on the country chart for some weeks. Its crossover success was due to label boss Sam Phillips, who heard Cash perform it as a ballad on the radio show Louisiana Hayride and insisted he speed up the tempo. It would, however, take Cash until 1959 to recruit a drummer, W. S. Holland, who would stay with him for 30 years.

1957

SKIFFLE CRAZY

Skiffle was the homespun British blend of high-tempo folk and blues that gave Paul McCartney, John Lennon, and the Rolling Stones their first experience of performing music. Tea-chest basses and other improvised instruments accompanied acoustic guitars played by the likes of Anthony "Lonnie" Donegan. His breakthrough recording of Leadbelly's "Rock Island Line" sold over three million copies and made the Top 10 in both Britain and the United States in 1956. He crossed the Atlantic, releasing albums entitled *An Englishman Sings American Folk Songs* (despite being born in Scotland), and *Lonnie Donegan Live,* in 1957. He appeared on Perry Como's TV show, making America aware of its musical heritage.

Anthony "Lonnie" Donegan, the man who inspired Lennon & McCartney. ▼

Where were you when?

"Everyone told us West Side Story *was an impossible project. They said the score was too rangy for pop music. Besides, who wanted to see a show in which the first-act curtain comes down on two dead bodies lying on the stage?"*

—Leonard Bernstein

"I saw the stage musical a long while before the film and although the sense of threat, and danger in the film is greater, the impact of the songs and the dancing was lost on the big screen. It really was a big landmark in the theater."

—Helen Schwarz, NYC

West Side Story

Leonard Bernstein and Stephen Sondheim's musical swam against the tide of traditional Broadway musicals, but became a modern classic.

With youth culture in its infancy, a musical updating the Romeo and Juliet story and setting it among the teen gangs in New York City was not a safe bet for Broadway success. But Arthur Laurents's all-singing, all-dancing *West Side Story,* with music by Leonard Bernstein and lyrics by Stephen Sondheim, would prove its worth over 732 performances.

Laurents and Jerome Robbins had started the project in 1949. The story went through several formats and titles, including *Gangway* and *East Side Story*. Originally the lovers were an Italian-American male and a Jewish female, but the wave of Puerto Rican immigration in the mid 1950s gave them new inspiration.

The public's initial reticence was overcome by such classic songs as "I Feel Pretty," "Maria," "Tonight," "Somewhere," and "America," inspired by the fated romance between Tony, leader of the white Jets, and Maria, sister of the leader of the rival Puerto Rican Sharks. But it was the dance music, so unlike anything heard on the musical stage before, that sparked its success, and it is this ebulliently memorable music that still makes it popular for revivals today, as well as inspiring the likes of *Grease* two decades later.

The London production of *West Side Story* outlived the first Broadway run, playing for 1,039 performances. Four years after it opened at New York's Winter Garden Theater the show was made into a movie. The film has earned its place alongside *The Sound of Music* and *My Fair Lady* as the third mega-hit musical of the late 1950s.

There are clear echoes of the plot in *Grease* and *High School Musical*, successes of the 1970s and the new millennium. Film star Jennifer Lopez, an American of Puerto Rican descent, has credited *West Side Story* with inspiring her to pursue her profession.

◄ Actress Chita Rivera takes the lead ahead of Llane Plane. Rivera played Anita, a role she reprised in the London run of the show at Her Majesty's Theatre.

ELVIS BUYS GRACELAND

In the year he bought his Memphis mansion, Graceland, Elvis Presley's domination of the charts continued. "Too Much" reached No. 2 in March behind Tab Hunter's "Young Love," while "All Shook Up," "Let Me Be Your Teddy Bear," and "Jailhouse Rock" all topped the pile for a combined 21 weeks over the year. He lost the services of sidemen Scotty Moore and Bill Black after a pay dispute with manager Colonel Tom Parker, but Elvis's continuing success suggested he would have little trouble meeting the maintenance costs of his new 23-room residence—even if Uncle Sam was threatening to keep him away from home in the near future.

Elvis stars in the 1957 movie *Loving You.* ▶

1957

TOP-SELLING SINGLES

"Love Letters in the Sand"
 —**Pat Boone**

"Jailhouse Rock/Treat Me Nice"
 —**Elvis Presley**

"All Shook Up"—**Elvis Presley**

"(Let Me Be Your) Teddy Bear"
 —**Elvis Presley**

"Tammy"—**Debbie Reynolds**

"Wake Up Little Susie"
 —**Everly Brothers**

"Little Darlin'"—**The Diamonds**

"Young Love"—**Tab Hunter**

"Bye Bye Love"—**Everly Brothers**

"You Send Me"—**Sam Cooke**

▲ The Everly Brothers in 1957, Phil (left)
and Don (right) aged just 18 and 20.

Buddy Holly

Buddy Holly's career almost ended before it had begun. Signed to Decca records for 1956 he ended the year without a hit and the record label dropped him.

The Crickets, led by bespectacled guitarist-vocalist Buddy Holly, became a model for the self-contained pop group when they found success this year. Future members of the Beatles, the Hollies, and countless other bands-to-be were watching and learning. Indeed, Paul McCartney once said, "If it wasn't for the Crickets, there wouldn't be any Beatles."

Holly began his career in 1949 as half of the country music duo Buddy and Bob. Introducing bassist Larry Welbourn into the mix, the band got exposure via a local radio show. In 1955 Holly recruited a drummer, Jerry Allison, and opened for trailblazing rock 'n' roll act Bill Haley and the Comets. Spotted by Nashville talent scout Eddie Crandall, Holly signed with Decca, but he ended 1956 hitless and Decca dropped him.

Undaunted, he headed for Clovis, New Mexico, where Norman Petty ran a studio. Given the time and encouragement to find their musical feet, Holly and his Crickets—Allison, bassist Joe B. Mauldin, and guitarist Niki Sullivan—put themselves on track for stardom.

Petty, who became Holly's manager as well as his producer, booked the Crickets on a couple of nationwide tours supporting the likes of Chuck Berry and Paul Anka. This exposure brought success. Million-seller "That'll Be the Day" was followed by a second million-seller, "Peggy Sue," while "Oh Boy!" would round out the hits hattrick the following January.

The "Chirping" Crickets, the only Crickets album to feature Buddy Holly during the singer's short lifetime, appeared in November 1957. Because Holly and the Crickets were constantly on the road, their recording sessions had to be fitted around live dates. Even the cover photo was taken on the roof of Brooklyn's Paramount Theater before a concert.

The Crickets perform on Ed Sullivan's CBS variety show, December 1, 1957. ▶

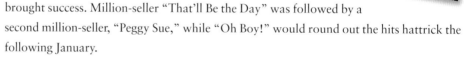

Where were you when?

"I think Buddy understood that this rock 'n' roll thing wasn't going to fade away...that a career could last many, many years."

—Phil Everly

"We like this kind of music. Jazz is strictly for stay-at-homes."

—Buddy Holly

FATS DOMINO

A big man in both body and talent, Antoine "Fats" Domino embodied the spirit of New Orleans music. He placed an amazing 40 titles on *Billboard*'s rhythm and blues Top 10 between 1950 and 1961, but his biggest U.S. pop hit at No. 2 came this year in the shape of "Blueberry Hill." While his rolling piano style and trademark right-hand triplets created the most distinctive sound around, Fats later admitted the lyrics were little more than nursery rhymes: "We didn't want to go over people's heads." Domino was as popular with the white pop audience as hardcore R&B fans: only Elvis outsold him in rock's first decade.

Fats Domino's classic hit "Blueberry Hill," sold more than 5 million copies worldwide between 1956 and 1957. ▶

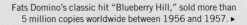

BEST-SELLING ALBUMS

Around the World in 80 Days
—**Original Soundtrack**

Loving You—**Elvis Presley**

Love Is the Thing—**Nat King Cole**

My Fair Lady—**Original Cast**

Oklahoma—**Original Soundtrack**

Elvis's Christmas Album
—**Elvis Presley**

Merry Christmas—**Bing Crosby**

A Swingin' Affair—**Frank Sinatra**

Here's Little Richard
—**Little Richard**

Close to You—**Frank Sinatra**

▲ Little Richard's debut album.

Ricky Nelson relaxes on the island of Kauai during location filming. ▼

Where were you when?

"I saw Ricky Nelson on American Bandstand *and became so obsessed by him that I made my then boyfriend (Arthur), answer to the name Ricky. Forty years later I'd totally forgotten until he reminded me at a class reunion. I blushed."*

—Trudi Hertl, Cincinatti

"I don't set trends. I just find out what they are and exploit them."

—Dick Clark

American Bandstand

Anchored by the country's "oldest teenager," *American Bandstand* was the launchpad for pop bands, teen idols, and a dozen dance crazes.

Although it had first aired locally several years earlier, Philadelphia's *American Bandstand* show, under genial host Dick Clark, became a national television phenomenon in 1957. Clark had replaced original co-host Bob Horn in 1956 and quickly charmed his way into viewers' affections as a kind of older brother figure.

The format combined bands miming to their latest recordings with a teenage audience of studio dancers who became the regular stars of the show. TV viewers identified with regular teen couples who were interviewed about their lives, loves, and opinions of the songs played on the show.

Advertisers piled in to take advantage of the estimated 20 million-strong audience, and the 90-minute daily show quickly became the best way for them and the record labels to reach American teens. Local Philadelphia acts such as Bobby Rydell, Fabian, Frankie Avalon, and Chubby Checker took advantage of their proximity to gain repeated airings. Dance crazes, like Checker's "Twist," were beamed across the nation, and what might once have taken a year to catch on became an overnight phenomenon.

American Bandstand proved groundbreaking television. It also catapulted Dick Clark to fame, though he was forced to surrender all music-related business interests in 1960 after suggested conflicts of interest; technically a TV station employee, he had diversified into record labels, management, and distribution to increase his earnings.

The arrival of British music groups, headed by the Beatles, loosened *American Bandstand*'s hold, and it slipped to a weekly timeslot on Saturday afternoons, but the show somehow weathered this as well as subsequent changes in music for many years. By the 1970s *American Bandstand*, having inspired other similar long-running music programs, such as *Soul Train*, was broadcasting from Los Angeles with Clark, "America's oldest-living teenager," still at the helm. The show ended in 1989.

◄ The face of American pop music, Dick Clark made Philadelphia a hot spot for teenage talent in the 1950s.

PAUL ANKA

Born in Canada of Lebanese parents in 1941, and a performer from the age of 12, teenager Paul Anka kick-started his career this year with the multi-million selling chart-topper "Diana," a song he wrote about the family childminder. His other major contribution to popular music would be penning the English lyrics to the Frank Sinatra signature tune "My Way," though he'd return to the top of the charts in his own right in 1959 with the movie-related "Lonely Boy." Anka, whose impressive run of 33 Top 40 hits came to an end in 1983, performed into the twenty-first century.

Paul Anka recorded his first single at age 14 and "Diana" at 16. ▶

1958

GREATEST HITS
BY JOHNNY MATHIS

Smooth-voiced San Franciscan Johnny Mathis was one of the most consistent popular performers of his generation. Only Frank Sinatra and Elvis Presley have registered more hit LPs in the States, while his *Greatest Hits*, the first ever such album in the popular music industry, was a chart staple for nearly a decade. Released in 1958, its 490-week run on the charts would only be eclipsed by Pink Floyd's *Dark Side Of the Moon* 15 years later. Johnny Mathis continues to perform and record in what is now a career stretching longer than 50 years.

▲ Owner of the "velvet voice," Johnny Mathis was raised in the Fillmore district of San Francisco.

Elvis Joins the Army

Many thought that Elvis Presley's army draft would put an end to his reign in the pop charts, but skillful planning kept him firmly in the public eye.

When the world's first rock 'n' roll icon hit the road for a European tour in March 1958, he didn't have a guitar or microphone in his hand. Instead, he had a gun. Elvis had been called up by the Memphis Draft Board to serve his country, and the patriotic Presley was not about to disappoint. "Whatever the Army people want to do with me is fine," he said, adding, "I don't expect any special privileges and favors. The officers expect discipline and respect and that's what I'll give them."

THE KING JOINS THE PEOPLE

The induction of Private 53310761 began with a medical check in January, which he passed; he would have joined up that month had manager Colonel Parker not secured a 60-day deferment to start filming on the movie *King Creole*. He also began a stockpile of recordings that he would augment while on leave, making sure the charts were not entirely without his input during his scheduled two-year absence. His basic training was carried out to the strains of No. 3 hit "Wear My Ring Around Your Neck," while his first Christmas in the army was celebrated by the double-sided "One Night/I Got Stung."

Tragedy struck the Presley family in August when Elvis's beloved mother, Gladys, died. But, having mourned, he left for Germany in September aboard the troopship *General Randall*. He served out his time on a base near Frankfurt, where he met his future wife Priscilla Beaulieu, daughter of an officer. She was just 14 at the time of their first encounter. They stayed in touch and married in 1967.

The impact Elvis Presley already had on popular music and culture was incalculable. Whether the King would still rule after Uncle Sam had finished with him was the million-dollar question.

◄ March 24, 1957, Elvis is sworn into the army by Major Elbert P. Turner in Memphis Tennessee. Elvis hoped he'd be treated "no different from the other boys in the army."

GIMMICK SINGLES

"The Purple People Eater" by Sheb Wooley and "The Chipmunk Song" and "Witch Doctor" by David Seville were just three of a rash of gimmick singles to reach the chart this year. All three made it to No. 1. Seville, real name Ross Bagdasarian, was a former actor who experimented by speeding up recordings of his voice on a tape machine to achieve comic effects. While Wooley's "Purple People Eater" remained a one-off, Bagdasarian's Chipmunk created a spin-off, *The Alvin Show*, which premiered on prime-time television in 1961 with all voices supplied by himself. It only ran for one year but was a success in a Saturday morning slot.

1958

STAND-OUT SINGLES

"Tequila"—**Champs**

"Johnny B. Goode"—**Chuck Berry**

"At the Hop"—**Danny & the Juniors**

"Get a Job"—**Silhouettes**

"Twilight Time"—**the Platters**

"It's All in the Game"
—**Tommy Edwards**

"Do You Want to Dance"
—**Bobby Freeman**

"Sweet Little Sixteen"
—**Chuck Berry**

"Rockin' Robin"—**Bobby Day**

"Tears on My Pillow"
—**Little Anthony and the Imperials**

"Summertime Blues"
—**Eddie Cochran**

"Fever"—**Peggy Lee**

"Yakety Yak"—**Coasters**

"Chantilly Lace"—**Big Bopper**

"Lonely Teardrops"—**Jackie Wilson**

"Good Golly Miss Molly"
—**Little Richard**

Danny and the Juniors started life in 1957 as The Juvenairs. Their classic 1958 hit "At the Hop" was originally titled "Do the Bop" to cash in on the success of a popular *American Bandstand* dance, The Bop. Dick Clark suggested they change the title to "At the Hop" and it became a No. 1 hit. ▾

Everly Brothers

Phil and Don Everly combined peerless harmonies with angelic good looks and sang songs for angst-ridden American teenagers.

The Everly Brothers' music—a marriage of country harmony, bluesy sincerity, and rock 'n' roll rhythm—would inspire and influence rock 'n' roll's second generation, from Simon and Garfunkel to Paul McCartney, who penned them a comeback hit in the 1980s.

In 1945 Don and his younger brother Phil made their first performance on KMA radio in Shenandoah, Mississippi, at ages eight and six, respectively. It was 13 years later that they became the biggest duo in pop. They kicked off the year with "This Little Girl of Mine," a rockabilly version of a Ray Charles classic that gave them a third Top 30 U.S. single. This was bested by "All I Have to Do Is Dream." "A country ballad with a Latin-ish beat," said *Billboard* of their second U.S. chart-topper, which also stayed seven weeks at the U.K. chart summit. It was backed with "Claudette," written by Roy Orbison, then a hopeful songwriter, and inspired by his wife. He was so keen to get the Everlys to record the song that he borrowed money to get to an Indiana gig to meet them. The nonsensical nursery rhyme "Bird Dog" became the Brothers' fourth million seller and third U.S. chart-topper in August. The B side, "Devoted to You," reached No. 10 in its own right. Rounding off a sensational year, the Bo Diddley–styled "Problems" ended 1958 at No. 2.

Another couple behind the scenes was instrumental in the Everlys' success. Former concert violinist Boudleaux Bryant and his wife, Felice, penned 11 hits that accurately reflected the teenage world of jealousy, insecurity, despair, and puppy love. Dates, movies, car borrowing, dealing with wrathful parents and teachers…the Bryants' creations were delivered with impeccable timing and distinctive harmonies by Don and Phil.

The brothers split following an on-stage row at Knots Berry Farm, California, in 1973, only to reconvene after ten years with a reunion show at London's Royal Albert Hall.

The Everlys, Phil on the left, older brother Don on the right. ▶

Where were you when?

"I don't think Elvis was as good as the Everly boys…and I don't think the Beatles were as good."

—Chuck Berry

"I was THE biggest fan of the Everlys but never got to see them play live till the early 1960s. Somebody at high school said they were playing town, and I wept when I found out it wasn't true."

—Laverne Power, Dayton

THE KINGSTON TRIO

Long before MTV made a virtue out of performing unplugged, California's Kingston Trio—Nick Reynolds, Bob Shane and Dave Guard—were smiling and strumming their way up the charts. The chart-topping "Tom Dooley" (a folksong written as "Tom Dula" and dating to 1868) put the Trio on the map with a vengeance this year, and while they put some folk purists' backs up, they inspired acts like the Brothers Four and the Highwaymen to follow their clean-cut, melodic example. By the time the Kingston Trio split in 1968, John Stewart had replaced Dave Guard, but they had already sown the seeds of the folk-rock explosion that happened when the Byrds picked up their electric guitars.

The Kingston trio, Bob Shane and Dave Guard (right) standing, Nick Reynolds kneeling. ▶

1959

BEST-SELLING ALBUMS

The Music from Peter Gunn
—**Henry Mancini**

The Kingston Trio at Large
—**Kingston Trio**

Here We Go Again!—**Kingston Trio**

Come Dance with Me
—**Frank Sinatra**

South Pacific
—**Original Soundtrack**

Heavenly—**Johnny Mathis**

Exotica—**Martin Denny**

Film Encores
—**Mantovani and his Orchestra**

Flower Drum Song—**Original Cast**

Kind of Blue—**Miles Davis**

It had been a major hit on Broadway when it debuted in 1949, running for five years and almost 2,000 performances. So when Rodgers & Hammerstein's *South Pacific* transferred to the big screen, success for the soundtrack album, which included "Bali Hai'i" and "Some Enchanted Evening," was assured. ▼

THE ENTERTAINMENT WORLD'S
MOST WONDERFUL ENTERTAINMENT!

OGERS & HAMMERSTEIN'S
SOUTH PACIFIC
COLOR by DE LUXE

SSANO BRAZZI · MITZI GAYNOR · JOHN KERR · FRANCE NUYEN

The Day the Music Died...

Buddy Holly had fashioned a future for himself beyond the Crickets, but to make money he had to go out on the road...

The name Buddy Holly surely will, to quote one of his hits, "not fade away" as long as popular music is played. The plane crash that claimed his life on February 3, 1959, near Mason City, Iowa, was described later by singer-songwriter Don McLean as "the day the music died." Yet his music lives on. Most of it was recorded in the year and a half between his first hit, "That'll Be the Day," and his death. Fellow musicians J. P. Richardson aka The Big Bopper and Chicano rocker Ritchie Valens also died when their single-engine Beechcraft crashed in a snowstorm.

FAREWELL PERFORMANCE

After tours of Australia and Britain (where they had four records in the Top 20 in a single week), the Crickets started on another marathon jaunt across the States. This 61-date Alan Freed's Big Beat Show was to be Holly and the Crickets' swansong.

Holly had married Maria Elena Santiago, a young Puerto Rican, and settled with her in New York—a long way from his Texas roots and the rest of the band. He was leaving the group to go out on his own, but he left them with the full rights to the Crickets name. Musically, too, he was pushing boundaries. At the end of 1958 he began recording with an orchestra. Pending ratification of his split from the group, royalties were frozen, and to make money he still had to tour. So fate decreed that this last road trip would bring down the curtain on his brief, bright, and hugely influential career.

HOLLY'S LEGACY

Even so, Holly's influence on popular music in Britain alone has been incalculable. The Hollies adopted their name in homage, while artists from Hank B. Marvin of the Shadows to Elvis Costello have donned his bespectacled look. The Beatles chose their insectlike appellation with the Crickets in mind—they were the Beetles before the Beatles—and Paul McCartney appointed himself keeper of the flame by buying up Holly's song copyrights.

Where were you when?

"Well, I'm either going to go to the top or I'm going to fall. But I think you're going to see me in the big time."

—Buddy Holly

"I went to visit the crash site in 2007, just to see it and be there for a time. There's a small silver monument to Buddy, Ritchie, and J. P. Richardson. I thought I'd be the only one there, but as I was leaving, someone from Germany pulled up."

—T. D. Owens, Des Moines

There is an annual Buddy Holly Week of shows and events in London to commemorate and celebrate his memory.

The long-running London stage musical *Buddy* and the successful 1978 big-screen bio-pic *The Buddy Holly Story* have also demonstrated the public's continuing appetite for Holly music. Add new recordings of the catalogue to tribute songs from artists as diverse as Alvin Stardust and Weezer, and it's clear Holly will never fade away.

In the corner of a snowy Iowa field, Buddy Holly, Ritchie Valens, and the Big Bopper met their untimely fate, thrown from the wreckage of the Beechcraft Bonanza aircraft. They had played the Surf Ballroom in Clear Lake, Iowa, and were heading for Fargo, North Dakota. ▼

RAY CHARLES BREAKS THROUGH

Ten years of struggle for blind pianist/singer Ray Charles ended this year when he scored the first of several million-sellers with a self-penned signature track "What'd I Say." He had spent most of the decade perfecting his recording technique while continuing to make a reputation as a dynamic performer, and this combined both aspects with a gospel-like call and response style that was genuinely exciting. It would prove his final hit for the Atlantic record label before moving on to ABC for more money and a guarantee of artistic freedom. "What'd I Say" took him to No. 6 in the pop listings, as well as topping the R&B charts; Elvis, Jerry Lee Lewis, and Bobby Darin were among those to record it.

1959

NO. 1 SINGLES

"The Chipmunk Song"
—**David Seville &
The Chipmunks**

"Smoke Gets in Your Eyes"
—**The Platters**

"Stagger Lee"—**Lloyd Price**

"Venus"
—**Frankie Avalon**

"Come Softly to Me"
—**The Fleetwoods**

"Kansas City"—**Wilbert Harrison**

"The Battle of New Orleans"
—**Johnny Horton**

"Lonely Boy"—**Paul Anka**

"A Big Hunk O' Love"
—**Elvis Presley**

"The Three Bells"—**The Browns**

"Sleep Walk"—**Santo & Johnny**

"Mack The Knife"—**Bobby Darin**

"Mr. Blue"—**The Fleetwoods**

"Heartaches by the Number"
—**Guy Mitchell**

"Why"—**Frankie Avalon**

Bobby Darin was born Walden Robert
Cassotto. He told reporters he took his
"Darin" surname from a malfunctioning
Chinese restaurant sign advertising
Mandarin duck. ▼

Where were you when?

"*Mary Martin found this property first and then invited us into it. We accepted the invitation because we liked the story very much…. Not only have we concocted this syrupy musical play, but we all love it and it has turned out a great success. This does not mean you should endorse it or like it. Nor are we obliged to agree with you that it is unadulterated treacle.*"

—Oscar Hammerstein

"*Take the basic story of* The King and I, *scrape the oriental spicing and substitute Austrian sugar-icing an inch thick. Add a little bit of drama at the end.*"

—W. A. Darlington, *Daily Telegraph*

The Sound of Music

Critics on both sides of the Atlantic lampooned it for its syrupy theme, but Mary Martin's project delivered a triumphant finale for Rodgers & Hammerstein.

The fictionalized story of Austria's Von Trapp family, making their escape from the Nazis with songs and ingenuity despite the oncoming threat of World War II resulted in a musical in 1959 that would become a classic. It also brought down the curtain on the brilliant partnership of Richard Rodgers and Oscar Hammerstein II, creators of *Oklahoma!*, *South Pacific*, *The King and I*, and *Carousel*, among others. Hammerstein died of cancer nine months after the premiere.

The original premise had been to use the family singing group's own repertoire in a play, adding just a couple of new songs. But by the time the production hit the stage at the Lunt-Fontanne Theater on November 16, a full complement of Rodgers and Hammerstein numbers had been assembled. And the songs the pair came up with— "Sixteen Going On Seventeen," "My Favorite Things," "Climb Ev'ry Mountain," "The Lonely Goatherd," "Do-Re-Mi," and "Edelweiss"— would easily stand the test of time.

A Broadway run of 1,443 performances followed, with Mary Martin in the role of the young governess Maria and Theodore Bikel as the widower Captain von Trapp. Martin called *The Sound of Music* a "triumph of audiences over critics," since it was not well reviewed in New York. The original Broadway cast album sold 3 million copies. The show then went on to take Britain by storm. Opening in 1961, it ran 2,385 performances, eclipsing *My Fair Lady*, *Oklahoma!* and *Annie Get Your Gun* in becoming the longest-running Broadway musical to play London. And there was more to come.

The movie that followed outgrossed every rival in the United States during the 1960s and produced a soundtrack album that spent 70 weeks at the top of the charts. *The Sound of Music* movie echoed the stage version's success, winning three Oscars in 1965 and confirming Julie Andrews, the movie's Maria, as a superstar. Bill Lee supplied the vocals for Christopher Plummer's Captain von Trapp in one of the greatest feel-good films of all time.

◄ Musical theater star Mary Martin played the first Maria. It had been her pursuit of the Von Trapp story that led to the stage adaptation, but at 46 she was considered by many to be far too old to play the role of a young novice.

TEEN IDOL

The Philadelphia music scene of the late 1950s, aided by its proximity to the *American Bandstand* studios, produced a number of stars manufactured by the music business to take advantage of the TV show's national exposure. Frankie Avalon's path to overnight fame was followed by Fabian and Bobby Rydell, undoubtedly the most talented of these Philly teen idols. While Fabian imitated Presley, Avalon and Rydell's performing style harked back to the pre-rock age. In all cases their chart success was relatively brief. Avalon, who scored No. 1s with "Venus" and "Why," moved into movies; Fabian (biggest hit "Tiger") faded fastest, while Rydell, whose million-sellers included "We Got Love," "Wild One," "Volare," and "Sway," headed for the cabaret circuit. But the teen idol concept was here to stay.

Local boy made good, Bobby Rydell. ►

1960-1969

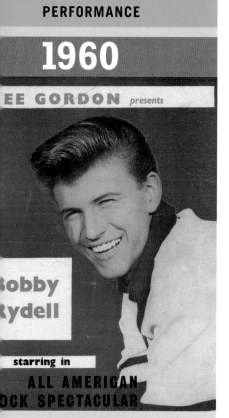

EE GORDON presents

Bobby
Rydell

starring in

ALL AMERICAN
OCK SPECTACULAR

TOP-SELLING SINGLES

"The Twist"—**Chubby Checker**

"Beyond the Sea"—**Bobby Darin**

"Are You Lonesome Tonight?"
—**Elvis Presley**

"Wild One"—**Bobby Rydell**

"Volare"—**Bobby Rydell**

"I'm Sorry"—**Brenda Lee**

"Money (That's What I Want)"
—**Barrett Strong**

"This Magic Moment"
—**the Drifters**

"It's Now or Never"
—**Elvis Presley**

"Wonderful World"
—**Sam Cooke**

▲ One of the original Teen Idols—others
included Frankie Avalon, Fabian, Johnny
Tillotson, Jimmy Clanton, and Bobby
Vee—Bobby Rydell was only 18 when his
single "Wild One" reached No. 2 on the
Billboard Hot 100 chart.

Chubby Checker— Let's Twist Again

Chubby Checker's No. 1 smash hit, "The Twist," sparked a dance craze that took America, and then the world by storm.

For a short while, as the 1950s turned into the 1960s, the dance crazes were the be-all and end-all of pop. The phenomenon was fostered by *American Bandstand*, a nationally broadcast U.S. TV show in which the dancing teenage audience were the real stars. New steps were created overnight, with new solo singers and short-lived groups emerging briefly to sing to the new beats.

Chubby Checker, born Ernest Evans, was a Philadelphia novelty singer whose first minor hit, "The Class," in 1959 showcased his gifts as a musical impressionist. In 1960 he recorded a Hank Ballard B side, "The Twist," as his fifth release. Demonstrated on *American Bandstand*, it made No. 1 and sold 3 million copies worldwide. Many other dance-craze singles followed, including the chart-topping "Pony Time" and the platinum "Let's Twist Again."

MUSIC HISTORY

But "The Twist" was to make music history when it returned to the U.S. top spot for a second time after the dance was adopted by the trendsetting clientele of the Peppermint Lounge nightclub in New York. The craze also spread to Britain where "Let's Twist Again" proved even more popular because it was actually easier to twist to.

Checker reacted by cutting the duet "Slow Twistin" with female singer Dee Dee Sharp and was rewarded with a U.S. No. 3 hit.

After Checker and record company Cameo Parkway milked the craze to its conclusion, Hollywood got in on the act with cash-in movies *Twist Around the Clock* and *Don't Knock the Twist*. The fact that a good dance craze never dies was underlined in 1975 when the British northern soul circuit embraced "The Twist" and put it back in the U.K. Top 5 and again in 1988 when Checker partnered with rap trio the Fat Boys in their version of his historic hit, "Yo Twist."

Checker demonstrates the Twist at an EMI party in London. ▶

Where were you when?

"Justin Timberlake, Britney Spears, all the rappers, they're doing my dances and they're making billions doing my dances. When they do that little thing with their hands, that's The Fly and The Pony."

—Chubby Checker

"Chubby and the Twist got adults out and onto the dance floor for the very first time. Before the Twist dance phenomenon, grownups did not dance to teenage music."

—Clay Cole, host of U.S. music program *The Clay Cole Show*

JOAN BAEZ AT NEWPORT FOLK FESTIVAL

The hit of the first folk festival at Newport, Rhode Island, in 1959, Joan Baez returned as a solo act that year with a Vanguard Records contract in the bag. Her eponymous debut album would appear in November, the month she made her New York City concert debut. She met Bob Dylan at Gerde's Folk City in April 1961, and would frequently introduce the singer-songwriter (and future boyfriend) over the years to come, including at Newport in 1963. Her second album *Joan Baez No. 2* became her first U.S. chart entry that year at No. 13, indicating the rising popularity of the folk and protest movement of which she and Dylan were the uncrowned royalty.

Her 1960 album, *Joan Baez*, made the singer a folk superstar. ▶

1960

2 GREAT SONGS

STAND-OUT ALBUMS

This Is Brenda
—**Brenda Lee**

Encore of Golden Hits
—**The Platters**

Unforgettable
—**Dinah Washington**

Gunfighter Ballads and Trail Songs
—**Marty Robbins**

Time Out
—**The Dave Brubeck Quartet**

It's Everly Time
—**The Everly Brothers**

String Along—**The Kingston Trio**

Joan Baez—**Joan Baez**

That's All—**Bobby Darin**

Belafonte at Carnegie Hall
—**Harry Belafonte**

Elvis Is Back!—**Elvis Presley**

Sketches of Spain—**Miles Davis**

Giant Steps—**John Coltrane**

Muddy Waters at Newport
—**Muddy Waters**

▲ The Everlys are the most successful U.S. rock and roll duo on the *Billboard* Hot 100. *It's Everly Time* is considered to be one of the finest rock 'n' roll albums of the pre-Beatles era.

Where were you when?

"We figured Elvis Presley for just another lightweight. But he's never angled himself into anything easy and he shows exceptionally good judgment for a kid worth a few million dollars. This guy Elvis has made it popular to be a good soldier."

—Unknown U.S. Army officer

"The next thing I knew, I was out of the service and making movies again. My first picture was called GI Blues. I thought I was still in the army."

—Elvis Presley

Elvis Leaves the Army

Elvis returned to civilian life with an exemplary military record, only to find that the next movie he was cast in would be *GI Blues*.

Elvis Presley hung up his fatigues and returned to his throne on March 5, having completed his allotted two-year U.S. Army stint in Germany. It would be the only time he was to spend outside the United States because his manager Colonel Parker, unbeknownst to either his charge or the general public, was an illegal Dutch immigrant and lacked the papers necessary to travel abroad.

Presley was stationed at a U.S. Army facility at Friedberg, near Frankfurt, where his father and grandfather joined him. Although he ducked the spotlight by living outside the base, he played a full role in military life. Presley left the service a sergeant, having risen through the ranks to lead a three-man reconnaissance team in the 32nd Scout Platoon.

His only public appearance during his 15-month European stay was when he was dragged on stage from the audience at the famous Paris Lido. Hits had continued during his absence at home, however, via stockpiled recordings, like "A Fool Such As I" and "Big Hunk of Love," which kept his name on the charts in 1959.

KING OF ROCK 'N' ROLL

The post-army Elvis was trimmer, shorter-haired, and calmer, and well on the way to becoming an all-around entertainer. Against the odds, Presley had actually broadened his appeal during the two years spent out of the spotlight. This was important in terms of his future, film-based career.

While rivals like Paul Anka, Frankie Avalon, and Ricky Nelson, had prospered with the teenage audience in his absence, no one had replaced him as King of Rock 'n' Roll. His popularity with the great American public appeared undamaged—a point proved when his first post-army release, "Stuck on You," soared to No. 1 as if he'd never been away.

◄ Sgt. Elvis Presley, speaking at a press conference in Fort Dix, New Jersey, in March 1960. The rock 'n' roll idol arrived from Germany after an 18-month tour of duty overseas.

DJ ALAN FREED ACCUSED OF PAYOLA

Alan Freed's career as a top disc jockey effectively ended this year when he was implicated in the pay-for-airplay "payola," scandal. The policy had been rife in the U.S. industry, but Freed appears to have been the high-profile scapegoat. Another payola technique was to credit DJs as co-writers of the songs, thus encouraging them to promote the record. In March 1963 he pleaded guilty to accepting $2,700 from two companies to promote their records. He left New York for California where he faced charges of tax evasion and died in 1965, aged just 42. His pioneering work was eventually acknowledged when he became one of the first inductees into the Rock and Roll Hall of Fame on its inauguration in 1986.

The pioneering DJ, who helped to promote R&B music, referred to himself as the "Father of Rock and Roll." ►

1961

MMY DEAN · BIG BAD JOHN

NO. 1 SINGLES

"Are You Lonesome Tonight?"
—**Elvis Presley**

"Wonderland by Night"
—**Bert Kaempfert**

"Will You Love Me Tomorrow"
—**The Shirelles**

"Calcutta"—**Lawrence Welk**

"Pony Time"—**Chubby Checker**

"Surrender"—**Elvis Presley**

"Blue Moon"—**The Marcels**

"Travelin' Man"—**Ricky Nelson**

"Running Scared"—**Roy Orbison**

"Moody River"—**Pat Boone**

"Wooden Heart"—**Joe Dowell**

"Take Good Care of My Baby"
—**Bobby Vee**

"Hit the Road Jack"—**Ray Charles**

"Runaround Sue"—**Dion**

"Bristol Stomp"—**The Dovells**

"Big Bad John"—**Jimmy Dean**

"Please Mr. Postman"
—**The Marvelettes**

"The Lion Sleeps Tonight"
—**The Tokens**

▲ Jimmy Dean's much parodied hit, "Big
Bad John," won a Grammy Award in 1962
for Best Country & Western Recording.
The country singer went on to found the
Jimmy Dean Food Company.

Where were you when?

*"It's like asking me in the
Cavern, 'Are you gonna make
it?' In the back of my mind
I thought I'm gonna make it,
but I couldn't lay it on the line."*

—John Lennon

◄ Ringo Starr was drumming with Rory
Storm and the Hurricanes before he joined
the Beatles.

Birth of the Beatles

By the end of 1961, Brian Epstein had discovered the Beatles, who were about to change the face of popular music. But not before a few significant changes...

The smoky subterranean Cavern Club on Liverpool's Mathew Street is enshrined in history as the birthplace of Mersey Beat—and the Beatles, the group that used the genre as their springboard to world fame. They played their first date there in March 1961 to support the Bluegenes (later the Swinging Blue Jeans).

The band had been off their hometown radar for a while, playing Hamburg clubs for the latter part of 1960, until 17-year-old guitarist George Harrison was deported in December for underage drinking. Their stage act was now finely honed, and they returned as conquering heroes.

At this point Paul McCartney was playing guitar along with Harrison and John Lennon, and Pete Best (drums) and Stuart Sutcliffe (bass) made up the rhythm section. But after returning to Hamburg for more work at the Top Ten club in April, Sutcliffe elected to stay to live with girlfriend Astrid Kirchherr and study art. McCartney moved to bass, Ringo Starr replaced Pete Best, and by 1962 the classic Fab Four lineup was complete.

The band had yet to fill their set with the songs that would make them famous, playing mainly rock 'n' roll standards plus the occasional rocked-up show tune. And with leather jacket chic the order of the day, they had not yet adopted their trademark suits. They did, however, have a road manager in Neil Aspinall who would eventually take over as head of their Apple empire.

Future songsmiths Lennon and McCartney had been playing music together since 1957, when a chance meeting led McCartney to join Lennon's skiffle—a revved up blend of folk and blues—group the Quarrymen. From there they tossed around such names as Johnny and the Moondogs and the Silver Beatles before settling on the Beatles.

Back in 1961, however, another important event took place at the Cavern. On November 9, record-shop owner Brian Epstein, intrigued when a young customer tried to buy a record the Beatles had cut with Tony Sheridan in Germany, saw them at a lunchtime show. The Beatles signed a management contract with Epstein a month later; fame was less than a year away.

◄ The original lineup, from left to right: Paul McCartney, Pete Best, George Harrison, and John Lennon.

LITTLE RICHARD GOES BACK ON THE ROAD

In late 1957, fans of Little Richard had been shocked when he quit music to enrol in Oakwood College Seminary to study theology. He made his decision while touring Australia, and legend has it that he confirmed the decision by throwing his trademark jewelry off Sydney Harbor Bridge into the sea. Having been ordained a minister of the Seventh Day Adventist Church, he returned to music and would go on to tour Europe with rising stars the Beatles and the Rolling Stones. This divide between rock and religion would continue to dog the God-fearing piano-thumper as he retired and returned several times through his career.

From left to right: Jet Harris of The Shadows, Little Richard, Gene Vincent, and Sam Cooke. ►

1962

THE BRILL BUILDING

An anonymous New York building at 1619 Broadway became the focus of attention this year as songs created there by the writing talents of Goffin and King, Leiber & Stoller, Bacharach & David, Barry and Greenwich, Neil Diamond and Neil Sedaka first became hits. This was the new Tin Pan Alley, but unlike the production line that cranked out pre–rock 'n' roll popular music, the Brill Building songsmiths were often barely out of their teens. The year's hits included Carole King's "It Might As Well Rain Until September," Neil Sedaka's chart-topping "Breaking Up Is Hard to Do," and Little Eva's equally successful "The Loco-Motion," also penned by King with husband Gerry Goffin.

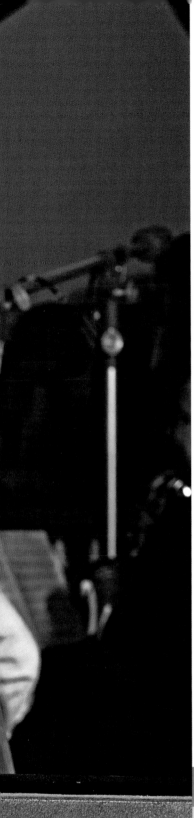

Ray Charles

The talented pianist, whom Frank Sinatra described as "the only true genius in the business," brought a soulful sound to pop music and helped shape R&B.

Born in Albany, Georgia, on September 23, 1930, pianist and singer Ray Charles started performing music professionally at 16 in Florida, where he was raised. But it was in 1962 that Charles broke new ground with the multimillion-selling single "I Can't Stop Loving You" and a Top 5 album, *Modern Sounds in Country and Western*.

Although the single was a relatively obscure Don Gibson song until the "Genius" gave it his unique treatment, the album found Charles, a black jazz and soul musician, performing a dozen country classics. It was his first venture into a genre with which he was to become increasingly comfortable. More important, it broke an unspoken color bar and took a significant step toward creating today's kaleidoscopic music scene.

Born Ray Charles Robinson, he dropped his surname to avoid confusion with the boxer Sugar Ray Robinson. He lost his sight at an early age due to untreated glaucoma. At age 22 Atlantic Records signed him, and he spent the 1950s establishing a reputation as a dynamic R&B performer.

BEST MALE JAZZ VOCALIST

Happily, his fans stayed with him no matter which musical route he chose. Jazz magazine *Downbeat* voted him best male singer five years in a row beginning in 1961, even though he'd long since strayed into other musical fields. He was ninth best-selling artist in the States in the 1960s, a decade that brought never-before-seen changes in musical fashion. His ability to push through musical boundaries placed him alongside the likes of Presley, Dylan, and the Beatles.

Charles was much honored in his lifetime and was one of the first musicians inducted into the Rock and Roll Hall of Fame, and a bio-pic, titled simply *Ray*, won its star Jamie Foxx an Oscar after its 2004 release. Acolytes Stevie Wonder, Van Morrison, Joe Cocker, and Billy Joel, to name but a few, mourned his death in 2004.

◄ Ray Charles performing in Los Angeles in 1961.

LIVE AT THE APOLLO

James Brown, the "godfather of soul," had his first R&B chart-topper in 1958 with "Try Me." Its success helped him fund a steady backing band, which gave him the idea of cutting a live album. So rare was this tactic in 1962 that he had to fund the venture himself. *Live at the Apollo* was recorded in 1962 and released by a skeptical King Records in 1963. It went on to reach No. 2 in *Billboard*'s album chart. From then on, until his death in 2006, a James Brown concert ticket was a much sought-after item.

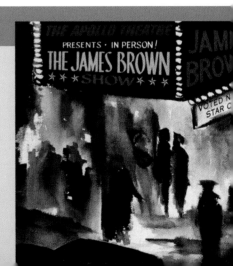

1962

TOP-SELLING SINGLES

"I Can't Stop Loving You"
—**Ray Charles**

"The Twist"—**Chubby Checker**

"Big Girls Don't Cry"
—**The Four Seasons**

"Roses are Red (My Love)"
—**Bobby Vinton**

"Sherry"—**Four Seasons**

"Peppermint Twist"
—**Joey Dee and the Starlighters**

"Stranger on the Shore"
—**Acker Bilk**

"Soldier Boy"—**The Shirelles**

"Johnny Angel"—**Shelley Fabares**

"Return to Sender"
—**Elvis Presley**

"Stranger on the Shore," originally written for a U.K. TV show, made Acker Bilk an international star. Bilk was the first British musician to have a song in the No. 1 position on the U.S. *Billboard* singles chart. ▼

Where were you when?

"*My records are built like Wagner opera. They start simply and end with dynamic force, meaning, and purpose. It's in the mind, I dreamed it up. It's like art movies.*"

—Phil Spector

"*He was always trying to create more and more, and I think it finally ate him up at the end, because the technology was not able to keep up with him.*"

—Larry Levine, Phil Spector's musical engineer

Phil Spector's Wall of Sound

As the pioneer of the "Wall of Sound," Spector's epic, radio-friendly pop songs began to score major successes for his roster of girl groups.

Few record producers have had the impact Phil Spector achieved in just six years. Yet he was as reclusive and secretive as his records were brash and overstated.

Arriving on the New York recording scene in 1960, Harvey Phillip Spector, a one-hit wonder with the singing group the Teddy Bears in 1958, actually found fame on the West Coast by creating a crack studio team of writers, arrangers, and musicians to work with largely unknown artists. His Wall of Sound involved pushing studio technology to its limits, creating three-minute mini operas that layered strings and vocals onto a backing track made big by the Gold Star Studios' famed echo chamber.

He achieved his first No. 1 in 1962 with "He's a Rebel" by the Crystals, five Brooklyn schoolgirls who hit even greater heights when session star Darlene Love was installed as their lead vocalist. Other successes included the Ronettes, whose main singer, Veronica Bennett, would later become Mrs Spector. The Righteous Brothers were a rare male group in his studio, while his last success would be Ike and Tina Turner's "River Deep Mountain High." Released in 1966, this typified his everything-but-the-kitchen-sink approach but would be a hit only on re-release several years later. Its apparent rejection by the public hurt him deeply, and he closed down his Philles Records imprint.

Phil Spector would emerge from self-imposed retirement in the late 1960s to work with the Beatles on the controversial *Let It Be* album. He also worked with Lennon and Harrison on solo records, but other projects, such as recording the Ramones and Leonard Cohen, were sporadic and less successful. In 2006 he was charged with the murder of actress Lana Clarkson, but a retrial was ordered in late 2007.

Spector's way of working proved a template for the writing and production teams that followed, from Motown's Holland-Dozier-Holland to Britain's Stock, Aitken, and Waterman.

◄ The Ronettes pose with Phil Spector while recording at Gold Star Studios in Los Angeles .

BEATLES FAIL DECCA AUDITION

The year of 1962 dawned inauspiciously for John, Paul, George, and Pete Best when, on January 1, they were auditioned and turned down by Decca in London. They cut 15 songs in a morning, but the label elected to sign the group that followed them into the recording studio, Brian Poole and the Tremeloes. In mitigation, Brian Epstein told them to minimise the self-penned numbers to concentrate on standards, but a third of the songs performed were chart hits for other artists. Fortunately, George Martin at EMI identified the potential that Decca A&R manager Dick Rowe failed to spot, and their career continued its upward trajectory six months later. Rowe's apocryphal comment that "guitar groups are on the way out," has never been officially confirmed.

The Beatles performing in 1962. ►

1963

ROLLING STONES FIRST SINGLES

Rock rebels the Rolling Stones made their first grooves in black vinyl this year when they recorded and released two singles. The first, "Come On," was a sneering version of a little-known Chuck Berry song, while the second, "I Wanna Be Your Man," was gifted to them by John Lennon and Paul McCartney of the Beatles when they bumped into their southern "rivals" in London's Denmark Street, home of the U.K. music publishing business. Manager Andrew Loog Oldham cheekily asked them if they had any songs to spare and the result reached an impressive No. 9, 12 places higher than its predecessor.

▲ The Rolling Stones performing "I Wanna Be Your Man" in 1963. On the vinyl recording Brian Jones played a bottleneck steel guitar, the first time this was done on a U.K. pop record.

Surf Music

The Beach Boys made waves on the charts with their close vocal harmonies and carefree lyrics that encapsulated the California youth lifestyle.

The California idyll of sun, surf, and sex appeal proved a potent mix long before television's *Baywatch* introduced it to a later generation. Back in 1963 the Beach Boys and friends were bringing their sun-kissed music to the charts. They started with a form of Chuck Berry–styled rock 'n' roll and overlaid it with the close harmonies of doo-wop to create an irresistibly catchy sound.

Their debut album, *Surfin' Safari*, reached No. 32, but it was their second album, *Surfin' USA*, which would climb to No. 2, with the single peaking just one place lower. By the end of the year Brian Wilson had taken the controls and produced his first Beach Boys album, *Surfer Girl*. Ironically, the only one in the group who was a bona fide wave rider was Brian's brother Dennis.

Jan Berry and Dean Torrence were the embodiment of sun-bronzed Californian youth and, as Jan and Dean, would blaze brightly—if briefly—after *American Bandstand* discovered their combination of looks and talent. Brian Wilson gave them the line: "Two girls for every boy" and they came up with a song to fit: "Surf City" would become not only a chart-topper but also a worldwide million-seller.

For 1963 at least Jan and Dean were untouchable, alternating songs about surfing with the American male's prime preoccupation—cars. "Drag City," "Dead Man's Curve," and "The Little Old Lady (from Pasadena)" were all Top 10 entries.

The Beach Boys, who ended the year with the classic "Little Deuce Coupe," evolved to create the classic *Pet Sounds* and *Smile* albums, which placed them firmly at the cutting edge of the U.S. musical mainstream. Jan and Dean hung on until an auto crash in 1966—a real-life echo of "Dead Man's Curve"—caused Jan's retirement.

The Beach Boys pose with Honda mopeds for this 1963 photo shoot. ▶

Where were you when?

"Brian (Wilson) and I got along really well. I always appreciated his stuff. It always had that tongue-in-cheek humor. Brian had an odd little way of looking at life, differently than the average person did. And I appreciated that."

—Dean Torrence

"The whole surf music thing came kinda late. I saw the movie Gidget *in 1958 and that turned me on to surfing. The Beach Boys just hooked up to surfing. They didn't look like the kind of guys that hung around Newport Beach."*

—Lori Taylor, Huntingdon, California

"BLOWIN' IN THE WIND"—PETER, PAUL & MARY

Peter, Paul & Mary emerged from New York's beatnik district, Greenwich Village, to take folk and protest to the chart. They shared management with Bob Dylan, so it was logical for the trio to cover his anti-war opus, "Blowin' in the Wind," which came within a whisker of giving Dylan his first chart-topper when it reached No. 2 in the summer of 1963. It had been preceded by the far less contentious "Puff the Magic Dragon" (another No. 2 hit). Peter Yarrow, Paul Stookey and Mary Travers signed off in style in 1969 with their one and only chart-topper, "Leaving on a Jet Plane," which gave another young singer-songwriter, John Denver, some much-needed exposure.

"PP&M" were one of the most successful folk-singing groups of the 1960s. ▶

1963

introducing...
THE BEATLES
NGLANDS No.1 VOCAL GROUP

FEATURING
WIST AND SHOUT
LEASE, PLEASE ME

STAND-OUT ALBUMS

In the Wind—**Peter, Paul & Mary**

Please Please Me—**The Beatles**

*Little Stevie Wonder/
   The 12-Year Old Genius*
   —**Stevie Wonder**

The Ventures in Space
   —**The Ventures**

Call Me/That's The Way Love Is
   —**Bobby Bland**

Live at the Apollo—**James Brown**

Meet the Searchers
   —**The Searchers**

The Freewheelin'—**Bob Dylan**

Surfer Girl—**The Beach Boys**

Ingredients in a Recipe for Soul
   —**Ray Charles**

Jazz Samba
   —**Stan Getz/Charlie Byrd**

Days of Wine and Roses
   —**Andy Williams**

▲ "Please Please Me" was, eventually, the Beatles' breakthrough record in the United States. When the single was first released in February 1963 (with "Ask Me Why" on the B-side), it disappeared without a trace. However, when it was re-released in January 1964 (with "From Me to You" on the B-side) it reached No. 3 in the U.S. Hot 100.

Where were you when?

"I consider myself a poet first and a musician second. I live like a poet and I'll die like a poet."

—Bob Dylan

"There was a lot of space to be born in then. The media were onto other things. You could develop whatever creative interests you had without having to deal with categories and definitions. It lasted about three years."

—Bob Dylan, talking about the 1960s folk boom to *TV Guide*

Bob Dylan

Dylan reenergized the folk music genre with his album *Freewheelin'* as his songs became anthems of the anti-war and civil rights movements.

This was the breakthrough year for Bob Dylan, arguably the most complex and influential individual in rock music. Born Robert Zimmerman in Minnesota in 1941, Dylan hit his stride in 1963 with his second album, *The Freewheelin' Bob Dylan*. It combined his interpretations of traditional material with hard-hitting cold war commentaries ("Masters of War" and "A Hard Rain's A-Gonna Fall") and established him as the king of folk and protest.

Two months after the album's release, Dylan was a star of the Newport Folk Festival, and was joined on stage by the folk-pop trio Peter, Paul & Mary. They had taken *Freewheelin'*'s civil rights anthem "Blowin in the Wind" to No. 2, sugaring the protest pill with sweet harmonies; Dylan's voice, by contrast, was sandpaper-rough.

By October, Dylan had finished another album, *The Times They Are A-Changin'*, and it seemed his creative muse was unstoppable. But his personal life was a mess, having traded long-time muse, Suze Rotolo, for fellow performer Joan Baez, who'd introduced him at Newport. The romantic "Don't Think Twice It's All Right" hinted at his regret for that lost love.

The ensuing years would see Dylan embrace electric rock as his way forward, trading his folk audience for a wider one. But *The Freewheelin' Bob Dylan* saw him introduce protest lyrics into pop consciousness. Dozens of tracks were cut and discarded as he struggled to find his voice. *Freewheelin'* would peak at a modest No. 22 on the charts, but it crucially put down a marker for the man whom many would regard as spokesman for his generation.

◄ Bob Dylan performing "Talkin' John Birch Paranoid Blues" during rehearsals for the *Ed Sullivan Show* in New York on May 12, 1963. After the rehearsal, Dylan was asked to perform a different song for the broadcast—a request he refused. Instead, he walked out of the studio and never appeared on the show.

A&M RECORDS LAUNCHED BY HERB ALPERT

Californian trumpet player Herb Alpert had reached the top as a studio musician before he decided to form his own group, The Tijuana Brass, and also a record label (A&M) to release their recordings. First hit "The Lonely Bull," established the popularity of his Mexican-flavored instrumentals, entering the chart late in 1962 and peaking at No. 6 in early 1963. It was the first of a string of similar singles like "Tijuana Taxi" and "Spanish Flea" that would continue to buzz around the charts until Alpert went solo in 1968. The Carpenters would be A&M's biggest hitmakers in the 1970s.

Herb Alpert (left) with Burt Bacharach. Their single, "This Guy's in Love with You," became a U.S. No. 1 in 1968. ►

1963

NO. 1 SINGLES

"Telstar"—**The Tornadoes**

"Go Away Little Girl"
—**Steve Lawrence**

"Hey Paula"—**Paul & Paula**

"Walk Like a Man"
—**The Four Seasons**

"He's So Fine"—**The Chiffons**

"I Will Follow Him"
—**Little Peggy March**

"If You Wanna Be Happy"
—**Jimmy Soul**

"It's My Party"—**Lesley Gore**

"Sukiyaki"—**Kyu Sakamoto**

"Surf City"—**Jan & Dean**

"So Much in Love"—**The Tymes**

"Fingertips—Pt 2"
—**Little Stevie Wonder**

"My Boyfriend's Back"—**The Angels**

"Blue Velvet"—**Bobby Vinton**

"Sugar Shack"
—**Jimmy Gilmer & The Fireballs**

"I'm Leaving It Up to You"
—**Dale & Grace**

"Dominique"—**The Singing Nun**

▲ Paul and Paula's No. 1 hit, "Hey Paula," was followed later in the year by "Young Lovers," which reached No. 6.

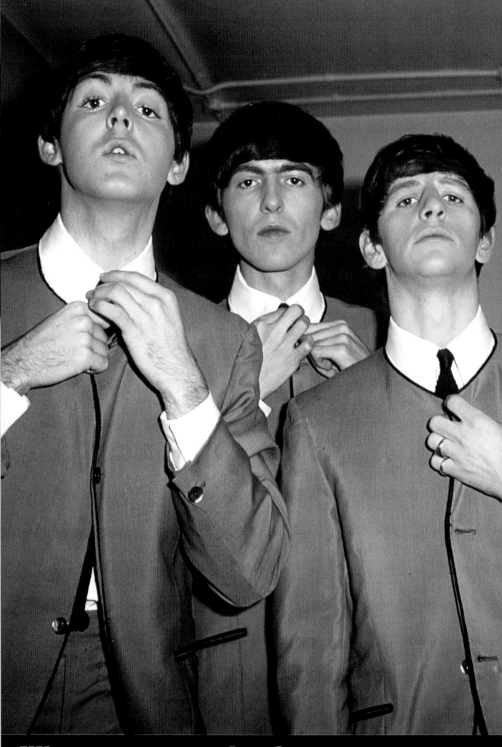

Where were you when?

"Lots of people have asked us what we enjoyed best…concerts, television, or recording. What we like to hear most is one of our songs taking shape in a recording studio, and then listening to the tapes afterwards to hear how it all worked out."

—Paul McCartney

"The Beatles saved the world from boredom."

—George Harrison

With the Beatles

The Beatles broke America with their second album and braced themselves for the unparalleled adoration and hysteria of their teenage fans.

When their second album, *With the Beatles,* went straight to the top of the British charts on its day of release, November 22, 1963, it emphasised that John, Paul, George, and Ringo stood at the very top of pop. Its American equivalent, *Meet the Beatles*, would be issued two months later, excluding five of the original tracks and adding the singles "I Want to Hold Your Hand" and "I Saw Her Standing There."

The album knocked its predecessor, *Please Please Me*, from the U.K. top spot and stayed there for 21 weeks. The Beatles held the U.K. No. 1 position for 51 consecutive weeks. *With the Beatles* had advance orders of half a million and sold another half million by September 1965, making it the second album ever to sell seven figures in the United Kingdom (the first was the *South Pacific* soundtrack).

"RATTLE YOUR JEWELERY"

Seven original Lennon and McCartney compositions provided the backbone of the album, and George Harrison debuted his first, "Don't Bother Me." The album's iconic cover, a monochrome photograph by Robert Freeman, would be much imitated in subsequent years.

The song "Not a Second Time" was analyzed in detail by William Mann, music critic of London's *The Times* newspaper, which added further respectability to the Beatles' music. They had played the Royal Variety Performance two weeks prior to the album's launch, where John Lennon advised the Queen and others to "rattle your jewelery" instead of applauding. The Beatles were bulletproof…and they knew it!

◄ The Beatles in their trademark collarless suits, photographed in 1963.

"MERSEY BEAT" ROCKS THE CHARTS

Following the Beatles' success, all roads led to Liverpool for record company talent scouts. Mersey beat—short, sharp songs performed with guitars and vocal harmonies—was the flavor of the year. The Searchers were first to hit the U.K. No. 1, even before the Beatles, with "Sweets For My Sweet" and followed up with "Needles & Pins," while Gerry and the Pacemakers revived Rodgers and Hammerstein show classic "You'll Never Walk Alone" and made it a Liverpool anthem. By 1966, Mersey beat had given way to more adventurous sounds, though many of the lesser groups continued in cabaret.

1964

THE SHANGRI-LAS

Named after a restaurant in their home district of Queens, New York, the Shangri-Las—Mary and Betty Weiss and Mary Ann and Marge Ganser—enjoyed 18 heady months of fame after "Remember (Walking in the Sand)" gave them a Top 5 single in late 1964. The follow-up "Leader of the Pack" became an all-time teen angst standard, with orchestration and sound effects courtesy of producer George "Shadow" Morton. The girls toured with the Beatles, Drifters, and James Brown, though Betty chose not to appear live until 1966.

The Supremes

They were the original "Dreamgirls," taking record label Tamla Motown to new heights of success and creating a superstar in Diana Ross.

Phil Spector may have created some legendary girl groups, but the Supremes from the Tamla Motown stable were the decade's most successful female vocal act. They registered 12 U.S. No. 1 hits, more than anyone except the Beatles and Elvis. Nineteen times they reached the Top 10 between 1964 and 1969. Their glamour and star quality inspired numerous acts, most recently Destiny's Child. And in lead singer Diana Ross they had a future solo superstar.

Mary Wilson and Florence Ballard formed the group the Primettes in Detroit and invited Ross to join when they graduated high school. They signed with Motown, but their first singles, written and produced by Smokey Robinson, failed. They were then teamed with Holland-Dozier-Holland whose writing and production led to a No. 1 hit in August with "Where Did Our Love Go?" "Baby Love" repeated the feat, and within months the Supremes had eclipsed Martha and the Vandellas and the Marvelettes to become the first ladies of Motown. Further U.S. chart-toppers (and H-D-H productions) included "You Keep Me Hangin' On," "Love Is Here and Now You're Gone" and "You Can't Hurry Love."

Label boss/Svengali Berry Gordy took a personal interest in the Supremes' development to the point of starting a relationship with Ross. The erratic Ballard left in 1967; her image simply didn't fit. Cindy Birdsong replaced her. Ballard died in poverty in 1976, unable to live a "normal" life. On Birdsong's arrival, the group became known as Diana Ross and the Supremes, presaging her inevitable solo career that began in 1970. The Supremes soldiered on with Jean Terrell, but further changes and lack of commitment from Motown led to a disappointing end to the story.

Mary Wilson's autobiography, *Dreamgirls*, told the behind-the-scenes tale, while Diana Ross remains a superstar with many solo hits and film appearances to her credit. *Dreamgirls* was made into a Tony-winning Broadway musical in 1981 and an Oscar- and Grammy-winning movie in 2006.

The Supremes (from left to right) Florence Ballard, Diana Ross, and Mary Wilson. ▶

Where were you when?

"Diana and I were the same kind of people. She wanted what I wanted. We saw it up there, we set out to get it and vowed never to let our personal relationship affect it."

—Berry Gordy

"I used to have an LP by The Supremes where they covered a whole load of Beatles songs. They called it something like The Supremes in Liverpool *and the group were dressed in bowler hats. Nobody in Liverpool has ever worn a bowler hat. It was like* The Beatles in New York, *with the Beatles wearing stetsons."*

—Nigel McLean, Kirby, Lancashire

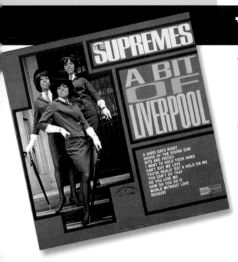

◀ The Supremes' take on Mersey Beat: *A Bit of Liverpool.*

BOSSA NOVA CRAZE

Astrud Gilberto, the Queen of bossa nova, has never been able to escape the hit that made her name in 1964. "The Girl From Ipanema" not only introduced the world to Astrud's talents, but also the treasure trove that is Brazilian music, and the love affair has continued. She had emigrated to the United States the previous year with musician husband Joao Gilberto, and sang on the recording at his suggestion, never having performed professionally before. The reward was a Grammy award-winning song, though she and Joao divorced soon after. Stage fright crippled her performing career, but she made a comeback in the 1980s with the help of son Marcelo Gilberto.

Brazilian chanteuse, Astrud Gilberto, pictured at the Grammys. ▶

1964

STAND-OUT SINGLES

"Twist and Shout"—**The Beatles**

"Under the Boardwalk"
   —**The Drifters**

"I Saw Her Standing There"
   —**The Beatles**

"I'm Into Something Good"
   —**Herman's Hermits**

"Viva Las Vegas"—**Elvis Presley**

"I Get Around"—**The Beach Boys**

"Pink Panther Theme"
   —**Henry Mancini**

"My Guy"—**Mary Wells**

"Fun, Fun, Fun"—**The Beach Boys**

"I Want to Hold Your Hand"
   —**The Beatles**

"Rag Doll"—**Four Seasons**

"She's Not There"—**The Zombies**

"Do Wah Diddy Diddy"
   —**Manfred Mann**

"Chapel of Love"—**Dixie Cups**

"You Really Got Me"—**The Kinks**

"The Way You Do the Things You Do"
   —**Temptations**

"Dancing in the Streets"
   —**Martha and the Vandellas**

"Oh, Pretty Woman"—**Roy Orbison**

Peter Noone (left) appeared in long-running British TV soap *Coronation Street* before going on to front Herman's Hermits at the tender age of 15. ▼

Where were you when?

"Now, something for the youngsters. Five singing boys from England who sold a lot of albums. They're called The Rolling Stones. I've been rolled while I was stoned myself. I don't know what they're singing about…but here they are."

—Dean Martin, introducing the Stones on TV show
The Hollywood Palace, June 13, 1964.

The British Invasion

The Beatles' early successes fueled a huge demand for British pop acts in the States. The Animals, Kinks, and latterly the Rolling Stones answered the call.

Up until this year the United States had dominated the popular music scene. But the arrival at No. 1 of the Beatles in February with "I Want to Hold Your Hand" began a British invasion that threatened U.S. pop music supremacy for the very first time.

Five more Beatles chart-toppers this year nailed the Union Jack to the top of the *Billboard* chart, while the Animals, Manfred Mann, and Peter and Gordon also had No. 1 hits. The Zombies, Dave Clark Five, Gerry and the Pacemakers, the Kinks, and Rolling Stones were also hit makers. The fact that London was fast becoming the center of the fashion world also worked in Britain's favor; the miniskirts and long, straight hairstyles of Patti Boyd and Jean Shrimpton became an immediate fashion statement, while future members of the Byrds and others took their cues from *A Hard Day's Night*.

Groups like Herman's Hermits, a second-division outfit in their native Britain, were launched in the United States after scoring a Christmas hit with "I'm Into Something Good." They became a sort of Beatles substitute, with music–hall derived songs like "I'm Henry VIII, I Am" and "Two Lovely Black Eyes." Other outfits, like Peter and Gordon and Chad and Jeremy, also offered an unthreatening variation on the British beat that was more popular Stateside than at home, the latter playing on their origins with Union Jack waistcoats.

The Rolling Stones and Animals were more durable talents, with wider-ranging appeal and threatening, surly frontmen in Mick Jagger and Eric Burdon respectively. The Animals rocked up a traditional American folksong, "House of the Rising Sun" and gained a transatlantic No. 1—a real coals-to-Newcastle story—while the Stones became the biggest televised sensation since Elvis Presley.

By 1967, America had struck back with the twin thrust of the Monkees and the hippie music movement, whose bells, beads, and kaftans made Swinging London and its sounds suddenly seem passé.

◄ April 8, 1964, the Rolling Stones appear on the bill for The Mod Ball held at the Empire Pool, Wembley, and televised by British pop program *Ready, Steady Go!*

SAM COOKE IS SHOT

Born in 1931, minister's son, Sam Cooke, was an important early figure in the creation and development of soul music; Otis Redding and Marvin Gaye were among his ardent fans. Sadly, he was to lose his life in a mysterious shooting incident in December 1964, aged just 33. Having booked into a Los Angeles motel with a girl he'd met at a club, Cooke was apparently enraged when she fled. Motel manageress Bertha Franklin shot him after he allegedly punched and threatened her: unproven rumors suggested he was robbed by the girl who fled with his cash and some of his clothes. Whatever the truth, music lost the hitmaker of "Wonderful World," "Bring It On Home to Me," and "Another Saturday Night," just three of the many classic songs that remain his legacy.

1964

TOP-SELLING ALBUMS

Meet The Beatles—**The Beatles**

A Hard Day's Night—**The Beatles**

Mary Poppins
   —**Original Soundtrack**

My Fair Lady
   —**Original Soundtrack**

Fiddler on the Roof
   —**Original Soundtrack**

The Barbra Streisand Album
   —**Barbra Streisand**

Money in the Horn—**Al Hirt**

Hello Dolly—**Louis Armstrong**

Beach Boys Concert
   —**Beach Boys**

▲ The original soundtrack of the movie *My Fair Lady*, starring Audrey Hepburn.

Though all songs on *A Hard Day's Night* are credited to Lennon and McCartney, John Lennon wrote the majority of the 13 tracks. ▼

Where were you when?

"We were sitting around at Twickenham studios having a little brain-storming session…. Ringo would do these little malapropisms, he would say things slightly wrong, like people do, but his were always wonderful, very lyrical…they were sort of magic even though he was just getting it wrong. And he said after a concert, 'Phew, it's been a hard day's night.'"

—Paul McCartney

"I made up my mind that this was the same sort of mass hit hysteria that had characterized the Elvis Presley days."

—Ed Sullivan speaking to *The New York Times* about his decision in late 1963 to book The Beatles.

Beatles—A Hard Day's Night

Their debut on *Ed Sullivan* had kick-started the Beatles' popularity in the United States, while their debut film helped confirm the impact of Beatlemania.

There had been rock exploitation films before, but *A Hard Day's Night* was different, not least because it starred the world's most popular group. First of a three-movie deal the Beatles inked with United Artists, it was produced over a period of 16 weeks in the spring of 1964. This relatively short time frame and the fact that it was shot in black and white reflected the studio's belief that Beatlemania would not last beyond the summer.

Its spoof documentary format about a group on the rise but trapped by their own fame inspired a generation of American youth to pick up guitars and aim for stardom, eager to follow the Fab Four's example: David Crosby said, "I came out (of the theater) and swung around a post arm's length going, 'Yes!' I went into that movie and came out knowing what I wanted to do with the rest of my life." An unprecedented number of prints were made, allowing 500 movie theaters to screen it simultaneously after its August 12 premiere at New York's Beacon Theater.

The title was allegedly Ringo's invention, but some say the phrase, which indicates the relentless nature of fame, had already appeared in a John Lennon poem. The song of that name became a transatlantic chart-topper in the summer of 1964 and won a Grammy for the year's best vocal group performance. The LP was not only the Beatles' first soundtrack album but the first album to consist entirely of Lennon and McCartney songs.

The film also represented a satire on the image of rock 'n' roll music as rebellious, portraying the Beatles as simple lads amazed at the attention they received.

A Hard Day's Night proved an international success, bringing in almost $14 million on its initial release. The film's director, Richard Lester, was retained to work on the Beatles' 1965 film, *Help!*

◄ Ed Sullivan introduces the Beatles on his TV variety program, February 9, 1964, their first live appearance on American TV. They went on to play their first gig at the Washington Coliseum on February 11.

"YOU REALLY GOT ME"

The Kinks' breakthrough single from 1964 radiated excitement from the very first distorted riff, a sound created by guitarist Dave Davies taking a razorblade to his amp's speaker and almost electrocuting himself in the process. Dissatisfied with the first recorded version, his singer-songwriter brother, Ray, had threatened to quit music altogether unless the band were allowed to re-record it—and was rewarded when it opened their chart career with a No. 7 hit (topping the chart at home). The song is often credited with inventing heavy metal but Dave Davies prefers to think of it as "the first heavy guitar riff rock record." It has been recorded by Van Halen, Mott the Hoople, Robert Palmer, and many more but never bettered.

The Kinks, with singer-songwriter Ray Davies second from left. ►

1965

"I CAN'T EXPLAIN" —THE WHO

While it would take an incendiary performance at 1967's Monterey Pop festival to initiate American chart success, the Who were making waves in their home country. "I Can't Explain" gave them their first U.K. Top 10 entry and would be followed up the charts by "Anyway Anyhow Anywhere" and "My Generation," each noisier and more rebellious than its predecessor. Pete Townshend's guitar smashing, Roger Daltrey's mike-swinging, and Keith Moon's manic drumming were already marking them down as a band going places, and this was recognized when the American TV program *Shindig Goes to London* featured them in performance in December. They first played the United States in March 1967 on a Murray the K show.

▲ The Who's first album, *My Generation*, was released in the United States under the title *The Who Sings My Generation*. The title song was inducted into the Grammy Hall of Fame in 1999.

Dylan Goes Electric

Dylan turned his back on the acoustic guitar—a controversial move that sent ripples through the folk and rock music scene.

Bob Dylan's rise to fame as the tousle-haired poet of folk and protest had understandably led to that musical movement taking a proprietary interest in him. Unfortunately, the marriage was to be dissolved in very public fashion at the 1965 Newport Folk festival. Dylan had graced the stage before, acoustic guitar in hand. But if the folk establishment had been shocked when his "Subterranean Homesick Blues" single had charted and he'd recorded rock tracks for his album *Bringing It All Back Home*, they could not have been prepared for his Newport appearance.

The previous day, Alan Lomax sneeringly introduced Paul Butterfield's Blues Band— "Let's see if these Chicago boys know what the blues are all about"— and had been punched by Dylan's manager, Albert Grossman, for his trouble. Now, on July 25, they, along with keyboardists Barry Goldberg and Al Kooper, turned in an electrified and electrifying set behind Dylan, who howled his forthcoming Top 10 hit "Like a Rolling Stone" as if his life depended on it. Legend has it that folk doyen Pete Seeger grabbed an axe and threatened to cut the power. The combination of Dylan's lyrics and electric music—showcased later in 1965 on *Highway 61 Revisited*—would open a new chapter in his career.

Far from selling out, as the die-hard folk "mafia" claimed, Dylan was now going to influence popular music from the inside and not rely on other people's recordings to spread his message. (The Byrds' version of "Mr. Tambourine Man" sat atop the charts as he played.) And his message annoyed the folkies because, unlike them, he didn't believe the big bad world could be changed. Pete Seeger had opened the Newport Festival with the words "we shall overcome." Dylan's world view was somewhat bleaker.

Picking up with the Band as his back-up musicians, he was to enjoy another year of influence until he was stopped in his tracks by a motorcycle accident. Immediately prior to that, he had famously endured the taunt of "Judas" from an audience member at London's Royal Albert Hall. After Newport he was, at least, prepared for it.

Dylan performing at the Newport Folk Festival July 25, 1965. ▶

Where were you when?

"From the moment the group swung into a rocking electric version of 'Maggie's Farm,' the Newport audience registered hostility. As the group finished 'Farm,' there was some reserved applause and a flurry of boos."

—Journalist Robert Shelton

"I had no idea why they were booing…. I don't think anybody was there having a negative response to those songs, though. Whatever it was about, it wasn't about anything that they were hearing."

—Bob Dylan

PHILIPS INTRODUCES THE TAPE CASSETTE

The compact cassette made its debut in 1963 as a recording medium, but it was soon apparent that it had possibilities as a player of music, too. With narrow $1/8$-inch ferric tape moving at a slow $1\,7/8$ inches per second, sound quality was not good, but portability was the main attraction. This year Dutch firm Philips, who had invented the concept, made licenses available to manufacturers of tapes and machines, and pre-recorded music cassettes would become available from 1966 onward. Further landmarks came in 1970 with the Dolby B noise reduction system and 1979 with the introduction of the Walkman. The equally portable and considerably higher-fidelity compact disc began to kill off the format in the 1980s.

A 1965 Grundig C100 cassette recorder. ▶

1965

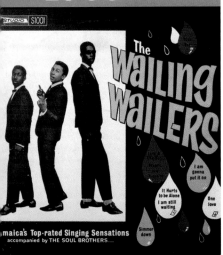

STUDIO S1001

The WAILING WAILERS

I am gonna put it on

It Hurts to be Alone
I am still waiting

One love

Simmer down

maica's Top-rated Singing Sensations
accompanied by THE SOUL BROTHERS...

TOP-SELLING SINGLES

"(I Can't Get No) Satisfaction"
— **The Rolling Stones**

"You've Lost That Lovin' Feelin'"
— **The Righteous Brothers**

"I Can't Help Myself (Sugar Pie,
Honey Bunch)"—**The Four Tops**

"Mrs. Brown You've Got a Lovely
Daughter"—**Herman's Hermits**

"Yesterday"—**The Beatles**

"Downtown"—**Petula Clark**

"Turn! Turn! Turn!"—**The Byrds**

"Stop! In the Name of Love"
—**The Supremes**

"Help!"—**The Beatles**

▲ The Wailing Wailers' 1965 LP featured a
young Bob Marley (center) but yielded no
monster-selling singles.

Manfred Mann's "Do Wah Diddy Diddy"
reached No. 1 in the United States. ▼

FEATURING "DO WAH DIDDY DIDDY"

The Five
Faces of Manfred Mann

Sonny & Cher

Husband and wife duo Sonny and Cher became the acceptable face of the hippie counterculture with their worldwide hit "I Got You Babe."

On the face of it, 30-year-old Italian-American Sonny Bono and his darkly glamorous Armenian-Cherokee wife, Cher, 11 years his junior, were an odd couple. But in 1965 they became pop's biggest duo since the Everly Brothers. They caught the mood of the moment with a sanitized version of West Coast bohemianism.

Bono began his music career working for producer Phil Spector in the early 1960s. One of his earliest songwriting efforts was "Needles and Pins," a hit for the Searchers. And while he couldn't persuade Spector to record Cher, whom he married in 1964, she did backup vocals for the Crystals and Ronettes. The couple's initial recordings as Caesar and Cleo, however, proved unpopular.

"I Got You Babe," a Sonny-penned declaration of love enhanced by Harold Battiste's flute and oboe orchestration deftly pastiching the Spector sound, hit the teen market with considerable force, reaching No. 1 in both the United States and Britain. And while they would never achieve the same heights again, solo singles "Laugh At Me" (Sonny) and "All I Really Want to Do" (Cher) were chart successes.

DO YOU BELIEVE IN LIFE AFTER LOVE?

A shift into movies backfired, and as groups with more charisma, like the Mamas and the Papas, seized their chart crown, Sonny and Cher slid sideways to the safety of the cabaret circuit. A syndicated TV show followed. They divorced in the mid 1970s, and Sonny (who died in 1998 in a skiing accident) went on to become a successful politician, while Cher managed to reinvent herself not once but three times. Her 1970s career as a reedy chart-topping pop singer with the likes of "Gypsies Tramps and Thieves" was followed by stints as a rock chick in the 1980s and a club diva in the 1990s. In 1998 her single "Believe" hit the No. 1 spot in 23 countries, including the United Kingdom and the United States. "I Got You Babe" remains an iconic single reflecting the innocent side of the 1960s and will probably be remembered most as the wake-up call for Bill Murray in *Groundhog Day*.

Sony and Cher pose for a 1965 photoshoot. ▶

Where were you when?

"People have said to me, 'You can't write songs. You can't play an instrument.' But I've got 10 gold records."
—Sonny Bono

"I'm still friends with all my exes, apart from my husbands."
—Cher

"Don't cling to fame. You're just borrowing it. It's like money. You're going to die, and somebody else is going to get it."
—Sonny Bono

JEFF BECK REPLACES CLAPTON IN THE YARDBIRDS

British blues band the Yardbirds provided a launchpad for three master lead guitarists—in chronological order, Eric Clapton, Jeff Beck, and Jimmy Page. After the early-1965 chart success of the poppy "For Your Love," blues buff Clapton headed for the comparatively purist ranks of John Mayall's Bluesbreakers, and Jeff Beck from the little-known Tridents was drafted in as his replacement. Beck's fretboard pyrotechnics would change the musical direction of the group and establish them as forefathers of the classic rock of the 1970s and beyond. "Heart Full of Soul," "Evil Hearted You," and "Shapes of Things" would widen their appeal, while the recruitment of Jimmy Page as second lead guitarist later confirmed them as the forerunners of Led Zeppelin—who, in the early days, were billed as the New Yardbirds.

The Yardbirds' mid-1960s lineup with Jeff Beck far left. ▶

1966

THE BEACH BOYS— *PET SOUNDS*

Having made their first impression four years earlier as a family-based group of all-American boys promoting surf culture, the Beach Boys now lent their name to an epic recording that was altogether different. *Pet Sounds* was a piece of uplifting mood music that in the words of Beatles producer George Martin "gives you an elation that is beyond logic." Indeed, it's said that not only was Brian Wilson inspired by *Rubber Soul* but that hearing *Pet Sounds* inspired Paul McCartney to respond with the Beatles' *Sgt. Pepper* the following year. The American public was confused by the Beach Boys' apparent change of direction. *Pet Sounds* reached only No. 10 but has since been recognized as one of the era's musical landmarks (it is No. 2 on *Rolling Stone*'s list of 500 Greatest Albums of all time). In June 2006 surviving members—Brian Wilson, Mike Love, Al Jardine, Bruce Johnston, and David Marks— reunited to celebrate *Pet Sounds*' fortieth anniversary.

Where were you when?

"*My wife was mad keen on Davey Jones when she was a teenager and when The Monkees played a concert in London she queued all day to make sure she was at the very front of the stage. The moment Davey Jones came on stage she fainted and had to be taken to the First Aid post. She missed the whole concert.*"

—John Heritage, North London

"*When they get it all sorted out, they might turn out to be the best.*"

—George Harrison

Hey, Hey, We're the Monkees

A Beatles-inspired TV show created real-life chart success for the madcap boy band The Monkees.

Linking the appeal of pop music to the power of television proved a winning formula for writer-producers Bert Schneider and Bob Rafelson when in 1966 they created a band to feature in "their own" TV series. Inspired by the success of the Beatles' spoof documentary *A Hard Day's Night*, they selected four of the 437 actors and musicians who applied, and instant stardom resulted.

I'M A BELIEVER

Record company mogul Don Kirshner backed the program with an advertising budget of $100,000—twice the amount with which Capitol Records had launched the Beatles two years earlier. By the end of the following year, Mike Nesmith, Davy Jones, Peter Tork, and Micky Dolenz would be worldwide stars, thanks to the power of the small screen. Their first single "I'm A Believer" and their debut album *The Monkees* topped the U.S. chart simultaneously, underlining their multi-media domination. But the quartet's ambitions would not let them remain puppets, and they demanded to create the backing on their records, replacing session musicians. Songwriter Tommy Boyce was not convinced, though. "Micky had the Paul McCartney voice, he could really sing. Davy had a passable ballad voice, Mike thought he was Merle Haggard and Peter had no voice at all." They toured with Jimi Hendrix as a support act, but it was a mismatch. As the hits faded, after early 1968's "Valleri," they created the film *Head*, a flop at the time but a major cult item since. The Monkees had grown up faster than their audience, and first Tork and then Nesmith would quit, leaving Jones and Dolenz to cut a ninth and final album under the name in 1970.

Reunions of various members of the so-called Pre–Fab Four have occurred in subsequent years, while affectionate recordings of their hits have come from the Sex Pistols ("I'm Not Your Steppin' Stone"), Blink 182, and others.

◄ Performing on the set of their TV show, *The Monkees*, in 1966.

SLICK JOINS AIRPLANE

When up and coming San Francisco bands Jefferson Airplane and the Great Society shared a bill at the city's Fillmore West in January, a connection was made that, in October, would lead to the latter's vocalist, Grace Slick, defecting. She brought with her two classic songs, "White Rabbit" and "Somebody to Love," that would hit the Top 10 in 1967 and establish Jefferson Airplane as leading members of the drug-influenced hippie counterculture. Slick made a particularly profound connection with guitarist Paul Kantner, and the result in 1971 was a daughter, originally christened God but eventually named China.

Grace Slick at a London reception for Jefferson Airplane. ▶

1966
HEY JOE
JIMI HENDRIX EXPERIENCE

CHAS CHANDLER DISCOVERS HENDRIX

When Briton Chas Chandler, bass player on Animals hits like "House of the Rising Sun," was introduced to flamboyant guitarist/singer Jimi Hendrix while in New York, he knew he had found the star to launch his managerial career. Chandler flew the former Little Richard sideman to London and, after unsuccessfully attempting to recruit Brian Auger's Trinity, signed up backing musicians Mitch Mitchell (drums) and Noel Redding (bass) to complete the Jimi Hendrix Experience. Initial recordings included garage-band classic "Hey Joe" (pictured above), which became the band's first single in December 1966. It shot to No. 6 in the U.K. chart and set up Hendrix to make 1967 his year with a triumphant return to his home country at Monterey.

Where were you when?

"They say the Beatles gave up touring because of the reaction in the United States, but they forget that there was a riot in the Philippines when they played in 1966. They refused an invitation to a State dinner with Imelda Marcos, so she got the television companies to film their empty chairs and disappointed kids like they hadn't shown up. At the airport the Beatles had to take shelter with nuns because of all the angry people. It was chaos."

—Tan Lanta, Quezon City, Manila

Beatles Outrage America

John Lennon's claim that the Beatles were more popular than Christ backfired spectacularly, while an ill-fated America tour sent them back to the studio.

The Beatles' love-hate relationship with both the United States and live performance would come to a head this year when they bowed out of touring altogether with a final August date at San Francisco's Candlestick Park.

The tour had started inauspiciously when an extract from a pretour John Lennon interview with London's *Evening Standard* was interpreted by teen magazine *Datebook* as a boast that his group was more popular than Christ. While this was not Lennon's intention, the removal of the Beatles' current album, *Revolver*, from radio playlists in the South and accusations of blasphemy from some quarters led manager Brian Epstein to try to cancel the Beatles' third American tour amid fears of a possible assassination attempt.

A contrite Lennon made peace at a press conference when the tour kicked off in Chicago on August 12, but stage appearances had long been unsatisfying for the quartet, who could not hear what they were singing or playing due to crowd noise. Performing behind six-foot fences with 200 police on hand to an audience of screaming fans had long since lost its luster. The *Hard Day's Night* scenario no longer appealed.

The final concert at San Francisco's Candlestick Park on August 29 was not advertised as such, or the stadium's 20,000 empty seats would surely have been filled. The Fab Four performed precisely 33 minutes of music to the assembled 25,000 crowd before bolting to an armored van that had been waiting behind the stage with its engine running.

As the Beatles flew out of San Francisco toward a studio-bound future, George Harrison remarked: "Well, that's it then. I'm not a Beatle anymore." As it transpired, he was wrong: Confining the band to the studio would yield stunning musical results, most notably the following year's *Sgt. Pepper*.

◄ The Beatles in their promotional video for the single "Paperback Writer" at Abbey Road, London, May 1966.

LENNON REGRETS "BEATLES BIGGER THAN JESUS" QUOTE:

"Christianity will go. It will vanish and shrink. I needn't argue with that; I'm right and I will be proved right. We're more popular than Jesus now; I don't know which will go first—rock and roll or Christianity. Jesus was all right, but his disciples were thick and ordinary. It's them twisting it that ruins it for me."

—John Lennon, published in England's *Evening Standard* newspaper (March 4, 1966) as part of an interview with writer Maureen Cleave

The Beatles at Chiswick House, London, during the making of a promotional film for "Paperback Writer," May 20, 1966. ▶

1966

NO. 1 SINGLES

"The Sound of Silence"
—**Simon & Garfunkel**

"We Can Work It Out"—**The Beatles**

"My Love"—**Petula Clark**

"Lightnin' Strikes"—**Lou Christie**

"These Boots Are Made for Walkin'"
—**Nancy Sinatra**

"(You're My) Soul and Inspiration"
—**The Righteous Brothers**

"Good Lovin'"—**The Young Rascals**

"Monday, Monday"
—**The Mamas & The Papas**

"When a Man Loves a Woman"
—**Percy Sledge**

"Paint It, Black"
—**The Rolling Stones**

"Paperback Writer"—**The Beatles**

"Wild Thing"—**The Troggs**

"Summer in the City"
—**The Lovin' Spoonful**

"Sunshine Superman"—**Donovan**

"You Can't Hurry Love"
—**The Supremes**

"Cherish"—**The Association**

"Reach Out I'll Be There"
—**The Four Tops**

"Last Train to Clarksville"
—**The Monkees**

"Poor Side of Town"
—**Johnny Rivers**

"You Keep Me Hangin' On"
—**The Supremes**

"Winchester Cathedral"
—**New Vaudeville Band**

"Good Vibrations"
—**The Beach Boys**

"I'm a Believer"—**The Monkees**

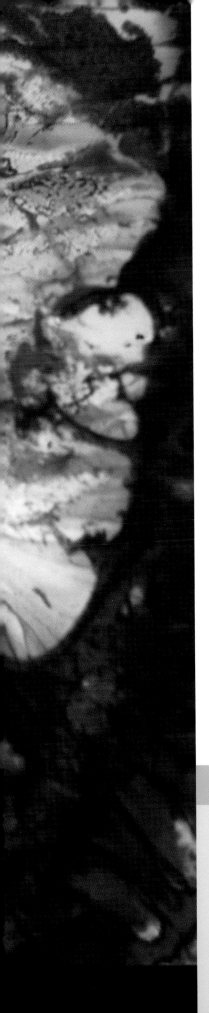

The Doors

The Doors' residency at Hollywood club, Whisky A Go Go, showcased Jim Morrison—one of the most charismatic figures in rock history.

The Doors' recording career was relatively brief—less than four and a half years. Yet their reputation as one of America's seminal bands, fronted by the enigmatic, charismatic, and often outrageous vocalist Jim Morrison, remains. And it was at the Whisky A Go Go nightclub on Los Angeles's Sunset Boulevard, where they played a four-month residency in the middle of 1966, that the first pages of the legend were written.

It was Morrison who suggested the name the Doors to keyboardist Ray Manzarek, referring to Aldous Huxley's *The Doors of Perception*, a description of the results of using the drug mescaline. Guitarist Robbie Krieger and drummer John Densmore completed the four-man lineup. Manzarek added keyboard bass in the absence of a bass guitar.

Their status as house band, which began in late May, allowed the Doors to play backup for established acts. Love main man Arthur Lee was so impressed when they supported his band that he recommended them to Elektra Records. Playing two sets a night forced the Doors to expand their repertoire, thus shaping the band's sound. "Repeat and stretch," said Manzarek, who explained that this was when their 1967 chart-topping single "Light My Fire" developed its extended guitar and organ solos.

Their first LP, simply titled *The Doors* and released in March 1967, was effectively the highlight of their stage act. Its double-platinum status suggests it touched a chord in the hearts and minds of a considerable army of listeners. Over 2 million copies were sold, winning it a lengthy U.S. chart residency of well over two years (beyond chart-topping successor *Waiting for the Sun*).

The Doors album kicked off a period of success mixed with controversy (Morrison was arrested several times for on- and off-stage misdemeanors) that was ended by the singer's mysterious death from a reported heart attack in Paris in 1971. Innumerable bands have been inspired by the Doors over the decades, and Manzarek and Krieger revived the name in 2003 with ex–Cult singer Ian Astbury filling Morrison's unfillable shoes.

◄ Morrison was renowned for his unpredictable stage persona.

BLONDE ON BLONDE—BOB DYLAN

Rock's first double album registered yet another career peak for Bob Dylan. *Blonde on Blonde* was created in eight days of sessions in February and March, backed by the cream of Nashville's session musicians. By May it was in the racks. Many of the songs were unfinished when he took them to the studio. "Sad Eyed Lady of the Lowlands" lasted an epic 11 minutes—the first song to fill an entire side of vinyl. Dylan's writing was consistently brilliant, and *Blonde on Blonde* retains its iconic status as an off-the-wall classic.

1967

ROLLING STONES' DRUG BUST

The jailing in London of Rolling Stones' Keith Richards and Mick Jagger on drug possession offenses made headlines in July following a police raid on Richards' Sussex mansion the previous February. While the duo were quickly bailed pending appeal, public concern as to whether they were being made scapegoats as representatives of the "alternative society" inspired an editorial in London's *The Times*, headed "Who Breaks a Butterfly on a Wheel?" Jagger's sentence was commuted to a conditional discharge and Richards' quashed altogether, but the episode prevented them from appearing at the Monterey Festival. In the longer term, an overdue debate on soft drugs and standards of morality in general had begun.

◄ Mick Jagger is mobbed as he leaves court in Chichester, Sussex, after being bailed on drug charges.

The Beatles Release Sgt. Pepper

The Beatles survived their "bigger than Jesus" controversy to release what many critics believe to be the album of the century.

When the Beatles turned their backs on live performance halfway through their career, they opened up groundbreaking studio possibilities. The massively influential *Sgt. Pepper's Lonely Hearts Club Band* was their magnum opus.

The album took six months to assemble at Abbey Road, clocking up 700 hours of studio time in contrast to their hurriedly recorded early works, and employing four-track technology pushed to its limits by producer George Martin and engineer Geoff Emerick.

The music was mainly Paul McCartney's brainchild: It was also his idea to name the album after the title song and reprise that song at the end. And while the result was not strictly a concept album, the combination of segued tracks (another innovation) with Peter Blake's groundbreaking collage cover has made it so. (The album cover also set new trends by having a gatefold sleeve and full lyrics to all the songs.)

Lennon's major contribution, "A Day in the Life," was inspired by a newspaper story, while "Being for the Benefit of Mr. Kite" came from a circus poster found in an antique shop. Inspiration was everywhere, and the Beatles picked up on it. As did the public; the album spent 15 weeks on top of the *Billboard* chart and won a Best Album Grammy.

Sgt. Pepper should be considered alongside the single "Penny Lane/Strawberry Fields Forever," which came out four months earlier but was not included on the album (both related to childhood memories of Liverpool, the album's original intended theme). The latter's druggy ambience was echoed by "Lucy in the Sky with Diamonds," a track its author Lennon unconvincingly insisted had nothing to do with LSD.

Critics claim the release of this album in June 1967 fired the starting gun for the Summer of Love. One thing is for sure: The Beatles had set the benchmark against which all rock albums of the future would be measured.

With no intention of touring to promote the album, the Beatles settled for the tried and tested routine of a promotional film. ►

TRACK LISTING

Side One
Sgt. Pepper's Lonely Hearts
   Club Band
With a Little Help From
   My Friends
Lucy in the Sky with Diamonds
Getting Better
Fixing a Hole
She's Leaving Home
Being for the Benefit of Mr. Kite!

Side Two
Within You Without You
When I'm Sixty-Four
Lovely Rita
Good Morning Good Mor
Sgt. Pepper's Lonely Hea
   Club Band (Reprise)
A Day in the Life

◄ The iconic album cover conceptualized by Peter Blake.

MONTEREY POP FESTIVAL

John Phillips, the leader of The Mamas and the Papas, was the prime mover behind 1967's Monterey Pop Festival in California. Stars of the event included Otis Redding—a last-minute replacement for the Beach Boys—whose stomping soul received an ovation from the almost exclusively white crowd, suggesting superstardom had he lived beyond the end of the year (he died in a plane crash), and Jimi Hendrix, playing on the final night, whose return to his home country after success in Britain raised his profile several levels. San Francisco bands like Jefferson Airplane and Canned Heat, along with the Grateful Dead and Big Brother and the Holding Company (featuring Janis Joplin), stole the show. This triggered a feeding frenzy, with record company A&R men swamping the city in an attempt to sniff out and sign the best talent.

PiNK FLOYD

STAND-OUT ALBUMS

Piper at the Gates of Dawn
—**Pink Floyd**

The Monkees—**The Monkees**

*Sgt. Pepper's Lonely Hearts
Club Band*—**The Beatles**

The Doors—**The Doors**

Surrealistic Pillow
—**Jefferson Airplane**

Vanilla Fudge—**Vanilla Fudge**

The Velvet Underground & Nico
—**The Velvet Underground
& Nico**

Are You Experienced?
—**Jimi Hendrix Experience**

Scott—**Scott Walker**

A Quick One—**The Who**

Buffalo Springfield Again
—**Buffalo Springfield**

Mr. Fantasy—**Traffic**

Days of Future Passed
—**The Moody Blues**

Disraeli Gears—**Cream**

Between the Buttons
—**Rolling Stones**

▲ Pink Floyd's debut album, *Piper at the Gates of Dawn*, had a major influence on psychedelic rock music. It was recorded at EMI's Abbey Road studios while the Beatles were laying down tracks for *Sgt. Pepper* in the studio next door.

Where were you when?

"Haight Ashbury was a ghetto of bohemians who wanted to do anything—and we did…. Yes, there was LSD. But Haight Ashbury was not about drugs. It was about exploration, finding new ways of expression, being aware of one's existence."

—Grateful Dead guitarist Bob Weir

"Drop out. Leave society as you have known it. Leave it utterly. Blow the mind of every straight person you can reach. Turn them on, if not to drugs, then to beauty, love, honesty, fun."

—"The Hippies: The Philosophy of a Subculture" (*Time* magazine, July 7, 1967)

Let's All Go to San Francisco

The Haight-Ashbury district of San Francisco became the center of the hippie revolution, which culminated in the flower children's "Summer of Love."

As the 1960s progressed, San Francisco overtook Los Angeles as not only the hub of American entertainment culture but the pulsing heartbeat of the "Summer of Love."

The popular style of music in the Bay Area was folk, and the likes of the Grateful Dead and Jefferson Airplane simply plugged into amplifiers, took drugs, and expressed the feelings that resulted in psychedelic rock music. There was a growing audience; venues like the Carousel Ballroom (renamed the Fillmore West by promoter Bill Graham) and the Avalon were hives of musical activity, their own light shows adding to the druggy effect, while bands like Quicksilver Messenger Service, Steve Miller, and Moby Grape were all signed by record companies seeking the "next big thing."

The growing hippie community centered itself around the Haight-Ashbury district. This group had succeeded the Beat poets as a significant cultural force as early as 1965. The hippie, with bells, beads, flowers, kaftans, and long hair, had become the latest stereotype, and with LSD still legal, it was possible to take the advice of Timothy Leary to "turn on, tune in, and drop out."

THE DREAM DIES

But the Summer of Love would prove both the climax and the end of the hippie movement. An influx of newcomers diluted the spirit that had made the Human Be In—held that January in Golden Gate Park—such a success, and the original "freaks" left.

Acid was reclassified as illegal, and with Vietnam and the draft on the agenda, peace and love couldn't last forever. So as songs like Scott McKenzie's "San Francisco (Be Sure to Wear Flowers in Your Hair)" topped the charts, the hippie dream was already on the wane. It would remain, however, a fashion statement for "straights" to adopt on weekends.

◄ Tom Wolfe (author of *The Electric Kool-Aid Acid Test*) talks with Jerry Garcia (center) of the Grateful Dead and the band's manager, Rock Scully, on the corner of Ashbury and Haight streets in San Francisco.

THE VELVET UNDERGROUND & NICO

The Velvet Underground were the darlings of New York art circles: the cover of their debut album was designed by Andy Warhol, while classically trained bassist John Cale added a dissonance and repetition to their work that would prove highly influential on electronic pop music in the 1970s. The deadpan delivery of singers Lou Reed (also chief songwriter) and Nico was in stark contrast to everything else on offer in the Summer of Love. Innumerable bands and artists from David Bowie through Roxy Music to Ultravox would take leaves from their style book. Andy Warhol would fade from the story as Reed took artistic control prior to his successful solo career, but there's an argument that it was *The Velvet Underground & Nico* that was the most influential album of the year, not *Sgt. Pepper*.

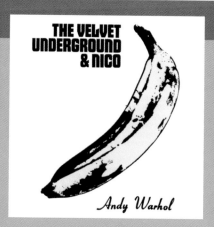

The record is sometimes referred to as the "Banana Album." ▶

1967

NO. 1 SINGLES

"I'm a Believer"—**The Monkees**

"Kind of a Drag"
—**The Buckinghams**

"Ruby Tuesday"
—**The Rolling Stones**

"Love is Here and Now You're Gone"
—**The Supremes**

"Penny Lane"—**The Beatles**

"Happy Together"—**The Turtles**

"Somethin' Stupid"—**Nancy Sinatra and Frank Sinatra**

"The Happening"—**The Supremes**

"Groovin'"—**The Young Rascals**

"Respect"—**Aretha Franklin**

"Light My Fire"—**The Doors**

"All You Need Is Love"
—**The Beatles**

"Ode to Billy Joe"—**Bobbie Gentry**

"To Sir With Love"—**Lulu**

"Daydream Believer"
—**The Monkees**

▲ Diana Ross. The Supremes' theme tune to flop movie *The Happening* reached No. 1 in April 1967.

Where were you when?

"I saw a touring version of Hair *in Ames, Iowa, in 1969, and even though the play had been out a year, it caused the biggest sensation of anything that visited."*

—L. Turner, Phoenix

"We knew this group of kids in the East Village who were dropping out and dodging the draft, and there were also lots of articles in the press about how kids were being kicked out of school for growing their hair long, and we incorporated that in the show too."

—Co-creator James Rado

Hair Debuts

The "Age of Aquarius" dawned with a controversial production that defined the rock musical and gave voice to the anti–Vietnam War movement.

The worlds of rock and theater were miles apart in the mid 1960s. Broadway was not anxious to confront the social issues that made up rock's typical subject matter—drugs, politics, sexuality, Vietnam—and any advances in incorporating these into stage productions were made by fringe theater groups. Not until *Hair*—promoted under the catch-all title "the American tribal love-rock musical"—opened off-Broadway in October 1967 at Joseph Papp's Public Theater did everything come together.

Written by Canadian composer Galt McDermot in collaboration with actors James Rado and Jerome Ragni, *Hair* did everything it could to be risqué. Song titles such as "Hashish," "Sodomy," and "Colored Spade" promised much, but the famous nude finale was added at the direction of businessmen Bernard Castelli and Michael Butler, whose backing took the show to Broadway. *Hair* also broke new ground in featuring a racially integrated cast and encouraging audience participation.

The rock-based musical score was performed by a band rather than the standard 30-piece orchestra, and while such gospel-inspired chants like "Aquarius" and "Let the Sun Shine In" may now seem dated, they captured the mood of the moment. A medley of those songs was a hit for the Fifth Dimension, while "Ain't Got No Grass" and "I Got Life" were taken to the charts by Nina Simone. *Hair* became the first off-Broadway musical to successfully make the transition to the Broadway stage when it opened there in May 1968, taking in about 7 million dollars from 1,750 performances, while its 1,999-show run in London was halted only by a roof collapse. A Los Angeles production featured such soon-to-be famous names as Jennifer Warnes and Meat Loaf.

The show's success paved the way for rock and theater's far closer relationship in the 1970s. Indeed, future *Rocky Horror Picture Show* creator Richard O'Brien and its star Tim Curry met as members of *Hair*'s London cast. But while the show itself is now seen to lack credibility—Galt McDermot later admitted that it was never intended to be more than "a tourist guide to the alternative society"— it retains at least a period charm.

◄ A scene from the off-Broadway production at Joseph Papp's Public Theater.

ROLLING STONE LAUNCHES

Rolling Stone—the brainchild of editor/publisher Jann Wenner—launched in San Francisco on November 9, 1967. Wenner had been encouraged by veteran music critic Ralph J. Gleason to create an underground music paper to reflect the increasingly serious popular music scene. It broke new ground in assuming that the lives of musicians were equally as interesting as politicians or businessmen, and treated them as such. *Rolling Stone* made the name of numerous writers, as well as photographer Annie Liebovitz. A move to New York in 1977 was gradually followed by the inclusion of lifestyle material, movie coverage, and political stories. But even if the focus moved away from music, *Rolling Stone*—now a glossy magazine rather than the original tabloid—remained a trendsetter and tastemaker.

The first issue of *Rolling Stone*, showing John Lennon in a still from the film *How I Won the War*. ▶

THE JIMI HENDRIX EXPERIENCE ELECTRIC LADYLAND

NO. 1 ALBUMS

Magical Mystery Tour—**The Beatles**

The Graduate—**Simon & Garfunkel soundtrack**

Bookends—**Simon & Garfunkel**

The Beat of the Brass—**Herb Alpert & The Tijuana Brass**

Wheels of Fire—**Cream**

Waiting for the Sun—**The Doors**

Cheap Thrills—**Big Brother and the Holding Company**

Electric Ladyland—**Jimi Hendrix Experience**

Wichita Lineman—**Glen Campbell**

▲ *Electric Ladyland* was Jimi Hendrix's only No. 1 album.

Cheap Thrills was the final Big Brother and the Holding Company album to feature Janis Joplin as a lead vocalist. ▼

Marvin Gaye

"I Heard it Through the Grapevine" gave Marvin Gaye his first No. 1 hit and became Motown's biggest selling single of the 1960s.

Among all the Motown legends, Marvin Gaye ranks alongside Stevie Wonder in having transcended his "hit factory" roots to create a more considered, self-composed music that crossed over to a new, sophisticated audience.

The church is the classic background for a soul singer, and since his father was a clergyman, Marvin began singing in the House of God at a very early age. He began at Tamla Motown as a session drummer but sought success as a singer and found it with only his fourth solo release: "Stubborn Kind of Fellow," the first of more than 20 hits. He found even greater success in tandem with Kim Weston and then Tammi Terrell, but Terrell collapsed in Gaye's arms on stage in 1967, and this affected the singer greatly. (She died three years later of a brain tumor at age 24.)

"I Heard It Through the Grapevine" was a song that had already been recorded by the Miracles and the Isley Brothers, but was never released, and Gaye took it and turned it into his first pop chart-topper. With the usual slow Motown pace, along with a string-laden backup track produced by cowriter Norman Whitfield and supporting vocals from the Andantes, the stage was set for Gaye to weave his magic, although it took two months to finalize the vocal. Until the release of the Jackson 5's "I'll Be There" twenty months later, it was the biggest hit single ever released by Motown, though Gaye felt he didn't deserve its 4 million sales success.

Ironically, a version of "Grapevine" by Gladys Knight and the Pips was released in the interim—Motown founder Berry Gordy preferred it to Gaye's—and it reached No. 2 in the pop listings. The annoyed Knight's departure from the label was therefore not unexpected, but Gaye, who married Gordy's daughter Anna, stayed with Motown until 1982.

Signing to CBS/Columbia, he returned to the Top 3 spot in 1983 with "Sexual Healing" but would die the following year at the hands of his father, a bullet bringing to a close both a glittering career and a troubled life. "I Heard It Through the Grapevine" was one of only a handful of Motown classics Marvin retained in his stage set to the end.

Marvin Gaye on the boardwalk in Atlantic City. ▶

Where were you when?

"Just back from an 8 month deployment in Vietnam, I went to a cafeteria to eat and heard Lady Madonna. First new music I heard in a long time and it was great. Nearly as great as the cheeseburger and chocolate malt I was having at the time."

—Ken Cruikshank, South Huntington, N.Y.

"The minute I heard 'Grapevine' on the radio I borrowed money to go out and buy it. His voice blended wonderfully with womens' voices, too. He didn't overwhelm them. He had British chart entries with four different ladies, Mary Wells, Kim Weston, Tammi Terrell and Diana Ross, which is quite an achievement."

—David Pinnel, Luton, England

ELVIS RELAUNCHES CAREER

Having spent the decade making ever more predictable movies, this year found the former King of Rock 'n' Roll taking the first step to regaining his crown. For two days Elvis Presley reunited with former band members Scotty Moore and D.J. Fontana, playing their hits to an appreciative audience. The loose jamming style sessions were edited by producer/director Steve Binder into a one-hour TV special. Broadcast in December 1968 on NBC, and simply titled *Elvis*, the result drew rave reviews and recorded the year's highest viewing figures for a musical special. Elvis was back—well, almost!

Elvis's "Comeback Special" aired on December 3, 1968. ▶

1968

TOP-SELLING SINGLES

"Hey Jude"—**The Beatles**

"I Heard it Through the Grapevine"
—**Marvin Gaye**

"Love Is Blue"—**Paul Mauriat**

"People Got to Be Free"
—**The Rascals**

"Love Child"—**Diana Ross
& The Supremes**

"Honey"—**Bobby Goldsboro**

"(Sittin' on) the Dock of the Bay"
—**Otis Redding**

"This Guy's in Love with You"
—**Herb Alpert**

"Mrs. Robinson"
—**Simon & Garfunkel**

"Judy in Disguise (with Glasses)"
—**John Fred & His Playboy Band**

▲ "(Sittin' on) the Dock of the Bay" was
recorded by Otis Redding three days
before his death. Redding, his manager,
the pilot, and four members of his backup
band, The Bar-Kays, were killed when his
chartered plane crashed into Lake Monona
in Madison, Wisconsin, on December 10,
1967. The posthumous release of "(Sittin'
on) the Dock of the Bay" reached No. 1 in
January 1968.

Where were you when?

*"Most people have formed the impression of us as three solo musicians clashing with
each other. We want to cancel that idea and be a group that plays together."*

—Eric Clapton

*"It wasn't a good gig…. Cream was better than that…. We knew it was all over.
We knew we were just finishing it off, getting it over with."*

—Ginger Baker on the Farewell Concert

Cream

After only two years together, the first "supergroup" of rock split, but their influence lived on in bands such as Led Zeppelin and Deep Purple.

As the less than modest name suggested, Cream comprised virtuoso rock musicians—guitarist Eric Clapton, bass player Jack Bruce, and drummer Ginger Baker, who had made their names and reputations with respected earlier bands, like the Yardbirds, the Bluesbreakers, and the Graham Bond Organization. But with such talents came egos to match, and the rock world's first "supergroup" was destined to have a short, incendiary life that ended with a 15-date tour and two soldout shows (the Farewell Concert) at London's Royal Albert Hall—the latter filmed by Tony Palmer for theatrical (and later DVD) release.

The decision to split was made in May 1968, halfway through a marathon U.S. tour, and reflected the stress caused by traveling long distances and putting on demanding shows night after night. Their career lasted just under three years, during which time the trio produced three seminal albums: *Fresh Cream* (1966), *Disraeli Gears* (1967), and *Wheels of Fire* (1968); a fourth, *Goodbye*, would appear posthumously.

Cream's blues-rock fusion influenced a generation, combining rocked-up blues classics like Robert Johnson's "Crossroads" and Junior Wells's "Lawdy Mama" (modified into "Strange Brew" with the help of producer Felix Pappalardi), with newly minted classics like "Sunshine of Your Love" and "Politician," penned by Bruce and lyricist Pete Brown. *Beat Instrumental* magazine's 1967 awards poll had Clapton, Bruce, and Baker at the top of their respective instrumental trees—and that was apt—their detractors claimed they tended to solo through each song!

No band members since the Beatles had enjoyed such high personal profiles, and all three would go on to make their mark in future years before Baker emigrated to Africa to breed polo ponies. Clapton overcame his reluctance to revisit history when, 37 years later, Cream followed four dates at the Royal Albert Hall with three at New York's Madison Square Garden in 2005.

◄ Cream pose in New York's Central Park in November 1968. From left to right: Eric Clapton, Ginger Baker, and Jack Bruce.

ROCK AND ROLL CIRCUS

The Rolling Stones Rock and Roll Circus was an all-star show in a Big Top filmed by Michael Lindsay-Hogg in December and intended for broadcast by the BBC. The cast included the Who, Marianne Faithfull, Jethro Tull and a one-off supergroup, the Dirty Mac, featuring Eric Clapton, John Lennon, and a black sheet-clad Yoko Ono, as well as the Stones themselves. The show was never broadcast—due, some claimed, to the fact that the Who stole the show from the headliners. Jagger and company relented in 1997, when a CD and video (later DVD) of the show were issued. *Rock and Roll Circus* is now considered most notable for being the last public performance of Brian Jones, who would leave the band and drown the following year.

In the back row, from left to right: Pete Townshend, John Lennon, Yoko Ono, Keith Richards, and Mick Jagger. ►

1969

STAND-OUT SINGLES

"Na Na Hey Hey Kiss Him Goodbye"
  —**Steam**

"Hot Fun in the Summertime"
  —**Sly and the Family Stone**

"A Boy Named Sue"—**Johnny Cash**

"Bad Moon Rising"—**Creedence Clearwater Revival**

"Polk Salad Annie"
  —**Tony Joe White**

"Time Is Tight"—**Booker T and the MGs**

"That's the Way God Planned It"
  —**Billy Preston**

"Pinball Wizard"—**The Who**

"Albatross"—**Fleetwood Mac**

"For Once in My Life"
  —**Stevie Wonder**

"Suspicious Minds"—**Elvis Presley**

"The Thrill Is Gone"—**B. B. King**

"Something in the Air"
  —**Thunderclap Newman**

"Space Oddity"—**David Bowie**

"Something"—**The Beatles**

"Many Rivers To Cross"
  —**Jimmy Cliff**

Following Sly and the Family Stone's high-profile performance at Woodstock, their single "Hot Fun in the Summertime" reached No. 2 in the summer of 1969. Sly and the Family Stone were inducted into the Rock and Roll Hall of Fame in 1993.▼

Where were you when?

"If everyone demanded peace instead of another television set, then there'd be peace."

—John Lennon

"At the time he was staying in the Queen Elizabeth Hotel (Montreal), I thought he was an indulgent, self-important rock star. But seeing the excesses committed by those that have come since, I now appreciate he was trying to do something."

—Todd Levine, Mount Royal, Montreal

Give Peace a Chance

John Lennon and Yoko Ono turned their honeymoon into anti-war performance propaganda by inviting the world's press to their Bed-In for Peace.

Two and a half years after their first meeting, Beatle John Lennon and Japanese artist/performer Yoko Ono married in Gibraltar on March 20, 1969. The problems they had to overcome to have their union recognized were documented in the song "The Ballad of John and Yoko," rush-released as a single in May when its predecessor "Get Back" was still at No. 1. (It reached only No. 8 because it included the phrase "Christ, you know it ain't easy," which restricted airplay.) The couple spent their honeymoon at the Amsterdam Hilton, where their Bed-In for Peace attracted the world's media like flies to a honeypot.

The press and much of the public had taken an instant dislike to the Tokyo-born Ono, who was seven years John's senior. She appeared to be riding to fame on the Beatles' coattails as well as destabilizing the group. The pair had recorded an album together, *Two Virgins*, which had to be distributed in a paper bag to obscure the deliberately controversial full-frontal cover shot.

By May, Lennon had changed his name by deed poll from John Winston to John Ono, and the couple had moved into a large estate near Ascot, Berkshire, called Tittenhurst House. This is where the *Imagine* album would come together once the Beatles split. Meanwhile, John and Yoko would travel to Canada later in the year to undertake another bed-in (at Montreal's Queen Elizabeth Hotel), record the anthem "Give Peace a Chance" and perform at a rock revival festival, while November would see Lennon return his MBE (Member of the British Empire) insignia to the Queen in protest at Britain's involvement in the Nigerian civil war.

Much to John's delight, "Give Peace a Chance" became the anti–Vietnam war song of choice, just as "We Shall Overcome" had been used in the civil rights movement. Lennon's increasing political activity, however, was to bring him to the attention of the U.S. authorities and cause problems in the 1970s when he sought to live and work in the States.

◄ Lennon and Ono photographed on March 25, 1969, at the Amsterdam Hilton.

BRIAN JONES—ROCK'S FIRST MAJOR CASUALTY

Having been unceremoniously ejected from the Rolling Stones, the group he had helped form in 1962, Brian Jones would be dead within a month. He was found at the bottom of the swimming pool at his Sussex farm in unexplained circumstances. He had been growing apart from the other members of the band, attending recordings only sporadically, while his drug convictions were an obstacle to their touring the United States. His press statement tactfully concluded: "I no longer see eye-to-eye with the others over the discs we are cutting." The Rolling Stones performed a scheduled free concert in Hyde Park, London, on July 5, two days after his death, where Mick Jagger read a poem by Shelley and liberated a box of butterflies in honor of his departed ex-bandmate.

The Rolling Stones' free concert in Hyde Park, London. ►

1969

CROSBY, STILLS, NASH & YOUNG

In echoes of Cream, this year brought the debut of supergroup Crosby, Stills, Nash & Young, virtuoso musicians who had made their names with other bands before joining forces. Stills and Young had played together in Buffalo Springfield, while Crosby was an ex-Byrd and Englishman Nash a refugee from the Hollies. Canadian Young, who would not appear on the band's first album, was persuaded to join them at their first major public date, the Woodstock Festival, and chart-topping second album *Déjà Vu* before striking out solo once more. The group trademark was stunning vocal harmonies that turned good songs into great ones, and major commercial success followed. As with Cream, however, four into one did not go and their subsequent career was sporadic.

▲ Singer Stephen Stills estimates that it took around 800 hours of studio time to record *Déjà Vu* in 1969. The band followed it up with *Four Way Street* in 1971.

Woodstock Nation

Despite getting double the numbers expected and jamming up the New York Thruway, the Woodstock Festival was a triumph for peace and understanding.

Pop festivals had been a recurring feature of the late 1960s, taking the formula pioneered by jazz and folk promoters and multiplying it in size by featuring the biggest crowd-pullers in mass-market music. Held on Max Yasgur's farm in New York State in August 1969, Woodstock was the pop festival to end them all, eclipsing forerunners such as Monterey by the fact that it reemerged the following year as a movie. Joni Mitchell's hymn to the event was also a hit for U.K.'s Matthews Southern Comfort, and Crosby, Stills, Nash & Young (U.S.), further ensuring its place in history.

While the first day, Friday, August 15, was dedicated to folk singers like Joan Baez and Richie Havens, it was the acts that rocked out on Saturday night and Sunday morning,

Where were you when?

"I was one of those Columbia University students who wound up at the right place at the right time, as original keyboard player for SHA NA NA! We played late Sunday night, or actually Monday morning. They kept bumping us; we were dressed in our rolled-up T-shirts, and it was cold in them mountains at night. I remember huddling in the back of a big panel truck behind the stage trying to keep warm and listening to the groups that were supposed to have gone on AFTER us! We finally got on next-to-last—just before Jimi!"

—Joe Witkin, Del Mar

notably The Who and Jefferson Airplane, that attracted most attention. The hitherto unknown Santana won kudos for their percussive Latin-flavored set, and Janis Joplin and Sly and the Family Stone won five encores between them. Jimi Hendrix closed the festival as a whole, delighting those of the 500,000 (over double the predicted number) who had stayed to celebrate the advertised "three days of peace and music."

Traffic gridlock, poor sanitation, bad weather, and food shortages bedeviled the event, but there were only two recorded fatalities—one a heroin overdose, and the other was someone in a sleeping bag in a hayfield who was run over by a tractor. The movie, which won an Oscar for best documentary, was a safer and acceptable substitute; a young Martin Scorsese worked on it as a film editor.

Woodstock held the record for the largest music audience in the world until eclipsed by the Summer Jam at Watkins Glen in 1973. It was replayed on its twentieth, twenty-fifth and thirtieth anniversaries, the first in a noncommercial way, but inevitably none of these revivals could recapture the vibe of the original.

Singer Grace Slick takes center stage with Jefferson Airplane. They began their set at 6 A.M. on Sunday morning, though they were technically last on the bill for Saturday night. The festival finally wound up on Monday morning. ▼

"I was at Woodstock. Just got out of active duty in the Navy. I was on the crest of the amphitheater. Country Joe McDonald started to sing, 'Next stop was Viet-nam.' I was a tad confused how to react."

—Ken Cruikshank, South Huntingdon, New York

There was rain throughout the Woodstock weekend, at one point causing the sound system to fail. By the end of the event, the stage was beginning to slide downhill. ▶

1969

BEST-SELLING ALBUMS

In A Gadda Da Vida
—**Iron Butterfly**

Hair —**Original Cast**

Blood Sweat & Tears
—**Blood Sweat & Tears**

Bayou Country
—**Creedence
Clearwater Revival**

Led Zeppelin —**Led Zeppelin**

Abbey Road —**The Beatles**

Nashville Skyline —**Bob Dylan**

Led Zeppelin 2 —**Led Zeppelin**

The Band —**The Band**

Let It Bleed —**Rolling Stones**

▲ Iron Butterfly's hit album title was supposedly a slurred version of, "in the Garden of Eden." The band was due to play at Woodstock but demanded a helicopter to avoid the traffic jam and that they go on stage as soon as they got there. The promoters didn't bother to phone them back.

Where were you when?

"Michael wasn't as outgoing and playful as the other guys. He was standing there, we were singing the song and all the time I was showing it to him I was thinking, 'Can he reach these notes?' Finally we took a try at it and he just hit it the first time."

—"I Want You Back" co-songwriter Freddie Perren

"The thing that made me catch my breath when I saw them on TV was how young they looked, yet how professional they acted."

—Louise McFadean, Toronto

I Want You Back

Father Joe Jackson schooled his five sons to become pop stars from an early age, but it was youngest son Michael who stole the show.

Motown was the black music success story of the 1960s—and as that decade closed, the torch was passed to a new generation of performers, a family group, the Jackson 5. The Indiana born brothers—Michael, Jermaine, Tito, Jackie, and Marlon—had been schooled for stardom by father Joe, and Berry Gordy was quick to see their potential. Diana Ross introduced them on national TV's *Hollywood Palace* showcase in October, and just a few weeks later "I Want You Back" had become the Jackson 5's first No. 1 single. They modeled themselves on the proven vocal group formula of the Four Tops and Temptations, but Michael, then just 10, was clearly the sibling with charisma to spare. His keening voice carried the day in a song written by a collection of top songwriters known as the Corporation that required a top E flat: Michael had that and more. With Motown's older groups running out of commercial steam, the Jackson 5 were crucial to Motown's future as the label prepared to relocate from Detroit to the West Coast. A string of specially written singles—"ABC," "Mama's Pearl," "The Love You Save," "Doctor My Eyes," and "I'll Be There"—proved profitable for both parties.

THE JACKSON 5 BECOME THE JACKSONS

Touring and recording continued, with live performances attracting a keen teenage following that encouraged a white family group called the Osmonds to follow in their footsteps. They even spawned a TV cartoon series. But while Jermaine and Jackie Jackson were launched as solo acts, only Michael would enjoy a consistently successful solo career; he would of course go on to eclipse the group in the 1980s.

The 5 left Motown in 1975 having sold 100 million records. The label retained rights to the name, forcing them to continue as the Jacksons until they disbanded in 1985. The group reunited in 2008, Jermaine explaining: "We feel we have to do it one more time. We owe that to the fans and to the public." After Michael's well-publicized problems, turning back the clock 40 years seemed an attractive option.

◄ December 14, 1969, Ed Sullivan shakes hands with Michael (right) and Marlon (second right) Jackson of the Jackson 5 after an appearance on *The Ed Sullivan Show*.

ALTAMONT

The feelings of hippie euphoria engendered by Woodstock this summer would last only a matter of months until a festival held at Altamont Speedway in December brought the generation to a close under a cloud. Headlined by the Rolling Stones, it had also featured the Flying Burrito Brothers, Jefferson Airplane, and Santana but failed to repeat the success of the Stones' earlier free concert in London's Hyde Park. Drugs and alcohol led to ugly scenes, and 18-year-old black youth Meredith Hunter lost his life after allegedly pulling a gun, stabbed to death by San Francisco Hell's Angels who were being used as security for the event.

The wreckage of Altamont where the hippie dream finally died. ►

1970-1979

1970

STAND-OUT ALBUMS

Fire and Water—**Free**

A Question of Balance
—**Moody Blues**

Paranoid—**Black Sabbath**

Bitches Brew—**Miles Davis**

Bridge Over Troubled Water
—**Simon/Garfunkel**

Chicago—**Chicago**

Sweet Baby James—**James Taylor**

Workingman's Dead
—**Grateful Dead**

Abraxas—**Santana**

▲ Carlos Santana's second album,
Abraxas, mixed rock, jazz, salsa, and
blues. The cover art features a painting,
The Annunciation, by Mati Klarwein.

James Taylor's *Sweet Baby James* featured
the poignant single "Fire and Rain" about
his friend Suzanne Schnerr who committed
suicide. ▼

Where were you when?

*"We were pretty good mates until the Beatles started to split up and Yoko
came into it. It was more like old army buddies splitting up on account of
wedding bells."*

—Paul McCartney

*"It was obvious the Beatles were going to split up. After Brian Epstein (their
manager) died in 1967, they had no one telling them what to do. Some of
Paul McCartney's decisions and a lot of his music since make me think that
having Lennon look over his shoulder was good for him."*

—Adam Bolland, Melbourne

Beatles RIP

Though the writing had been on the wall for some time, it was Paul McCartney who finally broke the inertia and dissolved pop's biggest-ever band.

The signs of a Beatles split had been in the air for a long time when, on the last day of 1970, Paul McCartney filed a lawsuit against Beatles & Co. seeking to dissolve his partnership with John Lennon, George Harrison, and Ringo Starr. The much praised *White Album* issued two years and a month before, had shown that the Lennon–McCartney songwriting partnership, upon which the group's reputation had relied since 1962, was now a partnership in name only: Indeed, several tracks didn't even feature the four members playing together. The album/movie *Let It Be*, the creation of which occupied the first part of 1969 before being abandoned, was an ill-tempered affair with Yoko Ono sitting in, a fact that added fuel to the flames, and while a truce was declared for the Abbey Road album, recorded "the way we used to do it," in the words of producer George Martin, sessions had to be fit in between the members' solo commitments between July and September 1969.

"Let It Be," the single and album, was to be the sole Beatles release of 1970 as all four members unleashed the first shots of their solo careers. The project had originally been christened "Get Back," but the change of title seemed symbolic of the Fab Four's wish to lay their collective past to rest and concentrate on their solo futures.

Paul McCartney's role as instigator of the split— "the man who broke up the Beatles," as the press had it—had been forced on him by the appointment of ex–Rolling Stones adviser Allen Klein. One of Klein's acts had been to commission producer Phil Spector to complete the abandoned *Let It Be* project, and for McCartney, messing with his music was the last straw.

◄ February 19, 1971, Paul McCartney and wife, Linda, leave London's Law Courts after petitioning for the break-up of the Beatles partnership.

BRIDGE OVER TROUBLED WATER

When Simon and Garfunkel released their masterwork *Bridge Over Troubled Water* they had, unknown to the public at large, already all but dissolved their profitable partnership. "We didn't say that's the end," Simon would later admit. "But it became apparent by the time the movie (Art's *Carnal Knowledge*) and the album (Simon's eponymous solo debut) was out that it was over." The album and single, both chart-toppers, would pick up four Grammy awards in March 1971, but it was perhaps fortunate that, instead of S&G performing the song at the awards, Aretha Franklin sang it.

Bridge was the final act in what was often a troubled partnership. ▶

1970

NO. 1 SINGLES

"Someday We'll Be Together"
—Diana Ross & the Supremes

"I Want You Back"
—The Jackson 5

"Venus"—The Shocking Blue

"Thank You/Everybody is a Star"
—Sly & the Family Stone

"Bridge Over Troubled Water"
—Simon & Garfunkel

"Let It Be"—The Beatles

"ABC"—The Jackson 5

"American Woman"
—The Guess Who

"The Long and Winding Road"
—The Beatles

"The Love You Save"
—The Jackson 5

"Mama Told Me (Not To Come)"
—Three Dog Night

"(They Long to Be) Close to You"
—The Carpenters

"Make It With You"—Bread

"War"—Edwin Starr

"Ain't No Mountain High Enough"
—Diana Ross

"I'll Be There"—The Jackson 5

"I Think I Love You"
—The Partridge Family

"The Tears of a Clown"—Smokey
Robinson & the Miracles

"My Sweet Lord"—George Harrison

"ABC" was The Jackson 5's second
single—and their second No. 1. ▼

Joni Mitchell and Neil Young

The seventies dawned bright for sensitive singer-songwriters such as James Taylor and Elton John and two Canadian artists with distinctive voices.

The year 1970 proved to be pivotal for Joni Mitchell and Neil Young, two Canadian-born artists who pursued very different musical paths in the years that followed but whose deeply personal observations of life and the human condition continue to resonate with audiences. Mitchell, who had been performing as a solo artist for several years, achieved the long-awaited breakthrough with her third solo album, *Ladies of the Canyon*, which featured several of her best-known songs, including "Big Yellow Taxi" and "Woodstock." *Ladies of the Canyon* hit the racks just as its predecessor, *Clouds*, earned Mitchell the Grammy for the Best Folk Performance of 1969. When compared to the earlier release, the new collection showed how well Mitchell was developing as a songwriter, and the album was featured heavily on FM radio shows throughout the summer. It spent just nine weeks on the *Billboard* charts and rose no higher than No. 27, but it sold steadily thereafter and eventually became her first gold album.

For Young the crucial release was not a solo album, but his first appearance with David Crosby, Stephen Stills, and Graham Nash in CSN&Y. *Déjà Vu* briefly topped the charts in May 1970 and went on to sell over 7 million copies. No surprise, then, that Young's third solo outing, *After the Gold Rush*, attracted far more attention than his earlier efforts. Not everyone was immediately impressed—*Rolling Stone*'s review of the album opened: "Neil Young devotees will probably spend the next few weeks trying desperately to convince themselves that *After the Gold Rush* is good music. But they'll be kidding themselves. For despite the fact that the album contains some potentially first rate material, none of the songs here rise above the uniformly dull surface."

Almost four decades on, Joni Mitchell and Neil Young remain among rock's most distinctive voices, two of the most highly regarded and influential performers of the last 50 years. *After the Gold Rush* regularly appears in rock Top 100 album lists.

First lady of the Canyon, Joni Mitchell. ▶

Where were you when?

"After the Gold Rush *was the spirit of Topanga Canyon. It seemed like I realized I'd gotten somewhere.*"

—Neil Young

"*My favorite song from* Gold Rush *was 'When You Dance You Can Really Love.' I wore that cut out through college. I only get nostalgic about it when I play the vinyl LP which I still have.*"

—Deanna Whittle, Macon, Georgia

Neil Young at a solo gig in 1970. ▶

JIMI HENDRIX DIES

On September 18, American guitar superstar Jimi Hendrix was found unconscious in his room at the Samarkand Hotel in London and shortly afterwards died from "inhalation of vomit due to barbiturate intoxication." The 27-year-old had jammed with Eric Burdon's band War on stage at Ronnie Scott's club just two days earlier, though his final major public performance had been at this year's Isle of Wight Festival. Hendrix's influence on the electric guitar lasts to this day—in 2003, *Rolling Stone* confirmed his status as No. 1 in their "100 greatest guitarists of all time." Given his arrival as an unknown in London in 1966, his impact in such a short time is remarkable.

Hendrix could play his Fender Stratocaster at any angle. ▶

STAND-OUT SINGLES

"Theme From Shaft"
—**Isaac Hayes**

"Nathan Jones"—**Supremes**

"Superstar"—**Carpenters**

"Won't Get Fooled Again"
—**The Who**

"Respect Yourself"
—**Staple Singers**

"Brown Sugar"—**Rolling Stones**

"Riders on the Storm"
—**The Doors**

"Black Magic Woman"—**Santana**

"Liar"—**Three Dog Night**

"The Night They Drive Old Dixie Down"—**Joan Baez**

"You've Got a Friend"
—**James Taylor**

"Me and Bobby McGee"
—**Janis Joplin**

Elton's 4-Album Year

Elton John proved he could master big orchestral ballads as well as kicking back his piano stool and getting the crowd on their feet.

For Elton John 1971 was an unforgettable year. As it began, all indications were that something big was about to happen, but the next 12 months exceeded all expectations, catapulting the shy 24-year-old Londoner to international superstardom. He had enjoyed an auspicious U.S. concert debut at the Troubadour club in Los Angeles the previous August, where his flamboyant performance wowed the critics and drew praise from fellow artists, including Quincy Jones and Bob Dylan. By the end of October, his self-titled U.S. debut album had entered the Top 40, and "Your Song," the second single to be lifted from it, charted soon after.

Billboard magazine greeted Tumbleweed Connection, issued in the opening week of 1971, enthusiastically, saying that it was "sure to be one of the biggest (albums) of the new year." It placed in the Top 5 right away and was awarded a gold record in March. That same month, the soundtrack album to an obscure film, Friends, that included only five new Elton John/Bernie Taupin songs was promoted as a new Elton John album, but record buyers weren't entirely fooled, and the album stalled at No. 36.

MADMAN ACROSS THE WATER

In between recording sessions, John toured extensively, playing 42 North American dates in April, May, and June, and another 16, including a seven-night stint at the Greek Theater in Los Angeles in August and September. A live album, 11/17/70, featuring material taken from a concert recorded for a radio station in New York the previous autumn, was released to tie in with his first U.S. tour.

Momentum was maintained with a new studio album, Madman Across the Water, in November, and it was no surprise that December's Billboard listed Elton John as the sixth most successful artist of the year. With four albums to his name, the artist formerly known as Reg Dwight, had enjoyed quite a year.

Elton with lyricist Bernie Taupin, or as they would later become, Captain Fantastic and the Brown Dirt Cowboy. ▶

Where were you when?

"I first saw Elton John on the Andy Williams Show *singing 'Your Song.' For about a year I thought he was American."*

—Brian More, Halesowen, England

"I heard the original radio broadcast of Elton's 11/17/70 *album which went out live on WABC-FM in New York. I still have an illegal bootleg copy. The quality is not good, but the vibe is fantastic."*

—Bill Mauger, Philadelphia

HARRISON AND LENNON RETURN TO THE CHART

George Harrison became the first solo Beatle to score a No. 1 with "My Sweet Lord," while his album *All Things Must Pass* was just as successful—much to his obvious delight, "I was only allowed to do one or two songs on Beatles albums, so I had a backlog. It was good to get them out of the way." Meanwhile John Lennon had followed his former bandmate to the top of the album charts with *Imagine*, whose anthemic title track stalled at No. 3 in the singles chart but arguably became the most significant solo song by any ex-Beatle.

Harrison with devotees from the Radha-Krishna Temple. "My Sweet Lord" was a celebration of his Hare Krishna beliefs. ▶

1971

NO. 1 ALBUMS

All Things Must Pass
—**George Harrison**

Jesus Christ Superstar
—**Various Artists**

Pearl—**Janis Joplin**

Sticky Fingers—**Rolling Stones**

Tapestry—**Carole King**

Every Picture Tells a Story
—**Rod Stewart**

Imagine —**John Lennon**

Shaft —**Isaac Hayes**

Santana —**Santana**

There's a Riot Goin' On
—**Sly & the Family Stone**

▲ *Tapestry* by Carole King remained on the album charts for almost six years.

Imagine, John Lennon's second solo LP. ▼

Where were you when?

"I could not be more fortunate and appreciative for the adoration I have received as a result of this show. I know this has influenced hundreds of thousands of people for years, and because of the fact that I was one of the players in that work, I am the luckiest man alive."

—Ted Neeley, the actor chosen to understudy Jesus Christ in the original Broadway production in 1971 and who was still touring the show, in the role of Christ, 37 years later.

"It seethes with pulsating tension and driving fury. Finally when those exulting chords of the title song sound the prelude for crucifixion, Jesus Christ Superstar *reaches a savage high."*

—*London Evening Standard*

Jesus Christ Superstar

The hit musical based on the last weeks of Christ's life had an inauspicious beginning—even its creators called it "brash and vulgar."

Perhaps inspired by *Tommy*, the Who's 1969 magnum opus, a new rock opera called *Jesus Christ Superstar*, made its debut in October 1970, initially as a concept album. Among the contributing artists were future Deep Purple vocalist Ian Gillan, playing Jesus, and Yvonne Elliman as Mary Magdalene.

Written by Andrew Lloyd Webber and Tim Rice, who had already enjoyed modest success with their stage musical *Joseph and the Amazing Technicolor Dreamcoat*, the new work was an almost instant hit, topping the *Billboard* charts within weeks. With sales in the United Kingdom remaining relatively poor, the producers decided to take the proposed stage production to Broadway. Meanwhile, hundreds of theater groups across America began to stage their own unauthorized versions, prompting legal action from the show's creators. The first officially sanctioned version of the show was a touring production that opened in Pittsburgh in July.

On October 12, 1971, *Jesus Christ Superstar*, directed by Tom O'Horgan, finally opened at the Mark Hellinger Theater on Broadway to mixed reviews. *The New York Times* described it as "heartless" and "overhyped," while Lloyd Webber himself, unhappy with the production, called it "brash and vulgar." The experience prompted him to form his own production company, Really Useful, some years later. The critics weren't the only dissenting voices—perhaps predictably, a musical dramatization of the final days of Jesus's life ruffled feathers among religious groups, some denouncing the show as "sacrilegious."

Despite this shaky start, *Jesus Christ Superstar* became an enormous success worldwide, changing the face of the musical forever. For Lloyd Webber it was the first of many phenomenally successful musical productions, including *Evita*, *Cats*, *Starlight Express*, and *The Phantom of the Opera*. Meanwhile, more than 30 years later, *Jesus Christ Superstar* is acknowledged as a classic and is still playing to packed houses around the world.

◄ Jesus surrounded by his disciples in the original Broadway run of the rock opera. Jeff Fenholt plays Jesus, but Ted Neeley, also in the cast, got to play him in the 1973 film.

ROD STEWART GOES SOLO

After years of struggle and manual labor, tousle-haired British singer Rod Stewart was in the fortunate situation of having a solo career that ran parallel to his exploits with his band, the Faces, which had risen from the ashes of a 1960s group, the Small Faces. His first mark on the charts came with single "Maggie May" and parent album *Every Picture Tells a Story*, which all simultaneously topped the transatlantic listings in October. He was fortunate that a radio DJ in Cleveland turned the single over from the original A-side "Reason to Believe" "or I could still have been digging graves." Stewart's rasping vocal delivery proved universally popular and laid the foundations of a career that was to continue successfully into the 2000s.

"Rod the Mod" turned into Rod the glam rocker in the 1970s. ►

BEST-SELLING SINGLES

"American Pie"—**Don McLean**

"Alone Again (Naturally)"
—**Gilbert O'Sullivan**

"Without You"—**Nilsson**

"Brand New Key—**Melanie**

"I Gotcha"—**Joe Tex**

"Daddy Don't You Walk So Fast"
—**Wayne Newton**

"Let's Stay Together"—**Al Green**

"The First Time Ever I Saw
Your Face"—**Roberta Flack**

"Brandy (You're a Fine Girl)"
—**Looking Glass**

"Lean on Me"—**Bill Withers**

▲ Harry Nilsson's single "Without You"
was taken from his most successful
album, *Nilsson Schmilsson.* The singer
would endure tragedy throughout his
career. Singer Cass Elliot and The Who's
drummer Keith Moon both died in his
London flat. Pete Ham and Tom Evans, the
writers of "Without You," both committed
suicide, and his good friend John Lennon
was gunned down in New York.

Marc Bolan: The Birth of Glam Rock

Once a part of the alternative music scene, Marc Bolan and his band T.Rex developed a commercial sound and an image that would transform pop.

Marc Bolan and his band T.Rex may not have had stellar success in North America, but their influence on music fashion was profound. After Bolan took to wearing top hats and feather boas on stage, as well as putting drops of glitter on each cheekbone, Glam Rock was born. Friend and sometime collaborator David Bowie picked up the androgynous theme, and soon the U.K. concert halls were awash with silver suits and glitter boots, and even performers such as Rod Stewart, Mick Jagger, and Elton John started to raid rock's dress-up box.

Bolan had started out as guitarist in psychedelic folk duo Tyrannosaurus Rex and in 1968 played live at a free concert in Hyde Park headlined by Pink Floyd. After a U.S. tour in which his percussionist was busted for drugs, Bolan recruited new drummer Mickey Finn, and the pair suddenly swapped their hippie audience for screaming teenage girls. The breakthrough single was "Ride a White Swan," produced by Tony Visconti, which reached No. 1 on the U.K. singles chart early in 1971. Follow-up singles included "Hot Love," "Bang a Gong (Get It On)," and "Jeepster."

By 1972 Bolan, aided by Visconti, had established his own distinctive sound, and he scored No. 1s with "Telegram Sam" and "Metal Guru," which kept Elton John's "Rocket Man" off the top spot. Two live appearances at the Empire Pool, Wembley, filmed by Ringo Starr for his ill-fated movie *Born to Boogie*, proved to be the high-water mark of his career. As Bolan's popularity declined in 1973, his friend David Bowie began to take over the charts as *Ziggy Stardust* won rave reviews.

Bolan would die in a car accident in 1977. Returning from a party, the car his wife was driving hit a tree at the edge of Barnes Common in South West London. Bolan died instantly, while his wife, the singer Gloria Jones, suffered a broken arm. The spot is still visited by fans who have erected a statue to Marc on the site and continue to leave flowers.

◄ Marc Bolan radically transformed himself from a hippie flower child, to a teen pop idol. Close friend David Bowie would step in and help when his career flagged.

IAN HUNTER—*DIARY OF A ROCK 'N' ROLL STAR*

Mott the Hoople's rapid ascent from also-ran status to supergroup had come courtesy of David Bowie giving them an anthem, "All the Young Dudes," that finally got them onto the charts. Singer Ian Hunter decided to chronicle the U.S. headline tour that followed, and the result was *Diary of a Rock 'n' Roll Star*, the definitive on-the-road account of life in a band. His eye for trivial detail and laconic humor made the book a must-read (he was already into his thirties), but given his evident distaste for the group lifestyle and the years of struggle already endured, it was little surprise that he went solo in 1974. Mott the Hoople are one of the few bands of the era never to re-form.

OSMOND

DON McLEAN— "AMERICAN PIE"

"The death of Buddy Holly in a plane crash in 1959 had a silver lining for teenager Don McLean, then a 13-year-old paper boy in New Rochelle, New York. Years later he turned the event into the theme for his biggest hit, "American Pie," which lamented "the day the music died." The single went to No. 1 in the U.S. *Billboard* chart for four weeks in January 1972. In 1972 an eight-minute single with a stream-of-consciousness lyric was headline news, and some of the imagery of the song has left itself open to interpretation: Mclean himself dodges the questions with the classic quote: "What does it mean? It means I don't have to work again." Madonna made her own version of the song in 2000, reenergizing McLean's career and establishing it as one of the greatest pop singles of all time.

Where were you when?

"*I looked younger than I was. I was 21, playing 16.*"
—David Cassidy on his *Partridge Family* role

"*I can remember being glued to the screen for every second of* The Partridge Family. *Nobody was allowed to speak when David Cassidy was on screen. That was MY moment of worship every week.*"

—Cheryl Chesney, Buffalo

The Osmonds and David Cassidy

Donnie and David were the perfect all-American, clean-living boys, scoring big hits at home but even greater success in Europe.

Two families ruled the teenage roost as the 1970s got into its stride—David Cassidy and his manufactured-for-TV *Partridge Family*, and real-life siblings the Osmonds. Between them they had the transatlantic teen market more or less sewn up.

Cassidy, son of actors Jack Cassidy and Evelyn Ward, graced the small screen from 1970–74 as Keith Partridge, topping the charts with "I Think I Love You" in *The Partridge Family* show's debut year. He launched as a solo artist in 1971, going Top 10 with "Cherish," then found even greater fame in Europe as the show was aired over there. But disaster struck at a 1974 concert at London's White City stadium when 30 fans were taken to hospital after a hysterical crowd got out of control. One fan, 14-year-old Bernadette Whelan, tragically died of her injuries four days later, and Cassidy, now 24, quit both *The Partridge Family* and touring in a vain attempt to reshape his career as an adult entertainer.

The Osmonds came to public notice in the 1960s as guests on the *Andy Williams Show* but were signed in 1971 by MGM as the label's answer to the Jackson 5. Brothers Alan, Merrill, Donny, Jay, and Wayne topped the charts for five weeks with "Down by the Lazy River," while Donny, Marie, and even youngest brother Little Jimmy registered solo hits. A total of 18 gold records adorned the walls of the family's Utah home by early 1974, an impressive display of musical success.

The family's Mormon religion had not only informed their act—no suggestive lyrics or movements were allowed—but was also the basis of a concept album, *The Plan*. But singles were the Osmonds' strength, and they continued scoring hits in Europe, where, like Cassidy, their popularity was now greatest, until 1975.

Donny made a comeback in the 1990s doing 2,000 performances in *Joseph and the Amazing Technicolor Dreamcoat*, while his brothers performed without him as a country act.

◄ Like the Jackson 5, there might have been five brothers in the group, but the focus of attention was inevitably on the youngest, Donnie, second from left.

CONCERT FOR BANGLADESH

George Harrison set the blueprint for Live Aid two decades earlier when he organized a star-studded event to help the refugees of the newly-created Asian state of Bangladesh. Two shows staged in one day at New York's Madison Square Garden on August 1 featured Ravi Shankar, Billy Preston, Eric Clapton, Leon Russell, Badfinger, Ringo Starr, and Bob Dylan, the last-named making his first live appearance for several years. An initial sum of $250,000—then a significant amount—was raised before a triple album and movie added significantly to the total.

From left to right, Jeff Beck, George Harrison, and Eric Clapton. ►

1973

NO. 1 ALBUMS

No Secrets—**Carly Simon**

Don't Shoot Me I'm Only the Piano Player—**Elton John**

Dueling Banjos—**Eric Weissberg and Steve Mandel**

Lady Sings the Blues—**Diana Ross**

Billion Dollar Babies—**Alice Cooper**

Dark Side of the Moon—**Pink Floyd**

Houses of the Holy—**Led Zeppelin**

Beatles 1967-1970—**The Beatles**

Red Rose Speedway—**Wings**

Living in the Material World—**George Harrison**

Chicago VI—**Chicago**

A Passion Play—**Jethro Tull**

Brothers and Sisters—**Allman Brothers**

Goat's Head Soup—**Rolling Stones**

Goodbye Yellow Brick Road—**Elton John**

▲ Elton John's album, *Don't Shoot Me I'm Only the Piano Player*, contained his first U.S. No. 1 single, "Crocodile Rock."

Where were you when?

"If you didn't know the entire track listing of Dark Side of the Moon *in my class at school, you were either shunned or ridiculed or both."*

—Toby Veall, Leicester

"I always wondered how they wrote the music for the woman who yells and screams on The Great Gig in the Sky. *It's an amazing performance. Then I saw a TV program which said she did that on the first take and I was even more amazed thirty years later."*

—Brad Reece, Seattle

Dark Side of the Moon

For a band that had almost imploded after losing its inspirational songwriter, *Dark Side of the Moon* was a triumph on many different levels.

One of the most eagerly anticipated albums of the decade, Pink Floyd's *Dark Side of the Moon,* was released on March 24, 1973, and topped the *Billboard* 200 five weeks later. Incredibly, considering that it's the twentieth best-selling album of all time in the United States, it stayed there just one week, but the statistic is put into perspective by the fact that it spent no less than 741 consecutive weeks in the Top 200, finally dropping out in April 1988.

Widely regarded as a landmark album, and by many as the pinnacle of Pink Floyd's career, *Dark Side of the Moon* had a lengthy gestation period. The band started gathering material for the new album as early as December 1971, initially exploring ideas left over from earlier projects. The "eureka" moment came when Roger Waters suggested the new songs should all be segued, forming a coherent whole linked by a theme he'd been working on. "The concept was originally about the pressures of modern life," drummer Nick Mason later explained, although as things progressed, that concept gradually developed into a more wide-ranging exploration of the human condition.

Dark Side of the Moon ended Floyd's habit of developing new material on the road prior to release, after a good-quality bootleg of one of their 1972 shows featuring the new songs appeared. But these unofficial recordings did little to prepare the world for the finished article—it was a stunning marriage of technology and humanity, with carefully chosen sound effects and snippets of conversation woven skillfully into and around each and every track. The memorable concept album was wrapped in an equally striking sleeve by British design group Hipgnosis.

It was an eerily atmospheric creation of subtle textures and startling changes in mood, lush yet sparse, a record on which what was left out said almost as much as what was put in. Above all, the production set new standards for rock albums, and to this day *Dark Side of the Moon* remains the recording most stereo buffs will use to test a new system.

◄ Pink Floyd live. Graphic designer Storm Thorgerson was a friend of Floyd's Roger Waters and Syd Barrett and helped create one of the most iconic album designs in rock music (inset).

ROCKY HORROR SHOW OPENS

The *Rocky Horror Show* was created by Richard O'Brien as an homage to the horror film genre. Mixing stereotypes from science-fiction movies, Marvel comics, beach party movies, and rock 'n' roll of every vintage, its plot portrayed the sexual confusion of a very straight American couple from the Eisenhower era confronted by the "decadent" morality of the 1970s. It opened in London as a six-week workshop project in June 1973, but quickly transferred to a converted cinema in Chelsea. It would enjoy a virtually uninterrupted eight-year run in the capital. Music mogul Lou Adler snapped up the American theatrical rights.

Tim Curry (center) in his star role as Frank N. Furter. ►

1973

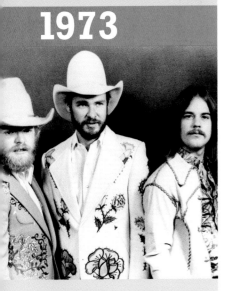

ZZ TOP

When it comes to paying dues, no band did more than Texas blues trio ZZ Top. Seven years of non-stop touring began in 1970, initially supporting Janis Joplin, Humble Pie, Ten Years After, and others, as well as opening for an all-black revue with Howlin' Wolf, Muddy Waters, and Freddie King. But 1973 was the year they turned from hopefuls into headliners, the catalyst being their third album *Tres Hombres*. Peaking at No. 8, a cool 96 places above its predecessor, it was ample reward for hard roadwork and set the tone for further success—though it would be 1983 before they next graced the Top 10 with *Eliminator*.

Ziggy Played Guitar

David Bowie had struggled to carve out a pop career in the late 1960s. Now, as superstardom in America beckoned, he decided to kill off Ziggy Stardust.

When *The Rise and Fall of Ziggy Stardust and the Spiders from Mars* was released in June 1972, David Bowie was barely known outside his native Britain. The new album not only confirmed him as a major talent, it also served as the inspiration for one of the greatest rock spectacles of all time. On stage Bowie became Ziggy, an alien, sexually ambiguous rock god who wore garish, provocative outfits and outlandish makeup at a time when the accepted rock 'n' roll uniform was a T-shirt and jeans. The musicians who'd played on the album also backed Bowie on tour, by default becoming the Spiders from Mars.

This was a new phenomenon, a daring mix of music and theatrical decadence that quickly elevated Bowie to international stardom. The success was richly deserved—by July 1973 he'd completed over 180 performances as Ziggy, toured for over a year without a significant break, and worked constantly to update the show by adding more costume changes and incorporating new songs. On July 3, he took to the stage at London's Hammersmith Odeon for the final date of a lengthy U.K. tour. There had already been talk of further European gigs in the autumn, and another U.S. tour, with perhaps 80 dates.

As the show reached its conclusion, Bowie dropped a bombshell: "This show will stay the longest in our memories, not just because it is the end of the tour but because it is the last show we'll ever do." The announcement came as a shock to almost everyone, including two of the Spiders. It transpired that Bowie had told only two people of his intention—his manager, Tony DeFries, and guitarist Mick Ronson. It was soon made clear that he'd simply decided to kill off his alter ego and fans across the globe breathed a collective sigh of relief.

Rock cinematographer D.A. Pennebaker captured Bowie's final performance as Ziggy at the Hammersmith Odeon. ▶

TUBULAR BELLS—MIKE OLDFIELD

Mike Oldfield's one-man instrumental masterwork *Tubular Bells* was the first release from Richard Branson's Virgin Records label. *Bells* built a reputation through word of mouth, and its success would force the reclusive guitarist, whose life's work it had been, to send the music out on tour, even if he got others—Steve Hillage and, later, a pre-Police Andy Summers—to play instead of him! *Tubular Bells* finally topped the U.K. charts 15 months after release, taking over from its follow-up *Hergest Ridge*, while its rise to the *Billboard* Top 3 was assisted when excerpts from it were used in hit movie *The Exorcist*: this also resulted in a bizarre No. 7 single in America.

◀ The Master of Ceremonies on the first *Tubular Bells* was the Bonzo Dog's Viv Stanshall. On *Tubular Bells II* duties fell to Alan Rickman, Professor Snape in the Harry Potter films.

1974

NO. 1 SINGLES

"The Way We Were"
—**Barbra Streisand**

"Come and Get Your Love"
—**Redbone**

"Seasons in the Sun"—**Terry Jacks**

"Show and Tell"—**Al Wilson**

"Love's Theme"
—**The Love Unlimited Orchestra**

"The Loco-motion"—**Grand Funk**

"Bennie and the Jets"—**Elton John**

"You Make Me Feel Brand New"
—**The Stylistics**

"Sunshine on My Shoulders"
—**John Denver**

"T.S.O.P. (The Sound of
Philadelphia)"—**MFSB featuring
the Three Degrees**

Robert Redford and Barbra Streisand star
in Sydney Pollack's film *The Way We Were*.
The film won Oscars for Best Music and
Best Song and the single release became
Streisand's first No. 1 *Billboard* hit, staying
on the chart for 23 weeks. ▼

Where were you when?

*"I remember seeing Abba on the Eurovision Song Contest when they won. They
were head and shoulders above everyone else. My dad said, 'Why aren't they
singing in Swedish, then?'"*

—Sara Rossiter, Milton Keynes, England

*"What people forget about Eurovison 1974—apart from Abba romping it—is that
the British entry was Olivia Newton-John. And she only came fourth."*

—John Bourne, Stockton-on-Tees, England

Made in Sweden

Abba were hailed as Sweden's biggest export after Volvo cars, and their songs, like the cars the company produced, have certainly stood the test of time.

Despite being ridiculed and criticized in equal measure, the Eurovision Song Contest, sponsored annually by active member countries of the European Broadcasting Union (EBU), is one of the world's longest-running television events, attracting audiences of more than 100 million watching from dozens of countries across the globe. Since the contest began in 1956, more than 1,000 songs have been chosen to represent the participating nations, and many more have been rejected, including some by writers who have since become household names.

Those whose efforts failed to make the cut include Elton John, Tim Rice, Andrew Lloyd Webber…and Abba, the most successful act ever to have risen from the ranks of Eurovision hopefuls. Abba's first shot at Eurovision success came in 1973, when they tried their hand with "Ring Ring," but the song came in third for that year's entry. The group got their name from the initials of members Agnetha Faltskog, Bjorn Ulvaeus, Benny Andersson, and sole Norwegian Anni-Frid Lyngstad.

Undeterred, the two couples tried again the following year, with "Waterloo," an unashamedly glam-style pop song with an unforgettable tune. The vast majority of Eurovision entries owed little or nothing to current trends in popular music, but here was a song with its finger firmly on the popular pulse, and it brushed the opposition aside. The fact that it was performed by a group with two young, attractive female singers certainly didn't hurt, but this was a good song.

"Waterloo" topped the singles charts in eight countries, reached the Top 3 in five more, and the Top 10 in another four. Success in the United States was unprecedented for a Eurovision winner and a good indication of the group's commercial appeal, but it would be a while before Abba fulfilled its early promise. The breakthrough came with single "Dancing Queen," which topped the U.S. charts in December 1976, and the album, *Arrival*, which reached the Top 40 shortly afterwards. Abba's success story continued until late 1982, by which time both the group and the two couples' relationships had dissolved.

◄ Abba (from left to right): Bjorn Ulvaeus, Agnetha Faltskog, Anni-Frid Lyngstad and Benny Andersson.

STEVIE WONDER

Soul superstar Stevie Wonder confirmed his recovery from serious head injuries suffered in a car crash in August 1973 by returning to live work. More than that, his *Fulfillingness' First Finale* album topped the U.S. album charts in September, proving a suitable follow-up to the classics *Talking Book* (1972) and the multi Grammy-winning *Innervisions*. Happily Wonder had rescinded his intention to retire and move to Africa to work with handicapped children (hence the title of the album), though he would continue to address issues close to his heart through his work. First single "You Haven't Done Nothin'," aimed at President Richard Nixon and featuring the Jackson 5 on backing vocals, was also a chart-topper.

Not content with writing his own material, in 1974 Stevie Wonder wrote and produced an album for Syreeta Wright. ►

1974

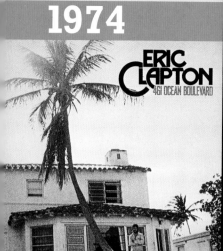

STAND-OUT ALBUMS

Autobahn—**Kraftwerk**

Caribou—**Elton John**

461 Ocean Boulevard
   —**Eric Clapton**

Kimono My House—**Sparks**

Before the Flood—**Bob Dylan**

Walls and Bridges—**John Lennon**

Sheer Heart Attack—**Queen**

Can't Get Enough—**Barry White**

AWB—**Average White Band**

Second Helping—**Lynyrd Skynyrd**

Phaedra—**Tangerine Dream**

▲ Clapton's No. 1 album was named after his address on Miami's Golden Beach.

The lyrics of Elton John's *Captain Fantastic* took a new autobiographical approach. ▼

Kiss

Glam rock on steroids—Kiss grabbed the mantle of "most outlandish rockers" with a band that cared as much about its appearance as its music.

Although they'd been active for almost a year, Kiss's bandwagon really started to roll on New Year's Eve 1973, when they were one of three acts supporting Blue Oyster Cult at an industry gig at New York's Academy of Music. It was immediately apparent that this was no ordinary rock band. Despite being bottom of the bill, they brought a 10-foot-high illuminated KISS logo with them on stage, much to the annoyance of the headliners, one of whom was heard to ask, "Who do these guys think they are?"

No one could have accused them of being understated. Gene Simmons, Paul Stanley, Ace Frehley, and Peter Criss wore outlandish costumes and striking makeup, appearing as if they were four comic-strip characters that had come to life. Pyrotechnics and other special effects also helped them make an impression, although bass player Gene Simmons' fire-eating routine, newly introduced to the act for this showcase gig, didn't go quite according to plan. His hair, liberally coated in hair spray, caught fire, and one of the roadies had to rush on stage to extinguish the hot-headed frontman.

Kiss started their first tour in February 1974, timed to tie in with the release of their self-titled debut album, on the new Casablanca label. They soon established a reputation as a first-rate live act, but their popularity didn't immediately translate into record sales. *Kiss*, and the follow-up, *Hotter than Hell*, failed to attract much interest, and their third album, *Dressed to Kill*, fared only slightly better.

With Casablanca facing bankruptcy and the band's future in doubt, something special was needed. The band's reputation was built on their live act, so a live double album was a logical step. *Kiss Alive* hit the racks in September 1975 and fortunately provided the much needed commercial breakthrough by reaching No. 9 in the United States.

More than 35 years and several lineup changes later, Kiss are still active, with more then 20 gold albums and record sales rumored to be approaching 100 million. They briefly ditched the makeup in the early 1980s but sensibly re-applied it and are still using the panstick today.

◄ Bass player Gene Simmons combined glam rock's fashion sensibilities with the dark theatricality pioneered by Alice Cooper.

PAUL McCARTNEY—*BAND ON THE RUN*

Having emerged from the biggest group in the world, ex-Beatle Paul McCartney hit his solo stride this year with *Band on the Run*. He was now nominally bass player and singer with his band Wings—yet the defection of guitarist Henry McCullough and drummer Denny Seiwell left him even more the musical focus of the depleted band as they decamped to Nigeria for recording sessions—and adversity stimulated some great music as McCartney doubled on drums. Wings, featuring Denny Laine and Linda McCartney, would endure until 1981, but this chart-topping album and its similarly successful title track single (other hits included "Helen Wheels" and "Jet") would remain their defining release.

1975

STAND-OUT SINGLES

"Laughter in the Rain"
—**Neil Sedaka**

"Pick Up the Pieces"
—**Average White Band**

"Only Women Bleed"—**Alice Cooper**

"Killer Queen"—**Queen**

"Jackie Blue"—**Ozark Mountain Daredevils**

"Before the Next Teardrop Falls"
—**Freddy Fender**

"Lady Marmalade"—**Labelle**

"Dance With Me"—**Orleans**

"Ballroom Blitz"—**The Sweet**

"Miracles"—**Jefferson Starship**

"Walk This Way"—**Aerosmith**

"Tangled Up in Blue"—**Bob Dylan**

"Roadrunner"—**Jonathan Richman & The Modern Lovers**

"Gloria"—**Patti Smith**

"Young Americans"—**David Bowie**

"Shame Shame Shame"
—**Shirley and Co.**

"Rock 'n' roll All Nite"—**Kiss**

▲ Alice Cooper's ballad, "Only Women Bleed," was about a woman trapped in an abusive marriage.

Where were you when?

"A lot of people have slammed 'Bohemian Rhapsody' but what can you compare it to? Name one group that's done an operatic single."

—Freddie Mercury

"Freddie asked me what I thought about Queen releasing 'Bohemian Rhapsody' as a single and I said, 'at that length—you've got to be joking.'"

—Elton John

Queen—Bohemian Rhapsody

It was an epic rock single not suited to radio play, but "Bohemian Rhapsody" changed pop music and helped usher in the age of the pop video.

Having built their career gradually through their first three albums, Queen made the jump to supergroup status in 1975 with *A Night at the Opera*, featuring the single "Bohemian Rhapsody," a six-minute epic that blended operatic vocals with heavy guitars and whose creation pushed recording technology to its limits. It was boosted by a groundbreaking film that would prove to be an outpost for the way pop music would henceforth be marketed—via the epic promotional video.

The film, the first music project for TV director Bruce Gowers, was put together at Elstree Studios in London in November 1974. Its creation was a desperation measure because the band's touring commitments made it impossible for them to promote their new single on television. The group members suggested that Gowers bring the head shot cover of their second album, *Queen II*, to life, and this was all done at a cost of $9,000, thanks to one of the band's managers owning an outside broadcast truck. The video's unique qualities have resulted in its often being referenced and parodied by later filmmakers.

"Bohemian Rhapsody" finally reached No. 9 in the United States in April 1976. Though the song was featured in the stage set, its complex operatic mid-section was played on a prerecorded tape, before Queen reentered the stage for the climax. The song had already climbed the British charts on its release, staying at No. 1 for nine weeks and bringing with it their equally extravagant fourth album, *A Night at the Opera*, to the U.K. chart summit. The album peaked at No. 4 in the States, Queen's second Top 20 album.

The song's North American fans included comic actor Mike Myers, whose decision to include "Bohemian Rhapsody" in the cult film *Wayne's World* saw it reenter the *Billboard* listing in 1992 and climb to No. 2.

◄ The song may have been operatic, but singer Freddie Mercury's outfit is balletic. Bassist John Deacon is mostly obscured by Mercury, while lead guitarist Brian May is to his left.

(BAY CITY) ROLLERMANIA

The Bay City Rollers were nothing less than a pop phenomenon. By 1975, the Scottish stars quickly established themselves as the biggest teen idols of the decade, developing strong "brand loyalty" from fans who decked themselves in the tartan clothing the band favored and, at the peak of Rollermania, sent their idols 11,000 fan letters a day! The Rollers set out for the States in October 1975 and were presented on television as the latest Scottish exports, bursting out of a huge tartan crate on one TV show playing "Saturday Night." The song reached No. 1, but concentration on the U.S. and Japanese markets left their British fans feeling abandoned. Rollermania, as fast as it had arrived, was seemingly already on the decline.

From left to right, Derek Longmuir, Stuart "Woody" Wood, an awed fan, Eric Faulkner, and singer Les McKeown. ►

DISCO RECORDS

In March, Johnnie Taylor's "Disco Lady" became the first but far from the last single with the word disco in its title to top the *Billboard* Hot 100. The latest musical trend was aimed at the dancefloor, and the worldwide charts were all set to reflect this. From 1975, many soul producers started to create records from scratch rather than recording performances, a process which led to vocals becoming less important; the 12-inch single encouraged mixes that increased the instrumental content, elongating songs to eight, nine, or ten minutes for the non-stop pleasure of the dancing audience. New names like Disco Tex, Silver Convention, Anita Ward, Boney M and Donna Summer appeared. The disco era had arrived, and *Saturday Night Fever* was around the corner.

▲ Donna Summer's breakthrough hit was "Love to Love You," recorded with influential disco producers Giorgio Moroder and Pete Bellotte.

"I Saw Rock 'n' Roll Future…"

Veteran *Rolling Stone* journalist Jon Landau had no doubts that he had found a rock messiah in Bruce Springsteen and the world eventually agreed.

When Bruce Springsteen left his blue-collar New Jersey roots in search of stardom in the early 1970s, he followed in the footsteps of Bob Dylan. The man who would later be nicknamed "The Boss" was signed to CBS/Columbia Records by John Hammond, the A&R man who discovered Bob Dylan. But while Springsteen's first two albums mined youthful experience on the boardwalks and in the amusement arcades of New Jersey, it was his incendiary live performances with the E Street Band that caused *Rolling Stone* critic Jon Landau to write: "I saw rock 'n' roll future, and its name is Bruce Springsteen."

By 1975 Springsteen was finally able to transfer that energy to his third album, *Born to Run*. Its release in October was heralded by an unprecedented appearance on the covers of both *Newsweek* and *Time* magazines. There seemed to be no doubt that the music justified the hype.

The songs and performances that brought Springsteen overnight success were built on tried and trusted foundations, echoing classic American singer Roy Orbison's emotive vocal delivery and Dylan's lyrical complexity, along with production that was reminiscent of Phil Spector's multilayered Wall of Sound. He was aided by larger-than-life saxophonist Clarence Clemons, who is featured on the album cover with Springsteen in a pose that has become an enduring rock image.

Millions of fans bought into Springsteen's version of the American Dream, and the album rocketed to No. 3 in the *Billboard* listings. But management problems brought his recording career to a halt soon after. A fourth album was delayed until mid 1978, keeping Bruce on the road to hone his stagecraft, premiere new songs, and build a fan base that would support him for even bigger things to come.

Bruce with long-serving guitarist Steve Van Zandt, who would go on to star in *The Sopranos* TV series. ▶

Where were you when?

"*I first saw Springsteen on the* Darkness on the Edge of Town *tour. The concert was a 3-hour plus powerhouse show with an unbelievable energy level that I had never experienced before. I still have the ticket stub from that night 30 years ago, and I remember the $9.00 ticket price stretched my financial resources to the limit.*"

—Jim Talbot, Toronto

"*Usually at arena gigs there will be some fans sitting down. The bored friends, girlfriends, etc. When I looked round the NEC during 'Born to Run,' nobody was sitting down, all 20,000 were dancing.*"

—Michael Pink, London

JIVE TALKIN' FROM THE BEE GEES

Having fallen from the charts as 1960s pop stars and even turned to cabaret in a bid to stay together, the Gibb brothers—Barry and twins Robin and Maurice—began a spectacular comeback this year with the album *Main Course* (their first Top 40 entry for three years) and hit single "Jive Talkin'." Producer Arif Mardin encouraged Barry to sing falsetto in black soul style. Though Gibb was unconvinced at first, the results were both spectacular and wildly different from the ballad style that had brought 1960s success. "Jive Talkin'" topped the charts, and the following year brought another soulful No. 1 in "You Should Be Dancing." The comeback was completed in 1978 with the *Saturday Night Fever* soundtrack.

The Brothers Gibb; Robin, Barry, and Maurice. ▶

1975

ROD STEWART GOES STATESIDE

After six years of success fronting the Faces, ex-gravedigger Rod Stewart finally left his part-time project. The ostensible reason was guitarist Ron Wood's defection to the Rolling Stones, but in truth Stewart was keen to base himself in the States and capitalize on his solo album *Atlantic Crossing* that had dominated the charts in 1975 with its attendant No. 1 single "Sailing." Stewart's cheeky demeanor and unapologetically sexist songs and "jack the lad" attitude would soften over the years, leading him to tackle the Great American Songbook in four best-selling volumes in the 2000s. In 1975, however, his laddish persona represented British pre-punk rock—a blonde on his arm and a beer in the other hand.

▲ Rod with trademark 70's blonde rinse. His move to the United States in 1975 helped him avoid punitive levels of British income tax and also helped in his relationship with U.S. based Britt Ekland.

Bob Marley— No Woman No Cry

Reggae artist Bob Marley had paid his dues gigging with the Wailers throughout the 1960s, but in the 1970s he found solo fame through a classic live album.

Reggae superstar Bob Marley's recording career began as far back as 1962. Eric Clapton's 1974 recording of his "I Shot the Sheriff" had raised the composer's profile when it topped the U.S. chart, but it wasn't until 1975, when he made a classic live album at the Lyceum ballroom in London, that the Jamaican made his long-awaited British Top 40 breakthrough.

Marley was now sole frontman of the Wailers, a role he'd shared until recently with Bunny Livingston and Peter "Tosh" McIntosh. Livingston and Tosh had fallen by the wayside, leaving Bob—like a Springsteen or a Jagger—the undisputed focus of attention. Most of the repertoire came from the classic Island Records LP trilogy of *Catch a Fire*, *Burnin'*, and *Natty Dread* from1972–75, though the anthemic "Lively Up Yourself" survived from the early Jamaican days when they were produced by Lee "The Upsetter" Perry. Indeed, it was Aston Barrett and brother Carlton on bass and drums, refugees from Perry's studio band, that powered the performance, with female vocal trio the I-Threes, including Marley's wife Rita, adding the gospel-style icing on the cake.

The Top 10 U.K. single "No Woman No Cry" stood out with its yearning quality, but as Marley's biographer Stephen Davis wrote 10 years later, "Every song seemed like an epiphonic poem of folk wisdom, and the band cracked like sheet lightning."

The audience that night, remarkably cosmopolitan in racial terms, included members of the Beatles, Rolling Stones, the Band, and Grateful Dead, plus Joni Mitchell and Cat Stevens—evidence of the impact Marley in particular (and reggae in general) now had. This popularity would continue until 1979, when during a tour of the States, Marley started to appear ill. He had been diagnosed with cancer in a toe in 1977 (described at the time as a football injury). Although he refused to have the toe and part of his right foot amputated, he seemed to be making a recovery. He died in 1981, at age 36, but this 1975 performance released as *Live!* remains one of the greatest live albums of all time.

Still the highest profile reggae artist, Bob Marley. ▶

Where were you when?

"I always associate 'No Woman No Cry' with going to secondary school for the first time in September 1975. It was all over the radio. What was so astonishing was that it was a live single. How many other live singles can you think of…? "

—Andy Stringfellow, Manchester

"I grew up thinking that the song 'No Woman No Cry' was Bob saying that if you don't have a woman in your life it's a lot less stressful. It's only when I saw a TV program recently that I realised it was an instruction 'No Woman Don't Cry.'"

—Lynval Stubbs, London

TOMMY THE MOVIE

The Who's rock opera *Tommy*, Pete Townshend's tale of the deaf, dumb, and blind kid that reached the Top 5 in 1969, finally emerged this year as a movie directed by Ken Russell. The band was augmented by guest stars Eric Clapton, Tina Turner (the Acid Queen), and Elton John as the Pinball Wizard, a part written specially for him that involved his playing a giant Bally machine. Townshend was nominated for an Oscar for his work in scoring and adapting the music for the film, the first and only movie to be recorded with a Quintaphonic soundtrack. *Tommy* would hit London and Broadway as a stage show in the 1990s.

Elton John dons some massive Doc Martens for his role as the Pinball Wizard. Elton got to release the track as a single, too. ▶

1976

STAND-OUT SINGLES

"Convoy"—**C.W. McCall**

"I Write the Songs"
—**Barry Manilow**

"Theme from Mahogany (Do You
Know Where You're Going To)"
—**Diana Ross**

"50 Ways to Leave Your Lover"
—**Paul Simon**

"Love Machine (Part 1)"
—**The Miracles**

"December, 1963 (Oh, What a
Night)"—**The Four Seasons**

"Disco Lady"—**Johnnie Taylor**

"Let Your Love Flow"
—**Bellamy Brothers**

"Welcome Back"—**John Sebastian**

"Boogie Fever"—**The Sylvers**

"Silly Love Songs"—**Wings**

"Love Hangover"—**Diana Ross**

"Afternoon Delight"
—**Starland Vocal Band**

"Kiss and Say Goodbye"
—**Manhattans**

"Don't Go Breaking My Heart"
—**Elton John & Kiki Dee**

"You Should Be Dancing"
—**The Bee Gees**

▲ Remarkably, Elton John had failed to
score a No. 1 single in the United Kingdom
until his 1976 duet with Kiki Dee.

Anarchy in the U.K.

**Inspired by the New York Dolls, the Sex Pistols set about changing the musical
landscape of the United Kingdom and banishing rock's indulgent "hippies."**

Punk pioneers the Sex Pistols and the Beatles' old label EMI, the bastion of pop
respectability, didn't make obvious bedfellows. But the band's Svengali manager Malcolm
McLaren signed his charges with EMI in October 1976 for a £40,000 ($80,000) advance.

It had been a whirlwind rise for Johnny Rotten, Paul Cook, Steve Jones, and Glen
Matlock, four wannabe musicans who got together at the London fashion store run by
McClaren and Vivienne Westwood. Taking their musical cues from the New York Dolls,
whom McLaren had briefly managed, they quickly became the face of punk with their
hand-me-down chic and safety-pinned clothing.

Their first interview with *New Musical Express* in February confirmed that what they
played was subordinate to their attitude: "We're not into music...we're into chaos!" The
cutup newsprint style of designer Jamie Reid, who created their record covers and posters,
was as much imitated as their basic garage-band sound.

Vocalist Rotten harangued his audience, while bassist Matlock, the only real musician
of the group (who would be replaced in February 1977 by the more punky but less able Sid
Vicious) marshaled Jones on guitar and Cook on drums. Attempts to tour Britain were
opposed by local councils, and the outrage they caused by their mere presence was reflected
by a gleeful tabloid press.

The Pistols' scheduled two-year contract ended in as many months when, after swearing
live on television in December, their behavior at London's Heathrow Airport en route to a
show in Amsterdam brought more unsavory headlines. Although the record label would be
commemorated by a track of that name on the Pistols' first album, EMI were undoubtedly
the losers in the affair. The withdrawn version of the group's first single, "Anarchy in the
U.K.," would become an instant collector's item.

The Sex Pistols finally imploded while on tour in America in early 1978, having
produced a classic album in *Never Mind the Bollocks* and two other anthemic singles in
"God Save the Queen" and "Pretty Vacant." Sid Vicious would die of an overdose in
February 1979 while facing charges that he murdered his girlfriend, Nancy Spungen.

The Sex Pistols helped put an end to 1970s mega-groups . ▶

Where were you when?

*"From the moment you heard the opening guitar run on 'Anarchy in the U.K.' you
knew this was a song with energy. Rock had got so lethargic and long-winded.
There were some really dire punk groups out there, but the Pistols had
everything; good songs and a wind-up merchant for a singer.* Never Mind The
Bollocks *helped me loosen all the light fittings in my student digs."*

—Geoff Keeble, Ontario

"I don't understand it. All we're trying to do is destroy everything."

—Johnny Rotten

PETER FRAMPTON COMES ALIVE!

Peter Frampton, ex-guitarist and singer with Brit bands the Herd and Humble Pie, had four good solo albums to draw on when he recorded the double live *Frampton Comes Alive!*—but few, including Frampton, expected the album to make him a big name overnight. It was not only the success of 1976 but his entire solo career. It topped the charts for 10 weeks, spawning Top 10 hit singles in "Show Me the Way" and "Do You Feel Like We Do." His inoffensive soft rock, topped off with the "talkbox" vocal effect that turned guitar riffs into "words," captured the imagination briefly, but the combination of a car crash and an ill-judged follow-up put Peter back in the also-ran bracket.

1976

STAND-OUT ALBUMS

Fleetwood Mac—**Fleetwood Mac**

Desire—**Bob Dylan**

Breezin'—**George Benson**

The Pretender—**Jackson Browne**

I Want You—**Marvin Gaye**

Station to Station—**David Bowie**

Fly Like an Eagle
   —**Steve Miller Band**

Hotel California—**The Eagles**

Ramones—**Ramones**

Songs in the Key of Life
   —**Stevie Wonder**

Boston—**Boston**

Arrival—**Abba**

Night Moves—**Bob Seger**

Chicken Skin Music—**Ry Cooder**

Joan Armatrading
   —**Joan Armatrading**

Small Change—**Tom Waits**

A New World Record—**Electric
   Light Orchestra**

Year of the Cat—**Al Stewart**

Diana Ross—**Diana Ross**

▲ Though Bowie would continue to change his image for the rest of his career, *Station to Station* featured his last character of "The Thin White Duke."

Where were you when?

"*When you're a fan you maybe look through things with rose-tinted spectacles. I saw the film when it was released in cinemas and thought it was better than the Woodstock movie. Now I'm able to own them both on DVD I can see that* The Last Waltz, *though lovingly shot, is not in the same league.*"

—Trent Chapel, Fairbanks, Alaska

"*The road was our school. It gave us a sense of survival; it taught us everything we know, and out of respect, we don't want to drive it into the ground.*"

—Robbie Robertson

The Last Waltz

The Band's Robbie Robertson couldn't imagine 20 years on the road. So after 16 they decided to call it quits with a farewell performance filmed by Scorsese.

Famed for backing Bob Dylan for over a decade, the Band decided to bow out of live performance after 16 years on the road with a farewell performance at San Francisco's Winterland ballroom on Thanksgiving Day 1976.

They were joined by more than a dozen special guests, including Paul Butterfield, Eric Clapton, Neil Diamond, Bob Dylan, Ronnie Hawkins, Dr. John, Joni Mitchell, Ringo Starr, Muddy Waters, Ron Wood, and Neil Young. The star turn of the evening was Van Morrison, whose entrance was described by rock writer Greil Marcus as "the catalyst that turned the show round." The performances were immortalized by filmmaker Martin Scorsese, who directed a movie of the epic four-hour final concert. A triple vinyl album of highlights also appeared that contained many songs not featured in the film.

The five-piece group—Rick Danko on bass, violin and vocals, Levon Helm on drums, mandolin, and vocals; Garth Hudson on keyboards and saxophone; Richard Manuel on keyboards, percussion, and vocals; and guitarist/songwriter Robbie Robertson—were impressive, but Helm believed the film concentrated too much on Robertson (Scorsese was Robertson's former roommate), whose decision to quit the road had prompted the disbandment. This would be the last time the five of them would appear on stage together.

The Band would re-form without Robertson in the 1980s, but their ranks were tragically depleted when Richard Manuel hanged himself after a 1986 show. Rick Danko died in 1999, while Robertson continued his musical career in soundtracks. The Band is credited with creating the Americana musical genre successfully mined by Wilco, Ryan Adams, Gillian Welch, and their like.

◀ Robbie Robertson takes center stage, with Rick Danko on bass to his right.

STIFF RECORDS

The brainchild of Dave Robinson and Jake Riviera, Stiff Records was a British indie label that more than punched its weight. It launched the careers of Nick Lowe, Ian Dury, and Elvis Costello, among others, with a welter of hype and some very clever slogans: "If it ain't Stiff it ain't worth a ****" being the most memorable. The Damned's single "New Rose" was the first punk single to achieve national distribution in the United Kingdom. A second chart assault was headed by the likes of Kirsty MacColl and the Pogues as the established stars headed for bigger contracts, but in ten years of existence Stiff carved a niche for itself as a witty footnote in pop history.

Elvis Costello (second left) was one of Stiff's main attractions. ▶

1976

"I FEEL LOVE"
—DONNA SUMMER

LaDonna Andrea Gaines arrived in Germany in 1970 after touring Europe with hippie musical *Hair*. Six years later she was sitting pretty atop the worldwide charts as Donna Summer with "I Feel Love," an electronic disco smash produced by Georgio Moroder. The sound of the "Munich Machine," created by Moroder and English guitarist Pete Bellotte, would dominate the discos for a while and, with its sequenced, synthesised beats, prove highly influential on the dance music of future decades. Summer would continue to find success for the rest of the decade, but later turned her back at least temporarily on her gay fans and disco roots.

Where were you when?

"Some of the wilder interpretations of 'Hotel California' have been amazing. It was really about the excesses of American culture and certain girls we knew. But it was also about the uneasy balance between art and commerce."

—Don Henley

"I used to think that the Eagles had a big feud with Steely Dan, but last year when the Eagles were touring I heard Glenn Frey say that they were friends and had the same management. Hence the song reference, '...they stab them with their steely knives.'"

—Mike Schmidt, Nashville

Hotel California

Founding member Bernie Leadon left The Eagles while Joe Walsh arrived to help create an album that would become one of the sounds of the 1970s.

Hotel California, the fifth album by West Coast supergroup the Eagles, featured an epic six-and-a-half-minute title track, the meaning of which is still hotly debated three decades later. The song has been interpreted as a statement on the hedonism of the Southern California music industry. Don Henley called it "our interpretation of the high life in Los Angeles."

The Eagles' off-stage excesses were also becoming news. Their hedonistic drug-fueled lifestyle led to critics claiming that art imitated life—much to their resentment. But the quintet were laughing all the way to the bank.

Ex-James Gang frontman Joe Walsh had joined the band in place of bluegrass fan Bernie Leadon prior to the recording of *Hotel California* and had a big influence throughout, writing and arranging many of the guitar parts and co-penning "Life in the Fast Lane" with Henley and singer Glenn Frey. The title track was one of two chart-topping singles the album contained; the other was "New Kid in Town."

WHEN HELL FREEZES OVER

The building on the album cover is the Beverly Hills Hotel, known as the Pink Palace, which is often frequented by Hollywood stars. The photographers sat in a cherry picker 60 feet above Sunset Boulevard to get the shot of the hotel at sunset from above the trees.

The *Hotel California* album reached No. 1 in the United States early in 1977, selling more than 9 million copies in that country alone and held at No. 2 in the United Kingdom. *Rolling Stone* magazine has since rated it No. 37 on their list of the 500 Greatest Albums of all time.

The Eagles would implode after taking two argumentative years to produce the difficult follow-up album *The Long Run*. Henley declared a reunion would take place only "When hell freezes over"—which it duly did in 1994. A new studio album, however, would take another 13 years.

◄ The Eagles in 1976, from left to right, Don Henley, Joe Walsh, Don Felder, Glenn Frey, and Randy Meisner.

TRACK LISTING

I had an auto accident all on my own because I was driving too fast with the stereo up loud, beating time on the dashboard with one hand. I didn't file on the report that I was listening to "Life in the Fast Lane."

—Erik Andersson, Milwaukee

Side One
Hotel California
New Kid in Town
Life in the Fast Lane
Wasted Time

Side Two
Wasted Time (Reprise)
Victim of Love
Petty Maids All in a Row
Try and Love Again
Last Resort

◄ *Hotel California* was the Eagles' fifth studio album and is one of the top 15 best-selling albums of all time.

1977

BEST-SELLING U.K. SINGLES

This was the year the U.K. chart was allegedly rigged so that Rod Stewart's single, "I Don't Want to Talk About It" was placed at No. 1 instead of the Sex Pistols' "God Save the Queen" to avoid embarrassment in Queen Elizabeth II's Jubilee week. Neither record made the end of year best sellers' chart, however.

"Mull of Kintyre"—**Wings**

"Don't Give Up on Us" —**David Soul**

"Don't Cry for Me Argentina" —**Julie Covington**

"When I Need You"—**Leo Sayer**

"Silver Lady"—**David Soul**

"Knowing Me Knowing You"—**Abba**

"I Feel Love"—**Donna Summer**

"Way Down"—**Elvis Presley**

"So You Win Again" —**Hot Chocolate**

"Angelo"—**Brotherhood of Man**

The King is Dead

Elvis Presley's sudden death at 42 was an event that stopped traffic and headed news bulletins all around the world.

There had been clear indications that Elvis Presley's health had been declining for some time, but the news of his death at the age of 42 still came as a shock to millions of fans across the globe. The King of Rock 'n' Roll had been found slumped on the floor of a bathroom at Gracelands on the afternoon of Tuesday, August 16. He was rushed to Baptist Memorial Hospital in Memphis but was declared dead on arrival. At 4:00 P.M., his death was announced to the world.

The news spread quickly. Radio and television programs were interrupted, and across the country people stopped what they were doing and tried to get any information they could. President Jimmy Carter paid tribute, saying: "With Elvis Presley a part of our country died as well," and former president Richard Nixon, who had a famous meeting with Elvis at the White House in 1970, asked all Americans to fly their flags at half mast. In Memphis the telephone network was jammed as many thousands of calls came flooding in.

PRESCRIPTION DRUGS

Initial reports gave the cause of death as heart failure and later reports said that the cause had not been determined, although Tennessee state pathologist Dr. Jerry Francisco was at pains to point out that no sign of drug abuse had been found. The truth was rather different: for several years before his death, Presley had become increasingly dependent on a mixture of prescription drugs, and these, coupled with his addiction to junk food, led to his early demise.

Although Presley had carried on performing right up to his death, the young, vibrant rock 'n' roller that had so galvanized the nation's teenagers 20 years earlier had become a dim, distant memory. His die-hard fans didn't seem to care, though. To them he was the King, come what may, and through them the memory of the man who brought rock 'n' roll to the world would continue to live on.

A sad day for Memphis as Elvis's coffin exits through the gates of Graceland. ▶

Where were you when?

"*I was 10 at the time and thought of him as an 'old' rock star. Now I'm coming up to the age that he died I realise he was truly very young.*"

—Madison Young, Scottsdale

"*I was at my parent's house in Memphis. I could tell my dad was upset about the news but he tried to shrug it off. The section of Highway 51 by Graceland was jammed for days afterwards.*"

—Mike Schmidt, Nashville

"*I heard the news on the tinniest of VW car radios traveling along the Pacific Coast Highway. It was so shocking I had to retune to a news program.*"

—Dan Parks, Fullerton

A RIOT OF MY OWN

The Clash, formed in the summer of 1976 by guitarist Mick Jones and bassist Paul Simonon and fronted by Joe Strummer, were the next most important punk band after the Sex Pistols. They took to the road after the release of first album, *The Clash*, which sold an unprecedented 100,000 on import after CBS Records refused to release it in the States. The band set out on the whirlwind White Riot tour of the United Kingdom, supported by the Jam and the Buzzcocks; this climaxed at London's Rainbow Theatre, when the audience tore the seats out of the venue in echoes of early rock 'n' roll. During the tour, CBS pulled "Remote Control" off the album as a single without the band's consent. In response, the Clash recorded "Complete Control" with reggae icon Lee 'Scratch' Perry.

The Clash's debut album, *The Clash*. ▶

1977

BEST-SELLING U.S. SINGLES

"You Light Up My Life"
—**Debby Boone**

"I Just Want to Be Your Everything"
—**Andy Gibb**

"Evergreen"—**Barbra Streisand**

"Undercover Angel"—**Alan O'Day**

"I Like Dreamin"—**Kenny Nolan**

"Dancing Queen"—**Abba**

"Torn Between Two Lovers"
—**Mary MacGregor**

"Higher and Higher"
—**Rita Coolidge**

"Southern Nights"
—**Glen Campbell**

"Best of My Love"
—**The Emotions**

▲ The Bee Gees' younger brother Andy Gibb also got in on the family act in 1977 with an impressive debut single. His first three songs would peak at No. 1 on the *Billboard* Hot 100.

Where were you when?

"For about six months I tried to emulate the walk that Travolta does at the beginning of the film. The killer walk. I was convinced that girls would find me irresistible if I could just get the walk right."

—Nathan Griffiths, Cardiff

"I can remember putting a lot of make-up on to get into the film. I was 16 and I had to look 18 to get in."

—Yvonne LaSalle, Charlotte

Saturday Night Fever

John Badham's gritty film about a young man struggling to escape a dead end job through his passion for disco music was not an obvious blockbuster.

When rock impresario Robert Stigwood purchased the rights to a movie project to be scripted by writer Nik Cohn in 1976, he knew it could be a winner. Stigwood, ex-manager of Cream, had been captivated by a Cohn article in a New York magazine entitled "Tribal Rites of the New Saturday Night," based on the city's burgeoning disco culture. The soundtrack of the film would be supplied by Stigwood's current charges, a British group called the Bee Gees.

Saturday Night Fever was a gritty, realistic look at life on the wrong side of town, although its darker side was toned down for a "family-friendly" edit, made to broaden the film's viewing demographic the following year. The lead role of upwardly mobile dancer Tony Manero was played by John Travolta, well known to U.S. TV audiences, thanks to his role in the sitcom *Welcome Back Kotter*. In the film he strutted his stuff under the mirror ball in an iconic white suit, and the box-office tills roared approval.

The soundtrack album combined six self-composed Bee Gees songs that appeared in the movie with other tracks, performed by soul groups Tavares, Trammps, and KC and the Sunshine Band. The album spawned four No. 1 singles: the Bee Gees' "How Deep Is Your Love," "Saturday Night Fever," and "Stayin' Alive," plus Yvonne Elliman's version of their "If I Can't Have You."

Not only was *Saturday Night Fever* a cultural phenomenon, it was an industry phenomenon, too. The film grossed an estimated $300 million and the album spent 24 weeks at the top of the charts. In fact, it went on to become the best-selling soundtrack album of all time.

◄ John Travolta as Tony Manero riding the subway all night after watching his friend, Bobby C., fall to his death from the Verrazano-Narrows bridge.

LYNYRD SKYNYRD

The story of legendary Southern rockers Lynyrd Skynyrd that began with a performance in a barbecue house in Jacksonville, Florida, in 1965, almost ended on October 20 when a plane crash near McCombe, Mississippi, deprived them of lead singer Ronnie van Zant—one of six fatalities among their entourage—and injured many band members. Their tour had been scheduled to peak two weeks later at Madison Square Garden, confirming their membership in rock's box-office elite. Ironically the cover of latest album *Street Survivors* depicted the band in a ring of fire. Skynyrd would re-form 10 years later and tour with van Zant's brother Johnny, but their legend still relies on the halcyon early-1970s years of "Freebird" and "Sweet Home Alabama."

Skynyrd's final album with Ronnie van Zant. ▶

1977

STUDIO 54

With disco at a peak of popularity, scenemaker Steve Rubell and partner Ian Shrager opened the most exclusive nightspot of them all in New York. Studio 54 at 254 West 54th Street would become a mecca for socialites, musicians, and wannabes—provided they could get past the club's elitist door policy that left many waiting frustratedly at the "velvet rope" should they not be selected for entry. The club would be namechecked in Chic's disco anthem "Le Freak" (above), which they wrote after being denied entry in 1977. It closed its famous logo-bedecked doors in 1986.

Brooke Shields and Steve Rubell at a gala re-opening of Studio 54. ▾

Rumours

Relations within Fleetwood Mac may have been tense, but the creative tension the problems generated helped create a behemoth of soft rock.

When Fleetwood Mac released the second self-titled album of the group's career in July 1975, they could hardly have anticipated what was just around the corner. The album sold slowly but steadily, setting a new record for the time it spent on the charts before reaching the No. 1 spot in September the following year. It eventually sold 4.5 million copies, spawned three Top 20 singles, and paved the way for the astonishing success of the band's follow-up, *Rumours*, released in February 1977.

Rumours was a cleverly crafted mix of catchy melodies, smooth harmonies, and surprisingly light instrumentation that catapulted the band to superstar status. It spent 31 weeks at the top of the *Billboard* 200—more than any other album since *West Side Story*, which notched up 54 weeks in the early 1960s—and provided the band with their only No. 1 single, "Dreams." As ever, there were dissenting voices, and some critics dismissed the album as inconsequential and lightweight, but its soft-rock style and essential simplicity seemed to have an almost universal appeal.

All the more amazing, then, that *Rumours* was written and recorded by a band in turmoil. In the 18 months leading up to its release, Mick Fleetwood's marriage had hit the rocks, and the two couples in the band—John and Christine McVie, and Lindsey Buckingham and Stevie Nicks—had each separated, but all of them remained members of Fleetwood Mac. Somehow the five of them managed to pull together, despite any anger or bitterness, to create a world-beating collection of songs.

The album's title, as Christine McVie later explained, came from the fact that they were all effectively writing about each other, and perhaps it was this raw, emotional dimension that broadened the album's appeal.

From left to right: John McVie, Christine McVie, Stevie Nicks, Mick Fleetwood, and Lindsey Buckingham. ▶

Where were you when?

"Rumours *was a great LP to put on when you took a girl back. There wasn't a weak track on it. It could have been longer though, it seemed like you were always turning the record over.*"

—Brent Baxter, Mobile, Alabama

"*A lot of our personal lives came through on this disc. The feeling, perhaps, was one of pain.*"

—John McVie

BAT OUT OF HELL

A quasi-operatic concept album produced by Todd Rundgren and the brainchild of writer Jim Steinman turned the former Marvin Lee Aday into a heavyweight rock name—and Meat Loaf's *Bat Out of Hell* album into a phenomenon. And while its No. 14 chart peak was moderate, it would become a consistent seller over the following decade, selling seven million in the United States alone. In Britain, bolstered by a series of gothic videos, it would notch up an amazing 471 weeks on the chart and pass 2 million sales. Two follow-ups to *Bat* were created, but neither they nor Steinman's solo album *Bad for Good* and later project *Pandora's Box* recaptured either the magic or the sales of the original.

Bat out of Hell continues to sell 200,000 copies a year. ▶

1978

SID VICIOUS KILLS NANCY SPUNGEN

When former Sex Pistols bassist Sid Vicious called police to the room in New York's Chelsea Hotel where his girlfriend Nancy Spungen had bled to death on October 12, he had no memory of having stabbed her. (Indeed, conspiracy theories as to possible killers have since abounded.) Both were drug addicts with a very shaky grasp on reality or lucidity. Bailed by manager Malcolm McLaren after a spell in Riker's prison, he soon attempted to take his own life by slashing his wrists, and returned to prison that Christmas after being involved in a fight. Released once more in February 1979, Vicious (real name John Ritchie), who had cleaned up in jail, died of a heroin overdose before he could be brought to trial. He was just 21.

Pretty vacant: Glen Matlock (left), the original bass guitarist of the Sex Pistols shares a settee with Nancy Spungen and his replacement bass guitarist Sid Vicious. Sid had previously been the drummer with Siouxsie and the Banshees and couldn't play his instrument. ▼

Grease is the Word

Robert Stigwood needed a follow-up to *Saturday Night Fever* and in a 1950s revivalist stage musical he found a vehicle that was greased lightning...

Apart from igniting the disco inferno, *Saturday Night Fever* revitalized the movie musical, a form that had been in decline for several years. During 1978 a wide variety of musicals hit the silver screen, including *The Buddy Holly Story*, *The Wiz*, *The Last Waltz*, *Thank God It's Friday*, and Bob Dylan's sprawling *Renaldo and Clara*, but head and shoulders above them all was *Grease*, Robert Stigwood's follow-up to *Saturday Night Fever*.

Based on the smash hit stage musical of the same name, *Grease* starred John Travolta and Olivia Newton-John as Danny and Sandy in a story of love and teenage rebellion set in Chicago at the end of the 1950s. Along the way, the storyline takes in adolescent sex, teenage pregnancy, and gang culture, but in stark contrast to the contemporary realism of *Saturday Night Fever*, this was an unashamedly lighthearted helping of nostalgia.

Several successful singles were lifted from the soundtrack, although only "Summer Nights" had featured in the original stage show, "You're The One That I Want," "Grease," and "Hopelessly Devoted To You" were all specially written for the film. Meanwhile, the soundtrack album, released shortly before the film, topped the *Billboard* chart for 12 of its 39 weeks in the Top 40.

THE FONZ

Had things worked out, John Travolta's character would have been played by Henry Winkler. The man who played the Fonz on TV's *Happy Days* auditioned for the part and got it, but he withdrew for fear of being typecast. Olivia Newton-John landed the part of Sandy after Marie Osmond turned it down, apparently unhappy that the character had to shed her "nice girl" image to get the guy.

While *Grease* simply confirmed John Travolta's superstar status, it revitalized Newton-John's career. After several successful years as a country singer, her star was in decline, and the movie offered a fresh challenge. In the wake of the film, Newton-John moved her musical career in a more mainstream direction.

Olivia Newton-John (Sandy) and John Travolta (Danny) put on the style on prom night. ▶

Where were you when?

"There's so many characters in Grease *that everyone can identify with someone in the cast."*
—Julie-Anne Duchesne, Montreal

"I feel like a part of history. I don't know if I would trade Grease *for anything."*
—John Travolta

1978

EVITA OPENS IN LONDON

Evita, the story of the rise of Eva Duarte from struggling actress to the wife of Argentine dictator Juan Peron and her subsequent death, made it to the stage this year. It opened in June at London's Prince Edward Theatre. Andrew Lloyd Webber and Tim Rice had completed the book and score in 1975 and the first recording was released in 1976 with Julie Covington as Eva and former Manfred Mann vocalist, Paul Jones, as Peron. The original production featured Elaine Paige as Eva (Julie Covington having declined the role), Joss Ackland as Peron and David Essex as Che and ran for well over 2,000 performances, ending in 1986. It opened in Los Angeles in May 1979 in a slightly modified form, transferring to Broadway four months later, and subsequently toured around the world.

Where were you when?

"After I heard 'Heart of Glass' on the radio I knew this was it. I would read my collection of Creem *magazine back to front for any small mention of Debbie Harry. I joined the Blondie fan club at 13 and got a plastic card with all the band's signatures. I wish I still had it, but you never keep the things you should."*

—Toby Ford, Portland

"As a kid, I always found blondes fascinating—that element of drama and tragedy was very attractive."

—Debbie Harry

Blondie

From punk came new wave, and out of new wave came a band playing power pop with a lead singer who held every teenage boy's attention.

While punk and the subsequent new wave genres had been sweeping established acts aside in the United Kingdom for almost two years, their impact in the United States had been limited until Blondie achieved a breakthrough in the autumn of 1978.

Fronted by former waitress and *Playboy* Bunny Debbie Harry, Blondie had been around since the mid 1970s, and early in their career she could be found playing gigs at such fashionable New York clubs as Max's and CBGB's. Harry was the perfect focal point—cool, sassy, and in control—and she attracted attention from the outset. But there was more to Blondie than a pretty girl. While the reaction at home remained muted, it wasn't long before the band's blend of 1960s power pop and new wave began to bring success overseas.

By the time *Parallel Lines* appeared in 1978, U.S. critics were beginning to take notice—*Rolling Stone* described *Parallel Lines* as "creating its own sound within a contemporary pop framework." Blondie abandoned their new wave credibility to embrace pure pop. The band's songwriting had developed steadily and now showed a remarkable consistency. Virtually any of the album's 12 tracks could have been released as a single, and six of them eventually were, although "Sunday Girl" was lifted only in Europe.

When "Heart of Glass" topped the Hot 100 singles chart in April 1979, Blondie's status as purveyors of top-quality mainstream pop was confirmed. Never afraid to absorb influences, their band's marriage of Giorgio Moroder electronica and *Saturday Night Fever* proved irresistible, and disco-pastiche became dance-floor classic.

Ushering in the band's most successful period, *Parallel Lines* went on to sell 20 million copies and is still widely regarded as Blondie's finest hour.

◄ Blondie was fronted by Debbie Harry. Though fans didn't realise it, she was already 33 when *Parallel Lines* was released.

PUNK MORPHS INTO NEW WAVE

While punk had undoubtedly revived the music scene with a much-needed infusion of energy, its spitting and safety pins were a little too extreme for some. So the term new wave was borrowed in an effort to market these new bands to an audience that didn't want to be threatened. Some say it was Sire Records boss Seymour Stein who coined the term, likening those who made the music to the French new wave of film in the 1960s. Certain sub-genres appeared, such as power pop, played by men with skinny ties and straight jeans like The Knack—most of whom were on at least their second stab at fame—while for others, like the Boomtown Rats, the Pretenders, and Elvis Costello it was a convenient marketing term.

The Knack had great success with the Punk-like "My Sharona." ▶

1979

STAND-OUT ALBUMS

Breakfast in America—**Supertramp**

Minute by Minute
—**Doobie Brothers**

Parallel Lines—**Blondie**

Cheap Trick at Budokan
—**Cheap Trick**

Slow Train Coming—**Bob Dylan**

Risqué—**Chic**

The Long Run—**The Eagles**

Tusk—**Fleetwood Mac**

Off the Wall—**Michael Jackson**

In Through the Out Door
—**Led Zeppelin**

London Calling—**The Clash**

Unknown Pleasures—**Joy Division**

Rust Never Sleeps
—**Neil Young & Crazy Horse**

The Wall—**Pink Floyd**

Metal Box/Second Edition
—**Public Image Ltd.**

The Specials—**The Specials**

Fear of Music—**Talking Heads**

Highway to Hell—**AC/DC**

Damn the Torpedoes—**Tom Petty
and the Heartbreakers**

The B-52's—**The B-52's**

▲ Supertramp's *Breakfast in America* was more successful in America than in the band's native Britain.

Where were you when?

"It was the corniest dance of all time, but you still see people doing the Y.M.C.A. at wedding parties. The Rick Astley 'Rick 'n' Roll' phenomenon means that you can never discount something goofy reappearing. I also saw some guys doing it in a museum on You Tube. "

—Roach Bailey, Indianapolis

"My favorite was the construction worker. I truly believe he started the trend for ripped Levis."

—Howard Martin, High Wycombe, England

Village People & D.I.S.C.O.

With its high-energy beats, disco music was the staple of gay clubs. So Jacques Morali got five guys to dress in "fantasy gear" and targeted the market.

The disco phenomenon, recognized by *Saturday Night Fever* in 1977, hit some sort of peak as the decade neared its close. And while the likes of Kool and the Gang, the Ohio Players, James Brown, and Earth, Wind, and Fire managed to jump on the gravy train, Bernard Edwards and Nile Rodgers of Chic turned their talents to producing and writing songs for others as well as scoring hits themselves.

In Europe, Giorgio Moroder and Frank Farian were making Germany an unlikely hotbed of disco creativity by launching the sounds of Donna Summer and Boney M. onto the world's dance floors. But the most curious creation of all was surely that of French producer Jacques Morali, whose Village People stormed the charts in 1979. The name was borrowed from the gay community based in New York's Greenwich Village.

Big Apple–based Morali wanted to create a group for the gay disco crowd to identify with, so he stitched together some stereotypes. Felipe Rose wore an Indian headdress, Randy Jones was a cowboy, Alex Briley was a GI, David Hodo was a construction worker, and Glenn Hughes, the last to join, wore leather from head to toe.

They followed up their debut Top 30 hit, "Macho Man," with a nursery rhyme–type singalong song called "YMCA," written as a filler to complete their first album. The Young Men's Christian Association at first objected to the appropriation of its name but would later ask to use the song in a commercial, so successful was the song and its accompanying dance routine. The feat was repeated with "In the Navy," which peaked at No. 3, one rung below its predecessor, but both songs topped charts worldwide.

Both remain floor fillers with enduring camp appeal today, but as the Village People's career burnt out—along with the money used to back their disastrous movie, *Can't Stop The Music*—so did disco.

◄ The first gay concept band, Village People arrived on the scene just as disco began to fade and introspective electronic bands came to the fore.

THE SONY WALKMAN

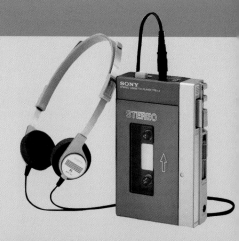

Invented in Japan in 1979, and considerably bulkier than subsequent versions, Sony's Walkman (or "Stowaway" in some markets) personal tape player offered entertainment on the move. It was created by removing the record function and speaker from a cassette recorder and equipping it with stereo circuits and headphones. Early versions had two headphone sockets so friends could share, but the manufacturer wanted everyone to own one so got rid of the extra socket. The original concept of a portable stereo came from Masaru Ibuka and Akio Morita, whose pocket-size plastic creation became an essential accessory to modern life. Radio and tape versions were released as well as sport and waterproof ones, and, while it has now been superseded by the digital iPod and MP3 player, the Walkman deserves its pioneering place in music history.

1979

STAND-OUT SINGLES

"My Sharona"—**The Knack**

"Le Freak"—**Chic**

"Do Ya Think I'm Sexy?"
—**Rod Stewart**

"Bad Girls"—**Donna Summer**

"YMCA"—**Village People**

"Reunited"—**Peaches and Herb**

"Ring My Bell"—**Anita Ward**

"I Will Survive"—**Gloria Gaynor**

"Too Much Heaven"—**Bee Gees**

"Hot Stuff"—**Donna Summer**

"Heart of Glass"—**Blondie**

"Tragedy"—**Bee Gees**

"Pop Muzik"—**M**

"Video Killed the Radio Star"
—**The Buggles**

"I Don't Like Mondays"
—**Boomtown Rats**

"Bright Eyes"—**Art Garfunkel**

"What a Fool Believes"
—**Doobie Brothers**

"Sultans of Swing"—**Dire Straits**

"Hold the Line"—**Toto**

"We Are Family"—**Sister Sledge**

Valerie Perrine stars with the Village People in the ill-fated movie *Can't Stop the Music*. The film took the honor of the first ever Worst Picture at the Golden Raspberry Awards of 1980. ▼

Where were you when?

"*We feel that in the future, groups are going to have to offer much more than just a pop show. They'll have to offer a well-presented theatre show.*"

—Syd Barrett (talking to *Melody Maker* in 1967)

"*I saw* The Wall *at Earls Court and it was so different from any other rock experience. The show works well in a big arena because you never get to see the band. So why not have a wall.*"

—Jerry Kelly, North London

The Wall

Pink Floyd's Roger Waters created the ultimate reclusive rock star performance. A wall was built between the band and the audience as they played…

The last major rock album of the 1970s came from a dysfunctional supergroup—Pink Floyd. *The Wall* was, in all but name, a Roger Waters solo effort on which the other members of the band acted as session men. Relationships within the band had deteriorated to such an extent that bassist vocalist Waters fired keyboardist Rick Wright during the album sessions, although he stayed to complete the recording and played on the subsequent tour as a hired musician.

Like *Animals* before it, *The Wall* dealt with society's ills, this time with a narrative structure and a central character, Pink, who suffers at the hands of an overprotective mother, vindictive teachers, and an unfaithful wife. Pink withdraws into himself, building a metaphorical wall around him to keep the world at bay. Madness and self-delusion follow, before Pink realizes he must escape and tear the wall down.

Live performances of the work broke new ground. During each show an enormous wall was erected in front of the band, gradually obscuring them from view. Animated films, created by artist Gerald Scarfe, were projected onto the wall, and several of the album's main characters appeared in the form of enormous puppets, also designed by Scarfe. The band's aim was to transform the album into a fully realized theatrical presentation, and in this they succeeded spectacularly, although the show was so complex and expensive to stage that performances were limited to short runs in each of a handful of major cities.

A film version followed in 1982, and Waters, who retained the rights to *The Wall* after he left Pink Floyd in 1985, performed it in Berlin with an all-star cast in 1990 to celebrate German reunification.

◄ Floyd's David Gilmour (left) and Nick Mason teeter on the edge of the stage in front of The Wall.

ELTON JOHN PLAYS IN RUSSIA

Having enjoyed an 18-month retirement from live performance, Elton John made history this month when he became the first non-classical Western musician to tour the still resolutely Communist Russia. The flower-strewn stage he left after climaxing his set with a full-on version of the Beatles' "Back in the USSR" attested to the fact that this was most definitely a case of to Russia, with love! A film crew followed him around as he played four concerts in Leningrad and a similar number in Moscow—and, as the tabloids back home proclaimed the coming of "Elton John Superczar," the veteran pianoman was clearly enjoying himself. "It was one of the most memorable and happy tours I've been on," beamed an invigorated Elton. "The hospitality was tremendous, the only negative experience, two or three vodka hangovers."

1980-1989

1980

STAND-OUT SINGLES

"Cruisin'"—**Smokey Robinson**

"Call Me"—**Blondie**

"Refugee"—**Tom Petty and the Heartbreakers**

"Another Brick in the Wall" —**Pink Floyd**

"Brass in Pocket"—**Pretenders**

"Geno"—**Dexys Midnight Runners**

"Fame"—**Irene Cara**

"The Rose"—**Bette Midler**

"Master Blaster (Jammin')" —**Stevie Wonder**

"Another One Bites the Dust" —**Queen**

"Love Will Tear Us Apart" —**Joy Division**

"Once in a Lifetime" —**Talking Heads**

"Ace of Spades"—**Motörhead**

"Going Underground"—**The Jam**

"I Will Follow"—**U2**

"Vienna"—**Ultravox**

▲ "Call Me," taken from the soundtrack to the film *American Gigolo,* was Blondie's biggest hit in the United States, reaching the top of the charts there and in the United Kingdom.

I Heard the News Today…

The shooting of John Lennon in New York on December 8 shocked music fans throughout the world who mourned the loss of one of rock's true geniuses.

The 40-year-old ex-Beatle had lived the previous five years out of the public eye, preferring to spend his time bringing up his son, Sean, with his wife, Yoko Ono. The silence had just ended in November with the release of *Double Fantasy,* an album that reflected a new philosophy. A single from the album, "(Just Like) Starting Over" was Lennon's first hit after six and a half years. To his fans' delight, Lennon had rediscovered the urge to make music, and the world awaited his next move with interest. Sadly, this move would never come. John and Yoko were approaching the Dakota, the elegant old apartment building where they lived, after a day at the recording studio when they were accosted by Mark Chapman, a 25-year-old security guard from Hawaii to whom Lennon had given his autograph earlier in the day. Chapman was obsessed with Lennon and had, it appeared, been stalking him for three days before shooting him five times at point-blank range.

Lennon was rushed to Roosevelt Memorial Hospital but was pronounced dead half an hour later. As the tragic news spread, crowds of grieving New Yorkers gathered outside the Dakota in the darkness. The day after his death, Ono issued a statement: "There is no funeral for John. John loved and prayed for the human race. Please pray the same for him." Three thousand miles away in John's hometown of Liverpool, fans held a silent vigil that would be repeated by millions worldwide on December 14 at the request of Yoko Ono. Fans reacted by buying his records in numbers unprecedented since the 1960s. Three different singles, "(Just Like) Starting Over," "Woman," and "Watching the Wheels," reached the Top 10 as the world mourned.

A fan's eye view of John Lennon and Yoko Ono in New York, January 1980. Lennon would regularly stop outside the Dakota, pose for photos, and sign autographs. ▶

Where were you when?

"We felt like we were going to be together for another 50 years or something."

—Yoko Ono

"I'm not afraid of death because I don't believe in it. It's just getting out of one car, and into another."

—John Lennon

"I woke up to the news and remember thinking, 'well, that serves him right for moving to a city where everyone owns a hand gun.' Which I regret now."

—Ashley Jennings, Swindon, England

FAME—REMEMBER MY NAME

Alan Parker's movie musical *Fame* followed four students at New York's High School for the Performing Arts from the time when they auditioned through to graduation. The unknown cast headed by Irene Cara made a big impression with their depiction of teenagers struggling to survive in a gritty, competitive, and stressful environment while they attempt to climb the ladder to fame and fortune. The title song won the Academy Award and the Golden Globe Award for Best Original Song. The show spun off into a successful TV series, *Kids From Fame*, in which a number of the original cast participated. The aspirational nature of *Fame*—not to mention the headbands and legwarmers—would strike a chord with a generation.

Leroy (played by Gene Anthony Ray) featured in the film and TV series. ▶

1980

BEST-SELLING ALBUMS

The Wall—**Pink Floyd**

The Long Run—**Eagles**

Off the Wall—**Michael Jackson**

Glass Houses—**Billy Joel**

Damn the Torpedoes—**Tom Petty & the Heartbreakers**

Emotional Rescue —**The Rolling Stones**

The River—**Bruce Springsteen**

The Game—**Queen**

Guilty—**Barbra Streisand**

Double Fantasy—**John Lennon and Yoko Ono**

Against the Wind—**Bob Seger & the Silver Bullet Band**

▲ *Off the Wall* was Michael Jackson's fifth solo album. Although it only reached the No. 3 spot, it sold 7 million copies and was his biggest selling album to date.

Where were you when?

"The trick was to keep the happening ingredients high energy, the reggae thing, emotional lyrics—and take them into new places."

—Stewart Copeland

"I worked in an office with 12 other women of about the same age and one day we all confessed to having fantasies about Sting. He was like the 'Diet Coke' guy of the 1980s."

—Sally Reynolds, Manchester, England

Don't Stand So Close To Me

The Police were No. 1 artists in the United Kingdom long before they enjoyed U.S. chart success. That all changed with singles taken from their 1980 album.

"Proto hippies on the other side of punk." That was one of many disparaging headlines describing the Police, an unusual group with an unusual name. Given the advanced age of guitarist Andy Summers, born in 1942 and active in the 1960s with the New Animals, and then later in jazz-rockers Soft Machine, they made unlikely punks. But the band, led by jazz-loving ex-schoolteacher Gordon "Sting" Sumner and completed by drummer Stewart Copeland, on the run from fading prog-rockers Curved Air, surfed to success with a mix of fast-paced rock and reggae rhythms.

Their bleached-blond image was also a factor as the MTV era approached; Sting's film star looks were a major selling point. While they were already a major success in Britain, it was their third album, *Zenyatta Mondatta*, and its associated singles that established the Police as a truly worldwide phenomenon. In the United States the nonsensical "De Do Do Do, De Da Da Da" stormed the airwaves to make the Top 10, and was closely followed by "Don't Stand So Close to Me" (which also won a 1982 Grammy award); the album reached No. 5 and paved the way for further success.

In Britain "Don't Stand So Close" was the biggest-selling single of the year. Written by Sting, their third chart-topping 45 told the tale of an illicit teacher-pupil relationship and featured a tortured rhyme between "shake and cough" and "Nabokov." Though Sting had worked as a teacher earlier in his life, he denied there was any autobiographical element in the lyric. The song re-charted in revised form in 1986 when a *Greatest Hits* album was released. At that point the band had been dormant for a couple of years.

It would be two decades before Sting's acting career and solo commitments permitted a reunion world tour for the Police, which took place in 2007 to general acclaim.

◄ From left to right: Stewart Copeland, Sting, and Andy Summers. Although The Police felt that the recording of *Zenyatta Mondatta* had been rushed, it became one of their most critically acclaimed albums.

BLUES BROTHERS

It could hardly have been predicted that a spin-off from TV's *Saturday Night Live* would become a musical phenomenon—but when John Belushi and Dan Aykroyd created their alter egos Joliet Jake and Elwood Blues they unleashed a monster. Their affectionate parody of the Stax soul phenomenon of the 1960s with black suits, fedoras, and sunglasses, turned into a touring band, then a live album, *Briefcase Full of Blues,* that in February 1979 topped the charts for a week. The next stage was the big screen, and Belushi and Aykroyd found themselves on a mission from God to save the Catholic home in which they had been brought up. Car chases, soul tunes, special effects, and cameos from James Brown, Ray Charles, and Aretha Franklin made the movie a classic.

The Blues Brothers' No. 1 live album went double platinum. ►

STAND-OUT ALBUMS

Ghost in the Machine—**Police**

Hotter Than July—**Stevie Wonder**

Moving Pictures—**Rush**

Hi Infidelity—**REO Speedwagon**

No Sleep 'Til Hammersmith
    —**Motörhead**

Bella Donna—**Stevie Nicks**

Tattoo You—**Rolling Stones**

Abacab—**Genesis**

Duran Duran—**Duran Duran**

Kings of the Wild Frontier
    —**Adam & the Ants**

Dare!—**The Human League**

The Poet—**Bobby Womack**

Stray Cats/Built for Speed
    —**The Stray Cats**

Heaven Up Here
    —**Echo and the Bunnymen**

Escape—**Journey**

Face Value—**Phil Collins**

Tin Drum—**Japan**

▲ Adam & the Ants' album *Kings of the Wild Frontier* reached No. 1 in the United Kingdom in January 1981. Their follow-up album, released in November of the same year, gave the band two No. 1 singles: its title track "Prince Charming" and "Stand and Deliver."

Where were you when?

"We were always able to sing and blend well together; that's our gift. But aside from that we're really two different guys."

—Paul Simon

"Paul has more, I think, of a feel for the stage. Whereas I have it more for the notes themselves. I love record making and mixing, arranging, producing. That I love. I love to make beautiful things, but I don't like to perform."

—Art Garfunkel

Feelin' Groovy

After six years apart, Simon and Garfunkel reunited for a free concert in New York's Central Park—an event that was watched by an audience of 500,000.

The on and off musical partnership of Simon and Garfunkel was very much on in September 1981 when the duo reunited to play to an audience of half a million in New York's Central Park, an event since commemorated on record and DVD. Both were New York residents, so when Simon was asked by Mayor Ed Koch to give the annual free concert in the Park, he was persuaded by friends to invite Garfunkel to participate.

Paul Simon and Art Garfunkel first met at elementary school in Queens, teaming up to minor success as Tom and Jerry in 1957. The pair then went their separate ways, reuniting in 1963 as part of the Greenwich Village folk scene. Their first album, *Wednesday Morning 3:00 A.M.*, flopped, and Simon left for England. In his absence producer Tom Wilson overdubbed a rhythm section onto the song "The Sounds of Silence" and turned it into a No. 1 hit.

Returning to America, Simon got back with his singing partner and recorded the album *Sounds of Silence*, followed by *Parsley, Sage, Rosemary, and Thyme*; *Bookends*; and 1970's *Bridge over Troubled Water*. The latter won an unprecedented six Grammy awards but was their last album together; they fell out during its creation.

A brief reunion took place at a benefit concert for Democratic presidential candidate George McGovern at Madison Square Garden in 1972. Three years later they performed together on TV's *Saturday Night Live* with "My Little Town," a song they recorded together, which also appears on both men's 1975 albums—Simon's *Still Crazy After All These Years* and Garfunkel's *Breakaway*.

The success of the free concert led to a world tour in 1982–83 during which tensions resurfaced. Simon's 1983 album, *Hearts and Bones*, was originally to have been a new Simon and Garfunkel project, but disagreements killed it. Relations have since thawed again, and they toured together in 2003 and 2004.

◄ After their world tour of 1982–83, Simon and Garfunkel did not appear together until 1990 when they performed at a ceremony to mark their induction into the Rock and Roll Hall of Fame.

PHIL COLLINS GOES SOLO

Balding, pullover-clad percussionist Phil Collins emerged this year as an unlikely but highly successful solo star. Having joined Genesis in 1970 as drummer, he'd taken on lead vocals six years later when Peter Gabriel left. His debut album *Face Value* was poles apart from Genesis's early progressive rock style and, with passionate lyrics inspired by the singer's recent divorce (as typified by lead single "In the Air Tonight"), appealed to millions of album buyers worldwide. It reached No. 7, and by 1985's *No Jacket Required* he would be a chart-topper in his own right. Collins, who also dabbled in acting, successfully juggled group membership and solo stardom until 1996 when he finally left Genesis; his solo career continued.

Phil Collins enjoyed many No. 1 singles, including "Against All Odds," "One More Night," and "Two Hearts." ►

1981

NO. 1 SINGLES

"(Just Like) Starting Over"
—**John Lennon**

"The Tide Is High"—**Blondie**

"Celebration"—**Kool & the Gang**

"9 to 5"—**Dolly Parton**

"I Love a Rainy Night"
—**Eddie Rabbitt**

"Keep on Loving You"
—**REO Speedwagon**

"Rapture"—**Blondie**

"Kiss on My List"—**Hall & Oates**

"Morning Train (Nine to Five)"
—**Sheena Easton**

"Bette Davis Eyes"—**Kim Carnes**

"Medley"—**Stars on 45**

"The One That You Love"
—**Air Supply**

"Jessie's Girl"—**Rick Springfield**

"Endless Love"—**Diana Ross &
Lionel Richie**

"Arthur's Theme (Best That
You Can Do)"—**Christopher
Cross**

"Private Eyes"—**Hall & Oates**

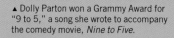

▲ Dolly Parton won a Grammy Award for "9 to 5," a song she wrote to accompany the comedy movie, *Nine to Five*.

Where were you when?

"I think MTV put a huge dent in the songwriting craft."
—Songwriter Christopher Cross

"I was 14 when I first saw an MTV video of Duran Duran, 'Save a Prayer.' I had been listening to their music but this video really transfixed me. From that time onwards, I just sat watching MTV hoping to see it. I didn't realise my husband was a fan until he came home one day with the CD of Duran Duran's greatest hits. Which has only confirmed my belief that I married the right man."
—Sharon, Leeds

I Want My MTV

Launched as a cable channel devoted to playing music videos, MTV went on to revolutionize the music industry.

Although cable channel MTV (the initials stand for Music TeleVision) would ultimately transform the way music was marketed and presented on television, the new station could boast only half a million subscribers when it launched on August 1, 1981. An advertising campaign using the slogan "I want my MTV" repeated by major stars like Mick Jagger, David Bowie, and Sting was instrumental in creating more demand. The station seemed to have arrived in 1985, when Dire Straits (with Sting) parodied the phrase in their No. 1 hit "Money for Nothing."

The Beatles had pioneered the use of promotional films in the 1960s when their global popularity and hectic schedule made it virtually impossible for them to appear in person on television. Queen upped the ante in terms of cost and visual effects with 1975's "Bohemian Rhapsody." By the early 1980s record companies began to realize the possibilities of using pop videos to sell music.

MTV's initial format was based on Top 40 radio, with 24-hour video broadcasts linked by VJs (video jockeys). It would ultimately take over radio's role as hitmaker. Its first superstars were visually attractive New Romantics like Adam and the Ants, Culture Club, and Duran Duran. Michael Jackson's groundbreaking use of video to promote his album *Thriller* opened the door to black performers, while other visually oriented superstars, like Madonna and Prince, began to realize the benefits that "heavy rotation" on MTV could confer on record sales.

Toward the end of the decade, MTV began to diversify its programming; VJs were phased out, and conventional TV formats such as news slots were introduced.

In February 2008, MTV hosted a live debate between Democratic presidential candidates eager to reach young voters, confirming that while it remains the dominant force in music television, MTV now plays a broader broadcasting role.

◄ MTV was instrumental in giving Duran Duran their first Top 5 U.S. single, "Hungry Like the Wolf."

DREAMGIRLS ON BROADWAY

Dreamgirls, telling the story of a female vocal trio from Chicago who become superstars, opened on Broadway in December, with Jennifer Holliday in the starring role of Effie. It won six Tony Awards in 1982, running for 1,522 performances. Two decades after that, and after many false starts involving Whitney Houston and Lauryn Hill, it was finally turned into a motion picture starring Jennifer Hudson, Beyoncé Knowles, Jamie Foxx, and Eddie Murphy. The plot of the theater production was loosely based on the story of the Supremes, whose Mary Wilson liked it so much she even named her 1986 autobiography after it— but Diana Ross, the apparent inspiration for the character of Deena, was not so happy.

The cast recording won a Grammy for Jennifer Holliday's vocal performance on "And I'm Telling You I'm Not Going." ▶

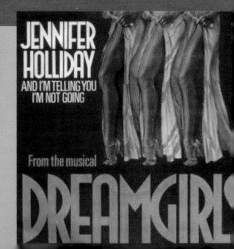

1982

CHARIOTS OF FIRE

Vangelis

Academy Award, Best Original Score 1981

NO. 1 ALBUMS

*For Those About to Rock
We Salute You*—**AC/DC**

4—**Foreigner**

Freeze Frame—**The J. Geils Band**

Beauty and the Beat
—**The Go-Go's**

Chariots of Fire—**Vangelis**

Asia—**Asia**

Tug of War—**Paul McCartney**

Mirage—**Fleetwood Mac**

American Fool
—**John Cougar Mellencamp**

Business as Usual—**Men at Work**

▲ Vangelis's soundtrack to the movie *Chariots of Fire* was an unexpected success. In a departure from most period movie scores, Vangelis used a primarily electronic, synthesizer-driven sound. The soundtrack won an Academy Award and stayed on the *Billboard* charts for 97 weeks. The main "Titles" track is often used in film and on TV shows for slow motion sequences.

Tainted Love

British pop duo Soft Cell made American chart music history with their infectious electro-pop recording of a classic soul "floor filler."

Setting a new record for the longest consecutive stay on the *Billboard* Hot 100—43 weeks— English electro-pop duo Soft Cell's "Tainted Love" peaked at No. 8 in 1982. Previously it had reached No. 1 in 17 countries, including the United Kingdom in August 1981.

The song was a new version of a soul classic first recorded in 1964 by Gloria Jones, who was later to marry English glam-rock star Marc Bolan. It was one of many 1960s American soul records that became popular at all-night dance clubs in the north of England during the mid 1970s, spawning a subculture known as northern soul. Written by Ed Cobb, member of the 1950s group the Four Preps and later a record producer, "Tainted Love" was recorded by Ruth Swan in 1975 in an obscure northern soul version that influenced Soft Cell in their radical reworking of the song in electro-pop style. The 12-inch single featured a medley of the song with the B-side, The Supremes' "Where Did Our Love Go?" By choosing to record another artist's song on the B-side Soft Cell lost the opportunity to earn songwriting royalties, a decision they lived to regret.

THE ART OF FALLING APART

Although Soft Cell enjoyed another five Top 10 hits in Britain and four successful albums (including *Non-Stop Erotic Cabaret* and *The Art of Falling Apart*), "Tainted Love" was to be their only U.S. hit, despite relocating to New York City for much of 1982. Flamboyant singer Marc Almond and taciturn keyboardist David Ball provided the template for later duos, like the Pet Shop Boys and Erasure. With his lyrics focusing on the sleazier side of life, the outspoken Almond was often a controversial figure. The band split up in 1984. Almond embarked on a sporadically successful solo career, and Ball formed an electronic dance outfit, the Grid. Soft Cell's reformation in 2001 was perfectly timed to coincide with the rise of 1980s nostalgia.

"Tainted Love" has been recorded many times. Marilyn Manson's 2002 version from the soundtrack of *Not Another Teen Movie* is the most famous. Soul singer Rihanna returned it to its soul roots four years later, using it as the basis for her hit "SOS."

Soft Cell (Marc Almond left, David Ball right) were unlikely pin-ups at a time when dashing New Romantic bands ruled the charts. ▶

Where were you when?

"David Ball and myself were both fans of 1970s disco, but having grown out of punk as well, we had this strange marriage of punk and disco and dance."

—Marc Almond

"The organ/synthesiser/klaxon sound at the beginning of "Tainted Love" is one of the most distinctive sounds in pop music. The second you hear it you know which record is coming on."

—Jed Carter, Ipswich, England

FIRST CD PLAYERS LAUNCHED

The five-inch compact disc had originated in 1969, the work of a Dutch physicist, but it would take more than a decade for the parameters to be agreed for an internationally recognized digital sound carrier. Philips, the originator of the cassette, and Walkman pioneer Sony were jointly instrumental in this. The first CDs went on sale this year, along with an all-important player. Initially manufactured in Germany and Japan, the CD first emerged from a U.S. factory in 1984, and Christmas 1985 saw the format take off at record shops, pushing annual sales past the 20 million mark for the first time. Worldwide sales had reached a billion by 1990 and the writing was on the wall for cassette and vinyl.

Philips' first CD player, which was launched in April 1982, cost more than $2,000 in today's money. ▶

1982

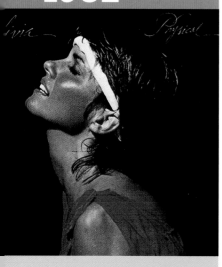

▲ "Physical" by Olivia Newton-John was one of the most successful *Billboard* Hot 100 songs of the 1980s. The single stayed at No. 1 for 10 weeks.

The Rise of Electro-pop

British synthpop band The Human League hit the top of the charts with their single "Don't You Want Me?" taken from their "perfect pop" album, *Dare!*

One of 1982's unlikeliest success stories was that of the British electro-pop outfit, The Human League, whose single "Don't You Want Me?" topped the *Billboard* Hot 100 in July. The original band gained a cult following in the United Kingdom for its somewhat dour electronic rock, but it split up acrimoniously in 1980, leaving the vocalist, Phil Oakey, with the rights to the name. He needed to find new band members for an imminent tour. Oakey's first recruits were two girl singers, Susanne Sulley and Joanne Catherall, whom he had seen dancing in a nightclub. The new lineup broke through in Britain, where "Don't You Want Me?" was No. 1 at Christmas 1981. Much of its success was ascribed to an atmospheric promotional video. Oakey later confessed that the song was inspired by a story in an American women's magazine and that he had lifted the opening lines almost word for word.

The album, *Dare!*, was also a staggering success, going double platinum in the United Kingdom and reaching No. 3 in the States. Its sound, largely crafted by producer Martin Rushent, would be hugely influential on the synthesized dance music that followed. The Human League scored a second U.S. chart-topping single in 1986 with "Human," written and produced by Jimmy Jam and Terry Lewis, who had previously worked with Janet Jackson. But a perfectionist attitude to their work, plus further lineup changes and disputes with record companies, resulted in their releasing only five more albums.

While British electro-pop groups such as Ultravox and Depeche Mode also gained success in the United States, The Human League was the first to reach No. 1. The band was at the forefront of the "Second British Invasion," which by November 1983 filled a third of the places in the *Billboard* Top 100 chart. A backlash against synthesized rock took place later in the decade, but The Human League survived to grace the new millennium. They played to an audience of 18,000 at the Hollywood Bowl in Los Angeles on October 24, 2006, as they celebrated *Dare!*'s quarter-century.

The Human League in their hometown of Sheffield. From left to right: Philip Adrian Wright, Phil Oakey, Ian Burden, Joanne Catherall, and Susan Sulley. ▶

Where were you when?

"*We desperately wanted to be Abba.*"
   —Phil Oakey, The Human League

"*Phil Oakey used to have this weird asymmetrical haircut which covered half his face and I thought it was really cool. One weekend I decided I would restyle my hair like that and came to school with 'the Human League look.' My friends thought I was trying to be Bryan Ferry (from Roxy Music) which was crushing.*"
   —David Salmo, Whitley Bay, England

MUSICAL—*LITTLE SHOP OF HORRORS*

When the musical *Little Shop Of Horrors* opened off-Broadway at the Orpheum Theatre in July, few would have predicted it would become the third longest-running musical and the highest-grossing production in off-Broadway history. It was based on a low-budget 1960 black comedy movie of the same name telling the story of a florist who raises a plant that feeds on human blood. Alan Mencken's deliberately retro-flavored score included such classics as "Skid Row (Downtown)," "Somewhere That's Green," and "Suddenly Seymour." A movie of the musical was made in 1986. Directed by *Muppets* man Frank Oz, it starred Rick Moranis, Ellen Greene, and the voice of Four Tops singer Levi Stubbs. The stage show finally made it to Broadway in 2003.

The original cast album of the off-Broadway production. ▶

1983

KAREN CARPENTER DIES

Brother and sister duo Carpenters (they insisted on leaving out the "the") had been the smiling face of easy listening since 1970, scoring an amazing 29 hits in 12 years. But unknown to most fans, Karen Carpenter had been battling anorexia nervosa. Her death on February 4, 1983, put the psychological eating disorder into the headlines when it was revealed that her body had been weakened from years of dieting. She suffered a fatal heart attack and was buried next to her father in Cypress, California. Brother Richard, who had overcome an addiction to sleeping pills, enjoyed a relatively low-key solo career but never sought to team up with another female singer and recreate the duo's songs.

▲ Karen and Richard Carpenter photographed in happier times in the 1970s.

Thriller

Michael Jackson's third solo album rewrote the record books, while his video for the title track *Thriller* was rumored to have cost a million dollars.

When Michael Jackson's *Thriller* was released in December 1982 there were high expectations for the album but probably not for 100 million units sold worldwide. *Thriller* became the biggest-selling album of all time.

A star since the age of 10 as a member of the Jackson Five and the Jacksons, and a millionaire at 14, Michael Jackson worked hard for the success of *Thriller*, which, like its multi-platinum predecessor *Off the Wall*, was produced by Quincy Jones. The lead-off single, "The Girl Is Mine," a duet with Paul McCartney, peaked at No. 2, but sales of *Thriller* began to soar when the international smash "Billie Jean" was released in March 1983. Another five singles followed, making a record seven (out of nine tracks) from the album. "Billie Jean" was followed by "Beat It," with Eddie van Halen's contribution on guitar confirming the album's crossover appeal, "Wanna Be Starting Something," "P.Y.T. (Pretty Young Thing)," "Human Nature," and finally "Thriller" itself in January 1984.

37 WEEKS AT NO. 1

The video for the title track reignited interest in the year-old album. A lavish horror spoof directed by John Landis of the *Blues Brothers* and *An American Werewolf in London* fame, it adroitly tapped into the expanding video market and was featured heavily on MTV. Jackson was said to have regretted making it when he was reportedly threatened with expulsion from the Jehovah's Witnesses because of its occult nature. The hour-long documentary *Making Michael Jackson's Thriller* was a record-breaker in itself, becoming the highest-selling home-video release at the time.

A special-edition CD was released in 2001, containing bonus tracks and interviews, and 2008's 25th Anniversary Edition featured more unreleased material, plus remixes. *Thriller* boasts impressive statistics: 27 times platinum in the United States, 80 consecutive weeks in the *Billboard* Top 10, 37 weeks at No. 1, and the best-selling album in two separate years, the only album to achieve this feat. Its blockbuster status is unlikely to be surpassed.

The "funk of 40,000 years..." Michael Jackson with his zombie cast for what was then the most expensive music video. ▶

TRACK LISTING

Side One
Wanna Be Startin' Somethin'
Baby Be Mine
The Girl Is Mine (with Paul McCartney)
Thriller

Side Two
Beat It
Billie Jean
Human Nature
P.Y.T. (Pretty Young Th
The Lady in My Life

◀ *Thriller*, the only album to be certified 27 times platinum.

Where were you when?

"*I saw that incredible* Thriller *dance recreation from the Filipino jail on YouTube. It just goes to show the impact of the music and the dance Michael created over 25 years ago.*"

—Louisa Humphries, Miami

"*I was a veteran before I was a teenager.*"

—Michael Jackson

"*I was six and my dad had recorded the* Thriller *music video for me and I watched it every day, dancing and singing my little heart out. One of the worst childhood memories I have is the day that my brother and I found out that Dad had recorded a Cliff Richard music clip over HALF of my* Thriller *tape. I was upset for weeks.*"

—Lee May Lim, London

1983

BEST-SELLING SINGLES

"Every Breath You Take"
  —**The Police**

"Flashdance…What a Feeling"
  —**Irene Cara**

"Say Say Say"—**Paul McCartney
featuring Michael Jackson**

"Billie Jean"—**Michael Jackson**

"All Night Long (All Night)"
  —**Lionel Richie**

"Total Eclipse of the Heart"
  —**Bonnie Tyler**

"Down Under"—**Men at Work**

"Beat It"—**Michael Jackson**

"Sweet Dreams (Are Made of This)"
  —**Eurythmics**

"Let's Dance"—**David Bowie**

▲ Dave Stewart and Annie Lennox
first collaborated in British band The
Tourists before leaving to seek artistic
independence. Their commercial
breakthrough came in 1983 with
"Sweet Dreams (Are Made of This)"
for which Lennox adopted her striking
ginger crew cut, also featured on the
cover of *Rolling Stone*.

Where were you when?

*"I saw Boy George on the Joan Rivers show and he was not like the typical pop star
interview. He had a lot of interesting things to say for himself. You could tell with
that kind of personality he'd have the chutzpah to dress and act the way he did."*

—Freda Kevi, Chicago

*"Seeing him clean up the streets of Manhattan, overweight and bald, it's hard to
think that anybody could have ever mistaken him for a woman."*

—Zachary Klein, New York

Culture Club

With the flamboyant Boy George to the fore, Culture Club topped the charts on both sides of the Atlantic, but was the lead singer really a boy…?

Singer Boy George was instantly outrageous. The latest in a line of androgynous English rock stars following in David Bowie's wake, George took gender-bending to new extremes, his appearance frequently causing genuine uncertainty as to whether he was male or female.

A member of the flamboyant New Romantic scene that sprang up in London in the early 1980s, George O'Dowd was briefly known as Lieutenant Lush before taking on his more familiar identity as lead singer of Culture Club. The band—George, Roy Hay (guitar), Mikey Craig (bass), and Jon Moss (drums)—became international stars with the reggae-inflected "Do You Really Want to Hurt Me" and achieved their only U.S. No. 1 single with "Karma Chameleon" in 1983. George's dreadlocks, wide-brimmed hat, and outrageous dress sense disguised a remarkable white-soul voice and acute musical sensibility.

Everything went downhill fast after Culture Club split in 1986. George turned to heroin, and his brother went public with the news of his addiction in an attempt to rescue him from the drug. The story was big news in both the American and British tabloid press during the summer of 1986, causing George to describe himself as "the world's most famous junkie." He renounced drugs after Michael Rudetsky, an American session musician, was found dead at his Hampstead home in October.

Boy George launched a solo career in 1987, but his initial U.K. success was not duplicated in the States, partly because his drug convictions caused him visa problems. Nevertheless, George remained very much a public figure. He was arrested for possession of cocaine in Manhattan in 2005, which resulted in his being ordered to do five days of community service. Media attention was intense. The balding, chubby figure picking litter off the sidewalk looked a long way from the glamorous figure that had once graced the cover of *Vogue* magazine.

Culture Club reformed in 1998 for a tour and studio album, while a musical based on George's life, *Taboo*, for which he supplied lyrics, was produced in London in 2002 and subsequently transferred to Broadway for a short run. He appeared in the original production but opted not to play himself.

◄ From left to right, Mikey Craig, Jon Moss and Boy George.

LET'S DANCE—DAVID BOWIE

Having successfully reinvented himself several times in the 1970s, David Bowie pulled off the feat again in 1983 on the album *Let's Dance*, which would catapult him into the major league of rock earners. Ever astute in choosing collaborators, Bowie recruited Nile Rodgers, co-creator of Chic's international disco hits, as producer. For the first time Bowie played no instruments, confining himself to singing in *Let's Dance*. The title track reached No. 1 on both sides of the Atlantic and the album went on to sell more than 6 million copies worldwide. Later Bowie distanced himself from it, claiming the album was "more Nile's album than mine." He seemed uneasy with its massive success. The follow-up albums, *Tonight* and *Never Let Me Down*, were lackluster in comparison.

Bowie's album cover for *Let's Dance*. ►

1984

NO. 1 SINGLES

"Say Say Say"—**Paul McCartney featuring Michael Jackson**

"Owner of a Lonely Heart"—**Yes**

"Karma Chameleon"—**Culture Club**

"Jump"—**Van Halen**

"Footloose"—**Kenny Loggins**

"Hello"—**Lionel Richie**

"Let's Hear It for the Boy" —**Deniece Williams**

"Time After Time"—**Cyndi Lauper**

"The Reflex"—**Duran Duran**

"When Doves Cry"—**Prince**

"Ghostbusters"—**Ray Parker, Jr.**

"What's Love Got to Do With It" —**Tina Turner**

"Missing You"—**John Waite**

"Let's Go Crazy"—**Prince & The Revolution**

"I Just Called to Say I Love You" —**Stevie Wonder**

"Caribbean Queen (No More Love on the Run)"—**Billy Ocean**

"Wake Me Up Before You Go-Go" —**Wham!**

"Out of Touch"—**Hall & Oates**

"Like a Virgin"—**Madonna**

▲ Jackson and McCartney's "Say Say Say" managed to score a No. 1 in both 1983 and 1984.

Where were you when?

"My daughter bought Purple Rain *and I took no notice of it until I heard that Tipper Gore (wife of Al) had taken her copy back to the record store complaining about the lyrics. I thought I have to adopt a parental role here and listen to the thing, too. And the long and short of it is that now my daughter is grown and we go to Prince concerts together."*

—LeeAnne Newton, Detroit

"Do I think I'm normal? Yes I do. I think I'm normal. I am normal."

—Prince

Purple Reign

It was an album, a film, a single, and a tour—Prince put out so much *Purple Rain* product in 1984 he could have applied for a trademark!

Twenty-six-year-old Prince Rogers Nelson hit the big-time in 1984 with his sixth album in a recording career that already stretched back as far as 1978. Its predecessor, the double set *1999*, had broken him into the mainstream and contained two of his most celebrated songs, "1999" and "Little Red Corvette." *Purple Rain*, the soundtrack to the movie of the same name, took his soul-rock fusion to new heights.

The project was an enormous success all around. The film, a vehicle for Prince's many talents, grossed nearly $100 million at the box office, and the album sold 19 million copies and spawned three massive hit singles—the title track, "Let's Go Crazy," and "When Doves Cry." At one point in 1984, Prince had the No. 1 album, single, and movie in the United States.

THE ARTIST FORMERLY KNOWN AS PRINCE

Purple Rain was a crossover of various styles: rock, pop, psychedelia, electronic music, urban R&B, funk, and dance. It featured performances with his band the Revolution. Some were recorded live, unlike the artist's earlier works, where he played all the instruments himself. Hyperactive as ever, he would average an album a year for most of his career. Prince had almost completed the follow-up album *Around the World in a Day* by the time *Purple Rain* was released, although fans had to wait until 1985 to hear it.

Rarely willing to toe the record company line, Prince became embroiled in a legal dispute with Warner Brothers in 1993. He was seen in public with "slave" written on his cheek as a protest. Claiming that Warners had trademarked the name Prince, he changed his moniker to a symbol. He dubbed this combination of the male and female sigils "the Love Symbol," but he became known as Symbol, The Artist formerly known as Prince, or The Artist for short. On the expiration of his contract with Warner Brothers, the enigmatic star reverted to his given name of Prince once more.

◄ Prince went out on the road to promote *Purple Rain* through 1984 and 1985. The album spent 24 consecutive weeks at the top of the *Billboard* album charts from August, holding at bay Springsteen's *Born in the U.S.A.*

BORN IN THE U.S.A.

This year marked Bruce Springsteen's return to rock 'n' roll action with the E Street Band after the acoustic interlude of *Nebraska*. *Born in the U.S.A.*, his first electric album since 1980's *The River*, spent the first of its seven weeks atop the chart in July, just after a 16-month world tour had kicked off in St. Paul, Minnesota. Long time Springsteen lieutenant Steve Van Zandt was replaced in the ranks by former Neil Young guitarist Nils Lofgren. Lead single *Dancing in the Dark* (with *Friend*-to-be Courteney Cox in the video) was first of seven Top 10 hits that would be spun off the album, making this the Boss's very own *Thriller*.

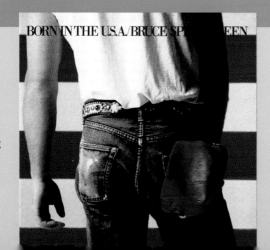

1984

STAND-OUT ALBUMS

Welcome to the Pleasuredome
—**Frankie Goes to Hollywood**

The Smiths—**The Smiths**

1984—**Van Halen**

Touch—**Eurythmics**

Love at First Sting—**Scorpions**

She's So Unusual—**Cyndi Lauper**

Private Dancer—**Tina Turner**

Sports—**Huey Lewis and the News**

Eliminator—**ZZ Top**

Madonna—**Madonna**

Born in the U.S.A.
—**Bruce Springsteen**

Zen Arcade—**Hüsker Dü**

Reckoning—**R.E.M.**

Run-D.M.C.—**Run-D.M.C.**

New Sensations—**Lou Reed**

Heartbeat City—**The Cars**

Climate of Hunter—**Scott Walker**

Building the Perfect Beast
—**Don Henley**

Paris, Texas—**Ry Cooder**

▲ Cyndi Lauper broke the mold for female rock stars and opened the door for many to follow, including Madonna and Gwen Stefani.

This Is Spinal Tap

If ever there were a subject waiting to be parodied it was the theatrics of heavy rock bands. *This Is Spinal Tap* **showed no mercy and rock stars loved it.**

Although it has since passed into folklore, *This Is Spinal Tap* was not initially a major success—some movie-goers mistook the spoof of the life of a touring rock group for an actual documentary. Released in March 1984, the movie was to find its audience when released on video, becoming required viewing on many rock bands' tour buses.

Spinal Tap was directed by Rob (*When Harry Met Sally*) Reiner, who in addition to appearing as manager Marti DiBergi, wrote the screenplay in collaboration with the principal actors Christopher Guest, Michael McKean, and Harry Shearer. The film followed the declining fortunes of the eponymous English heavy rock band. Much of the dialogue was ad-libbed and provided many notorious quotes (and misquotes), perhaps the best-known coming from guitarist Nigel Tufnel (Guest) when discussing the band's amplifiers: "The numbers all go up to 11...it's one louder."

SMELL THE GLOVE

Countless rock stars have claimed that incidents in the movie actually happened to them, including Ozzy Osbourne, Robert Plant, Aerosmith's Steven Tyler, Eddie Van Halen, Lars Ulrich of Metallica, and Judas Priest's Rob Halford. In reality Spinal Tap was not based on any one band but was a combination of observations and the writers' personal experience of touring in satirical reviews, although Shearer went on the road with British heavy-metal outfit Saxon for a couple of dates to prepare for his part.

Spinal Tap was made cheaply for $2.5 million, but its creators reportedly saw little of the profits it generated. In an effort to redress the balance Guest, McKean, and Shearer made an album in 1992. This was followed by live dates that featured the actors actually playing their instruments. *Spinal Tap* completed a nine-city North American tour in 2001 and appeared as part of the awareness-raising Live Earth gig in London in 2007.

In 2002 *This Is Spinal Tap* received the ultimate accolade of cultural acceptance when the Library of Congress's National Film Registry preserved it as being "culturally, historically, or aesthetically significant."

The Tap from left to right, Christopher Guest (Nigel Tufnel), Michael McKean (David St Hubbins), and Harry Shearer (Derek Smalls). ▶

Where were you when?

"I think our most Spinal Tap moment was when we were playing Wolverhampton Lafayette Club in 1979. It was a pretty important gig and about two seconds before we went on stage my trousers split right up the back. I had no option but to stand facing forward all night with gaffa tape holding them together."

—Joe Elliott, Def Leppard

"I loved the mini-Stonehenge moment. It's known amongst people of a certain age, so if you have a situation where someone's got a set of measurements completely wrong you just say 'a bit like mini-Stonehenge,' and people grin."

—Terry Kinsella, Dublin

CAN'T SLOW DOWN—LIONEL RICHIE

Motown were in need of a superstar as the 1980s progressed—and found one in the shape of Alabama-born Lionel Richie. His career in the Commodores on keyboards and main vocals had been relatively low key, and few soul stars have emerged from groups to become credible solo performers. But his self-titled solo debut reached No. 3 in 1982 and included the chart-topping single "Truly," so much was expected of Richie's second effort. *Can't Slow Down* did not disappoint, and would be a Top 5 fixture throughout 1984 after spending three weeks at the top. Its tenure was extended by trademark ballad "Hello" that followed lead single "All Night Long" to the top. Its schmaltzy video featuring a "blind" sculptress helped etch it into the memory.

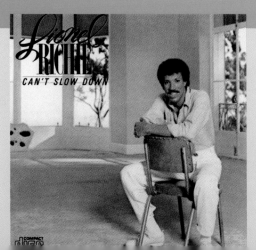

1984

MARVIN GAYE
SHOT DEAD

Soul superstar Marvin Gaye, whose songs were covered by everyone from the Rolling Stones through Michael Bolton to the Who, died in Los Angeles in April—shot in the chest by his preacher father after a family squabble. It was especially poignant since Gaye, 44, had conquered cocaine addiction to rebuild his career, recording an international hit, "Sexual Healing" in the process, and had only recently returned to the States from his adopted home in Belgium to promote it. His father, Marvin Sr., was found to be suffering from a brain tumor that contributed to the incident and was thus sentenced to five years probation for voluntary manslaughter.

▲ Marvin Gaye, whose death was referenced in the Commodores' single "Night Shift." Gaye had left Motown himself in 1982 after an argument over the packaging of his *In Our Lifetime* album.

Where were you when?

"I have earned the title Queen of Rock 'n' Roll."
—Tina Turner

"I bought a British Electric Foundation (B.E.F.) cassette with Tina singing 'Ball of Confusion,' which was easily the stand-out track amongst a whole number of different cover versions. You could tell she still had it from her 'River Deep' days. I could never hear Ike singing on 'River Deep' anyway, it sounded like her voice was all over it."

—Lance Price, Birmingham, England

Private Dancer

Tina Turner's record company thought her career was over, but after she released a version of Al Green's "Let's Stay Together," that all began to change.

The comeback of the year, perhaps the decade, belonged to Tina Turner thanks to the phenomenally successful album *Private Dancer*.

Tina hooked up with future husband Ike Turner in 1959. She was employed first as a backup singer before taking lead vocals on the Top 30 hit "A Fool in Love" in 1960. Ike and Tina enjoyed limited chart success for the remainder of the 1960s—their signature tune, the Phil Spector–produced "River Deep Mountain High," only reached No. 88 in America, while the duo's last chart success, "Nutbush City Limits," came in 1973.

With the duo's popularity in decline, Tina launched a solo career in 1974—Ike produced her first two albums—and she appeared as the Acid Queen in the movie adaptation of the Who's rock opera *Tommy* in 1975. Having endured Ike's physical and mental abuse long enough, Tina finally left him, mid-tour, in 1976. Two more unsuccessful solo albums followed before she took a five-year hiatus.

Her career was only revived when she was contacted by British group Heaven 17 to sing the vocal for "Ball of Confusion"on a music project. They followed this up with a version of Al Green's "Let's Stay Together" which was a surprise hit.

For *Private Dancer*, Turner moved away from her soul and R&B roots to a more mainstream rock sound. The album's winning formula comprised new material by the finest contemporary songwriters. Dire Straits' Mark Knopfler composed the title track. Five singles were lifted from the album, including the No. 1 "What's Love Got to Do With It?" Later this would be the title of Tina's biopic. Certified five times platinum in the United States, *Private Dancer* sold more than 20 million copies worldwide and won four Grammy awards.

◄ Turner's comeback was engineered by British producers Martyn Ware and Ian Craig Marsh who got her to record Al Green's "Let's Stay Together" in 1983.

POLICE SPLIT

There's much to be said for going out at the top, and supertrio the Police did just that after their fifth and final album *Synchronicity* hit No. 1 in both the United Kingdom and United States. The end of the Synchronicity tour in March 1984 effectively ended the band, who reportedly could barely stand the sight of each other. As well as launching a solo career, Sting branched out into acting in the Who's *Quadrophenia* and Dennis Potter's play *Brimstone and Treacle*, while drummer Stewart Copeland began a career in film music and guitarist Andy Summers reverted to jazz and instrumental recordings. The band had been compared with Cream in terms of influence and record sales—and, like Clapton, Bruce, and Baker, they would put differences aside to enjoy a brief reprise in the 2000s.

By the end, Copeland (left) and Sting (center) were not seeing eye to eye. ►

1985

STAND-OUT SINGLES

"Careless Whisper"—**Wham!
Featuring George Michael**

"Private Dancer"—**Tina Turner**

"The Boys of Summer"
—**Don Henley**

"Don't You (Forget About Me)"
—**Simple Minds**

"Can't Fight This Feeling"
—**REO Speedwagon**

"Crazy for You"—**Madonna**

"Smooth Operator"—**Sade**

"A View to a Kill"—**Duran Duran**

"Money for Nothing"—**Dire Straits**

"We Built This City"—**Starship**

"Into the Groove"—**Madonna**

"West End Girls"—**Pet Shop Boys**

"Running Up That Hill"
—**Kate Bush**

"Don't You (Forget About Me)"
—**Simple Minds**

"Addicted to Love"
—**Robert Palmer**

"Inbetween Days"—**The Cure**

"Freeway of Love"
—**Aretha Franklin**

"She Sells Sanctuary"—**The Cult**

"Road to Nowhere"
—**Talking Heads**

▲ Chris Lowe (left) and Neil Tennant of British synth duo The Pet Shop Boys.

Live Aid

***Live Aid** brought together the world's biggest rock stars for two concerts that raised more than $90 million for famine relief in Africa.*

Rock music had never been noted for its compassion, but in Live Aid—a one-day, globally televised event—one summer day in 1985 it showed that it could rally around when needed and, in the true sense of the old hippie ideal, change the world.

The story began in October the previous year when Bob Geldof, singer with Irish band the Boomtown Rats, saw a television report about the Ethiopian famine. It moved him to do something about the problem, but his own group's fortunes were on the wane. He decided to form a supergroup with the intention of scoring a Christmas No. 1 hit. This he did with "Do They Know It's Christmas," issued under the name Band Aid, featuring stars from Boy George to U2. Other countries followed suit with U.S.A. for Africa's "We Are the World" (Michael Jackson, Lionel Richie, etc.) and Canada's "Tears Are Not Enough."

An impressive £8 million ($16 million) was raised, but once Band Aid had set up an aid program, Geldof realized that the sum was not enough to make a difference. His next idea was to put the superstars of Band Aid and U.S.A. for Africa on the concert stage in London and Philadelphia, broadcasting the shows as a telethon and extracting money from a wordwide audience. The logistical problems were immense but on July 13 a roll call of rock greats, from Paul McCartney, the Beach Boys, and the Who to Wham! and Madonna, hit the stages at Wembley and JFK stadiums, plus Moscow and Sydney.

The stadium audiences numbered 72,000 and 80,000, but more importantly, an estimated 1.5 billion viewers across 100 countries watched the shows in what was one of the largest-scale satellite linkups and live television broadcasts of all time. The Prince and Princess of Wales were present at Wembley to confer establishment approval.

After performing his own set, Phil Collins flew by Concorde from London to Philadelphia to play drums for Eric Clapton and the re-formed Led Zeppelin. Mick Jagger's plans for a satellite-linked duet with David Bowie proved unworkable, so the Stones singer still appeared in Philadelphia with Tina Turner. Live Aid raised some $90 million worldwide, and its echoes are still being felt today. It may have heralded an era of socially responsible rock, but it was undoubtedly a historic event that would never be equaled.

The London finale including messrs McCartney, Mercury and Bowie. ▶

Where were you when?

"I so remember—Phil Collins playing both shows, Paul Shaffer being blamed for the satellite cutting out during the Who, *Madonna saying that she wasn't going to take her clothes off after those* Playboy *spreads appeared, sound coming from Nick Rhodes' keyboard before his fingers actually hit the keys during "A View to a Kill," Tom Petty looked awful, the awesome Led Zep reunion, rumors of a Springsteen appearance, Queen playing 'Radio Ga Ga,' Bono leaving the stage to dance with a girl, and Michael DesBarres looking like a total dork, and I taped the entire concert on Beta. Now, if only I could find a Beta machine…"*

—Barret Anderson, Fresno, California

"I was stationed in England in the U.S. Air Force at the time. I remember the buildup in the press before the concert was intense. The Sun *newspaper had the headline 'Beatles reunion for Live Aid' the day of the concert. We were having war games the day of the show, but I told my commander that I had a ticket. He said I could go. I had no ticket of course, but was able to scalp one with no problem. There was no Beatles reunion, but Queen stole the show."*

—Mike Ziegler, San Diego

Significant players on the Philadelphia stage; top row from left to right, Keith Richards, Darryl Hall, John Oates, Ron Wood. Front row; Tina Turner, Mick Jagger, Madonna, Bob Dylan. ▶

1985

LES MISERABLES OPENS IN LONDON

Based on a novel by Victor Hugo and set at the time of the French Revolution, *Les Miserables* opened in London and was still running in the West End in 2008—a record for a musical. The score was written in 1980 by French composer Claude-Michel Schönberg on a libretto by Alain Boublil. The show flopped in Paris and it was only when British producer Cameron Mackintosh began work on an English language version, with lyrics by Herbert Kretzmer, that the musical took off. Memorable songs include "I Dreamed a Dream," "Do You Hear the People Sing?" "One Day More," "Empty Chairs at Empty Tables," and "Master of the House." The Broadway production that opened in March 1987 ran until 2003 and was nominated for 12 Tony Awards, winning 8, including Best Musical and Best Original Score.

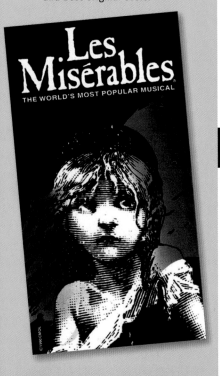

Like a Virgin

With a hit film, hit album, hit singles and a *Live Aid* performance, there was no avoiding Madonna in 1985.

Madonna Louise Veronica Ciccone introduced the concept of Girl Power to pop long before the Spice Girls. It was no coincidence her rise to fame coincided with MTV's popularity, and her many reinventions in the quarter-century that followed have succeeded in keeping her at music's cutting edge.

Having breached the U.S. Top 10 in 1984 with singles like "Borderline" and "Lucky Star," Madonna made 1985 her year. Her second album, *Like a Virgin*, not only contained five genuine Top 5 singles but also headed the album chart. The album's issue also coincided with the release of her first major movie, *Desperately Seeking Susan*, and her first series of concerts, the Virgin Tour, that included an appearance at *Live Aid*.

DESPERATELY SEEKING SUSAN

Madonna reveled in her racy image and the controversy the *Like a Virgin* album title created, knowing this would not only attract male attention but also persuade teenage girls to emulate her. Though her style consisted mainly of wearing underwear as outerwear and cutting the fingers off lace gloves, Macy's department stores opened a Madonnaland clothing concession to make imitation even easier. Nude pictures taken when she was a struggling starlet resurfaced in *Penthouse* and *Playboy*, bringing her even more risqué publicity, and her marriage to bad-boy film star Sean Penn in August became a media event.

The relentless series of singles that followed the title track helped put the album at No. 1. Each had a memorable video, most notably "Material Girl" but also "Angel" and "Dress You Up." A fifth single, "Crazy for You," was extracted from the movie soundtrack of *Vision Quest*, while U.K. chart-topper "Into the Groove," from *Desperately Seeking Susan*, was added to later pressings of *Like a Virgin*.

With her earlier material resurfacing as new fans discovered her, Madonna registered eight U.K. hits in the calendar year, making chart history by becoming the first singer since 1950s songbird Ruby Murray to have three records in the U.K. Top 15. Many more records, not to mention taboos, would fall to Ms. Ciccone over the coming years.

Madonna's "Boy Toy" look was intended to provoke. ▶

Where were you when?

"I saw Les Miserables *on its second night at the Barbican Theatre. There were rumors that half the barricade had got stuck during previews, but it all swung together on the night and Alun Armstrong stole the show as the most repulsive Master of the House. Ironically, 23 years later, my 16-year-old son, Theo, has become so addicted to the musical that he's read the 700-page Victor Hugo novel. I told him he should have read it in French."*

—Frank Hopkinson, Esher, England

"Madonna was my fashion idol. She was on everything in 1985. My folks hated me liking her, which only backed up the view that she was the perfect choice."

—Ellen Smith, Dallas

WHAM! HAVE BIG SUCCESS

Fresh-faced teen duo Wham! consisted of London schoolfriends George Michael (born Giorgios Panayoutou) and Andrew Ridgeley—one a singer and songwriter, the other an average guitarist. The unequal partnership seemed to work, as consecutive No. 1 hits such as "Wake Me Up Before You Go-Go," "Careless Whisper," and (this year) "Everything She Wants" proved. Further 1985 releases "Freedom" and "I'm Your Man" made the Top 3. Wham! was a worldwide success, becoming the first Western pop group to visit China before a spectacular farewell concert in 1986 left singer-songwriter Michael to go on to solo fame. While he made a successful transition from teen idol to stubble-chinned serious artist, Ridgeley recorded just one solo album before retiring to Cornwall on his royalties.

Andrew Ridgeley (left) gave George Michael the impetus to start his pop career. ▶

1986

BEST-SELLING SINGLES

"That's What Friends Are For"
—**Dionne Warwick featuring Elton John, Gladys Knight and Stevie Wonder**

"Walk Like an Egyptian"
—**The Bangles**

"On My Own"—**Patti LaBelle & Michael McDonald**

"Greatest Love of All"
—**Whitney Houston**

"Kiss"—**Prince**

"Kyrie"—**Mr. Mister**

"Rock Me Amadeus"—**Falco**

"Stuck with You"—**Huey Lewis & the News**

"Papa Don't Preach"—**Madonna**

"There'll Be Sad Songs (to Make You Cry)"—**Billy Ocean**

▲ Trinidad-born singer Billy Ocean had previously won a Grammy in 1985 for his single "Caribbean Queen."

The Bangles' 1986 line-up. ▼

Where were you when?

"It was one of those rare times when you go on an adventure, you're absolutely enthralled with what you find, and then everybody likes the photos you brought home!"

—Paul Simon

"I was at the Prince's Trust concert, right at the back of the first block with a big aisle behind. I can't remember who was on stage playing, but at one point I looked round and Tina Turner was in the middle of the aisle behind, dancing."

—Brian More, Malvern, England

Diamonds on the Souls of His Shoes

Paul Simon's *Graceland* album was a breathtaking mix of world music styles, but its release brought success and controversy in equal measure.

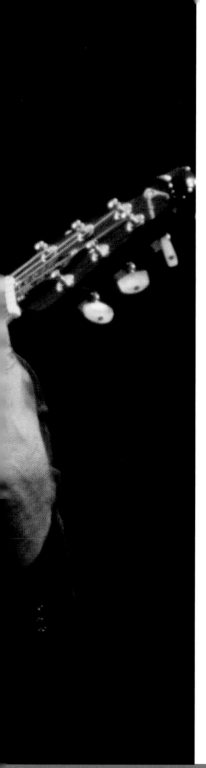

After a period in the doldrums, Paul Simon (of Simon and Garfunkel fame) reignited his career with the album *Graceland*, which achieved his highest-ever solo U.S. chart placement, No. 3, and sold 6 million copies. It was lauded by the critics and went on to win the Grammy award for Album of the Year. The title track was inspired by a visit to Elvis Presley's mansion. The lead-off single, "You Can Call Me Al," was promoted with a memorable video starring Chevy Chase.

Simon was so taken with a tape of South African township jive he was sent that he flew to Johannesburg to record part of the album there, but then found himself embroiled in controversy over the use of South African musicians. He was accused of breaching the UN boycott of South Africa and, because the sleeve notes failed to mention apartheid, it was rumored that he had signed an agreement with the South African government preventing him from criticizing them. The African National Congress urged people to stay away from his European and American tour.

Simon was forced to call a press conference in London to respond to the allegations. Flanked by exiled South African musicians Miriam Makeba and Hugh Masekela, who were touring with him, he explained that he was working to end apartheid in his own field and had not mentioned it in the sleeve notes, because he was operating from a cultural rather than a political point of view. He argued that the embargo applied to performance, not recording, and that the local musicians had voted in favor of him coming over.

Simon's work had often featured an eclectic mix of styles, from the Peruvian tune "El Condor Pasa" on *Bridge over Troubled Water* to the reggae of solo tracks "Mother and Child Reunion." On *Graceland* the African rhythms perfectly complemented the twists and turns of the songs and their often quirky subject matter, and the result encouraged a demand for South African music across the globe.

◄ Paul Simon's *Graceland* album introduced many fans to the world music styles of *isicathamiya* and *mbaqanga*.

THE PRINCE'S TRUST CONCERT

Prince Charles celebrated the tenth anniversary of his trust, set up to benefit deprived youngsters, with a gala concert at Wembley Arena that boasted a host of big names. Dire Straits, Status Quo, Joan Armatrading, Suzanne Vega, and Level 42 were invited to play along with Bryan Adams, Phil Collins, Elton John, and Rod Stewart, who were favorites of the Princess of Wales. This show marked Paul McCartney's return to the stage for the first time since Live Aid and he closed the show, duetting on "Get Back" with Tina Turner. Tina also sang with Eric Clapton on "Tearing Us Apart," while George Michael and Paul Young spontaneously duetted on "Every Time You Go Away" simply because Michael didn't know any other song.

The all-star line-up for the Prince's Trust album, Tina Turner takes the throne. ►

1986

NO. 1 ALBUMS

The Broadway Album
—**Barbra Streisand**

The Promise—**Sade**

Welcome to the Real World
—**Mr. Mister**

Whitney Houston
—**Whitney Houston**

5150—**Van Halen**

Control—**Janet Jackson**

Winner in You—**Patti LaBelle**

Top Gun—**Original Soundtrack**

True Blue—**Madonna**

Dancing on the Ceiling
—**Lionel Richie**

Fore!—**Huey Lewis and the News**

Slippery When Wet—**Bon Jovi**

Live 1975-1985
—**Bruce Springsteen and
the E Street Band**

▲ Bon Jovi's *Slippery When Wet* released
in 1986 went on to sell 26 million copies
worldwide. During the Slippery tour which
supported the release, lead singer Jon Bon
Jovi (center) damaged his vocal chords
and, like similar vocal casualty Elton
John, has subsequently tended to adopt a
lower pitch for live performance.

Where were you when?

*"In the 1970s Sarah Brightman was a leather-clad dance babe and Michael
Crawford was a bungling TV sitcom star. To see them on stage beautifully
transformed into these serious roles and in this operatic setting made the hairs on
your arm stand on end. I went 4 times before they changed the cast."*

—Muriel Phillips, Dartford, England

*"The least favorite question is the one that I'm asked, particularly in Japan, 'What's
the difference between theater and cinema?' and I think, 'About eighty bucks.'"*

—Andrew Lloyd Webber

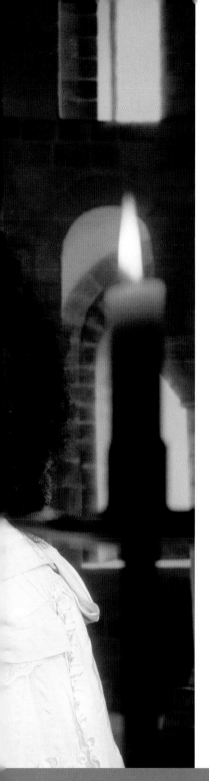

Phantom of the Opera

When Andrew Lloyd-Webber's latest and grandest musical was pasted in *The New York Times*, the omens for its longevity were not good.

Andrew Lloyd Webber's musical *Phantom of the Opera* opened in London's West End in October 1986, where it is still running. In January 1988 the show transferred to the Majestic Theater in New York, which has one of Broadway's largest houses. Initially, the principal members of the British cast—Michael Crawford, Sarah Brightman, and Steve Barton—recreated their roles for the American stage.

The Broadway version survived a panning in *The New York Times* to become the longest running and highest-grossing Broadway production ever, overtaking Lloyd Webber's *Cats* in 2006. It has been seen by more than 11 million people and has taken in $600 million at the box office. Worldwide it is the most profitable entertainment franchise of all time, having been produced in over 20 countries. The soundtrack album from the London show was ranked No. 1 in Britain but did not achieve the same level of success in the United States.

The musical was turned into a movie in 2004, directed by Joel Schumacher, while a shorter version, based on the film and re-titled *Phantom: The Las Vegas Spectacular*, opened at the Venetian in 2006. It plays in a theater custom-built to resemble the Paris Opera House, featuring state-of-the-art set design, technology, and special effects.

Originally a novel by Gaston Leroux that was first published in France in 1910, the story is set in the Paris Opera House and concerns the mysterious, disfigured Phantom's tragic obsession with a beautiful singer. *Phantom of the Opera* has become an enduring classic, prompting many variations. A 1925 silent movie starred horror legend Lon Chaney and was re-dubbed and partially re-shot for sound in 1929. A remake starring Claude Rains was released in 1943.

Untouchables director Brian De Palma adapted the story into a rock opera, *Phantom of the Paradise*, which starred songwriter/actor Paul Williams. This 1974 movie was a flop with critics and public alike but has since achieved cult status.

◄ Michael Crawford, the original Phantom, alongside the object of his affection, Christine Daaé, played by Sarah Brightman.

OZZY OSBOURNE BLAMED FOR YOUTH'S DEATH

Having suffered a blow in 1982 when guitarist Randy Rhoads tragically died in a plane accident while on tour, Ozzy Osbourne's fragile life took another battering this year. He was subpoenaed in January when the lyrics of his song "Suicide Solution" were cited as directly causing the death of a young fan, California teen John McCollum. The case was eventually thrown out of court in December, Judge John L. Cole stating the case involved areas "clearly protected by the First Amendment." The very same month, however, Judas Priest were hit by a similar lawsuit which would take until 1990 to resolve in their favor. Their music was said to contain subliminal messages.

The contentious song was released on the 1981 album *Blizzard of Ozz*, one of the rare LPs to achieve multi-platinum status without the benefit of a big chart single. ▶

1987

Heart abandoned their rock roots for a more playlist-friendly style. The result was the album *Heart* which would go multi-platinum and featured the chart-topping singles "Alone" and "These Dreams." ▼

The Joshua Tree

U2 were Irish rockers led by the soaring voice of Bono (vox). They had been building their audience steadily until the release of *The Joshua Tree*...

In April 1987 U2 achieved the notable feat of appearing simultaneously on the covers not only of *Musician* and *Rolling Stone* but also *Time* magazine, a sure sign that they had truly arrived. Backstage guests at their arena gigs included Mickey Rourke, Madonna, Sean Penn, and Jane Fonda. Bob Dylan joined them on stage. The Irish band brought traffic to a standstill in Los Angeles while filming a rooftop video shoot in homage to the Beatles' final public performance on the roof of their Apple offices.

The Irish quartet—Bono (vocals), the Edge (guitar), Adam Clayton (bass), and Larry Mullen (drums)—had come a long way since their first Stateside visit six years before, when they played clubs and colleges and worried whether their American record company would take up the option on their second album.

Their fifth studio album, *The Joshua Tree*, changed everything for them. Steeped in Americana, it found them exploring country, blues, and gospel music and demonstrated U2's new maturity in songwriting and performance, which added a widescreen element to the band's often anthemic material. Critically acclaimed, it spent nine weeks at No. 1 and yielded two chart-topping singles—"With or Without You" and "I Still Haven't Found What I'm Looking For." Both typified the album's themes of spirituality and soul-searching. It won two Grammies, including Album of the Year.

The Joshua Tree was quickly followed by *Rattle and Hum*, a part studio/part live double set that also served as the soundtrack to the movie of the Joshua Tree Tour. U2's next move, *Achtung Baby*, saw them shed some of their earnestness in a deliberate attempt to forge a new sound, embracing elements of dance and electronica that would culminate in 1993's ambitious *Zooropa*.

Three years later U2 completed the transition to post-modern rock band in Pop before returning to basics with *All That You Can't Leave Behind* and *How to Dismantle an Atomic Bomb*. Nevertheless, most fans and critics still rate *The Joshua Tree* their definitive statement.

From left to right, The Edge, Adam Clayton, Bono, and Larry Mullen. ▶

Where were you when?

"I think we have a love and an emotion without the flowers in our hair and we have an aggression without the safety pins in our noses."

—Bono

"I was totally wrapped up in The Joshua Tree. *'With or Without You' was like the perfect mirror for a relationship hiccup I was trying to reconcile. In the end I chose the 'without you' option. Now whenever I hear the song I regret the choice I made."*

—B. Sullivan, Halifax

HOORAY FOR DOLLYWOOD: THE DOLLY PARTON THEME PARK

When Dolly Parton was born to a tobacco farmer in 1946 and raised in a one-room cabin with six brothers and five sisters, it seemed long odds she would become an American icon and entertainment superstar. The most successful female country performer of all time, Parton placed 25 songs at No. 1 on the *Billboard* country charts. The cap was put on her career this year when she opened Dollywood, an 87-acre theme park in Pigeon Forge, Tennessee, near her birthplace in the Smokey Mountains. As well as this, Parton's other ventures have included a TV production company which produced *Buffy the Vampire Slayer* and a charitable Foundation, also named Dollywood.

Dolly Parton has worked more than 9 to 5 to achieve her astonishing success. ▶

1987

BEST-SELLING ALBUMS

Slippery When Wet
—**Bon Jovi**

License To III—**Beastie Boys**

The Joshua Tree—**U2**

Whitney—**Whitney Houston**

Bad—**Michael Jackson**

Faith—**George Michael**

Dirty Dancing
—**Original Soundtrack**

Tunnel of Love—**Bruce Springsteen**

Appetite for Destruction
—**Guns N' Roses**

Control—**Janet Jackson**

▲ *Control* was Janet Jackson's third album release following the relatively unsuccessful *Janet Jackson* and *Dream Street* and represented Janet taking "control" of her career away from her father who had also managed her brothers' early careers. Despite the album being launched in 1986 it easily made the best-sellers list for 1987.

I Wanna Dance with Somebody

Whitney Houston spent her teenage years learning "the family business" and with her 1987 album *Whitney* set about breaking records.

Whitney Houston emerged as a serious challenger for Madonna's crown as Queen of Pop in 1987. Her pedigree was impeccable: She was the daughter of Cissy Houston, cousin of Dionne Warwick, and her godmother was Aretha Franklin. She started singing in a gospel group at age 11 and spent much of her teens touring nightclubs with her mother. At 16, Whitney sang backup vocals for Chaka Khan's hit "I'm Every Woman," a song she would record herself in 1993.

Her self-titled first album was released in 1985 and was the biggest-selling debut by a solo artist at that time. Three singles from the album went to No. 1: "Saving All My Love for You," "How Will I Know," and "The Greatest Love of All." The 1987 album, *Whitney*, spawned another four chart-toppers—"I Wanna Dance with Somebody," "Didn't We Almost Have It All," "So Emotional," and "Where Do Broken Hearts Go"—setting a new record of seven consecutive U.S. No. 1 singles, beating the previous best of six held jointly by the Bee Gees and Beatles. With *Whitney* she became the first female artist to enter the *Billboard* album chart at No. 1.

The winning streak continued with 1990's *I'm Your Baby Tonight*, and the year after she became the first artist to turn "The Star Spangled Banner" into a chart hit with her rendition at Super Bowl XXV. Next she branched out into acting, appearing opposite Kevin Costner in *The Bodyguard*, as well as contributing six songs to the soundtrack album.

Things started to go awry in the new millennium as rumors spread of abusive behavior in her marriage to Bobby Brown and problems with drugs and anorexia. Record sales took a nosedive. Her public image took a hammering, too, as her behavior became increasingly erratic: canceling rehearsals and concerts on short notice and arriving hours late for interviews.

Houston's performance on single "I Wanna Dance With Somebody" won her a Grammy Award for Best Female Pop Vocal. ▶

Where were you when?

"God gave me a voice to sing with—and when you have that, what other gimmick is there?"

—Whitney Houston

"Listening to Whitney's songs today makes me even more emotional than I was back then. 'I Wanna Dance With Somebody' is my prom song. I gave the DJ special instruction that that song would be played, and it was."

—Valerie O'Neill, Boston

DEF LEPPARD—*HYSTERIA*

On the final day of 1984, Def Leppard drummer Rick Allen lost an arm when his car crashed during an impromptu road race. Just over a year and a half later, he made his stage return with a specially modified kit at the Monsters of Rock festival at Castle Donington, England. He had already laid down the tracks for 1987 album *Hysteria* with the aid of a Fairlight computer, but the ability to reproduce Leppard's earlier hits in a live environment gave the band extra incentive to continue and vindicated their decision to wait for Allen to convalesce. *Hysteria* became only the third rock album to chart seven singles in the *Billboard* Top 100.

From left to right: (back) Rick Allen, Joe Elliott, Steve Clark; (front) Rick Savage, Phil Collen. ▶

1988

STAND-OUT ALBUMS

Tracy Chapman—**Tracy Chapman**

Scenes from the Southside
   —**Bruce Hornsby and the Range**

Open Up and Say Ahh—**Poison**

Rattle and Hum—**U2**

Travelin' Wilburys Vol. 1
   —**Travelin' Wilburys**

Don't Be Cruel—**Bobby Brown**

Kylie—**Kylie Minogue**

Surfer Rosa—**Pixies**

Straight Outta Compton—**N.W.A.**

Nothing's Shocking
   —**Jane's Addiction**

Green—**R.E.M.**

I'm Your Man—**Leonard Cohen**

Bug—**Dinosaur Jr.**

Fisherman's Blues
   —**The Waterboys**

Bummed—**Happy Mondays**

And Justice for All—**Metallica**

▲ Little did Australian soap star Kylie Minogue realize that her first single with the hit-making team Stock, Aitken, and Waterman, "Loco-Motion," and debut album, *Kylie*, would eventually propel her to the status of "pop goddess." The apparent hat she is wearing on the cover of her debut album is in fact a felt ring.

Where were you when?

"In America I'm accepted as an adult, but in England it's still a bit dodgy. There's that stigma."

—George Michael

"To hear The Specials sing 'Free Nelson Mandela' in that atmosphere at Wembley was the most moving musical experience you can imagine. We'd previously had the death of Steve Biko and there was no guarantee the South Africans would release him. Jerry Dammers is a star."

—Jason Downing, London

Faith

The transition from "teen pop idol" to "serious artist" is difficult if not impossible to make. *Faith* helped George Michael cross the great divide.

George Michael made the difficult transition from teen idol to adult pop star in 1987 with the release of his debut solo album, *Faith*. In 1988 he consolidated that position with the Faith World Tour. The first single from the album, "I Want Your Sex," had been a statement of intent that was also featured on the soundtrack of the movie *Beverly Hills Cop 2*. The song was banned by many American radio stations because of its overtly sexual lyrics. The video featured celebrity makeup artist Kathy Jeung in a tight-fitting bodice that MTV refused to play in the daytime. Kasey Casem, host of *American Top 40*, even refused to say the title of the song on air. Despite, or maybe because of the furore, the single reached No. 2.

10-MONTH TOUR

By the end of 1988, *Faith* had gone seven times platinum and had spawned four American chart-topping singles. With the track "One More Try" Michael achieved the distinction of becoming the first white solo act to top the Hot Black Singles *Billboard* chart. The singer's massive 10-month tour to promote the album inflicted persistent throat problems and he told his record label Sony that he wouldn't be doing anything on that scale again.

As if to underline his determination to be taken seriously, Michael's next album was entitled *Listen Without Prejudice Vol. 1* (Vol. 2 was later scrapped), and he refused to undertake promotional duties or to appear in any videos. The single "Praying for Time" reached No. 1 in the *Billboard* Hot 100, but the album sold relatively poorly in comparison to its predecessor.

In the intervening years George Michael became a controversial figure, particularly after a run-in with the law in Beverley Hills for "engaging in a lewd act" in 1998 when his long-concealed homosexuality became public knowledge. He was later arrested on drug charges in London. It was a far cry from his wholesome image as one half of pop duo Wham! who enjoyed U.S. chart-toppers earlier in the decade.

◄ George Michael's love affair with the leather jacket continued in the *Faith* press and publicity photos.

NELSON MANDELA 70TH BIRTHDAY TRIBUTE CONCERT

Nelson Mandela had been jailed for life in 1962 for opposing South Africa's white minority government. His seventieth birthday was used by Artists Against Apartheid as an awareness-raising event to draw attention to his plight, and the result was an all-star Tribute Concert at London's Wembley Stadium in June. Jerry Dammers of The Specials was a key mover, having earlier recorded the joyous "Free Nelson Mandela" single. Artists participating included Dire Straits (featuring special guest Eric Clapton), Eurythmics, George Michael, Sting, Whitney Houston (who sang with her mother Cissy), Stevie Wonder, UB40 (with Chrissie Hynde guesting) and the Bee Gees. Mandela was finally released in 1990 and went on to become president of South Africa four years later in the country's first democratic elections.

The Mandela concert was an effective blend of pop and politics. ►

1988

INXS DOMINATE VIDEO MUSIC AWARDS

Australia's INXS, fronted by the irrepressible Michael Hutchence, hit a peak of worldwide popularity this year after the release of *Kick*, an album that yielded four Top 10 singles and several more international hits, including "New Sensation," "Never Tear Us Apart," "Devil Inside," and the No. 1 "Need You Tonight." The band toured heavily behind the album throughout 1987 and 1988, but it was their presence on the still comparatively new music channel MTV that really cemented their fame. The clip for "Need You Tonight," which paid homage to Bob Dylan's classic "Subterranean Homesick Blues" won five MTV awards this year, including Best Video. The band themselves performed "New Sensation" at the ceremony at LA's Universal Amphitheater in September.

▲ INXS with lead singer Michael Hutchence center.

Where were you when?

"I always thought of Slash as the heart of Guns N' Roses not Axl Rose. To be the perfect rock star you should look totally out of place in a supermarket. Slash looks like the kind of guy who doesn't do groceries. The video for 'November Rain' is the ultimate rock guitar fantasy. How many air guitar solos has that inspired?"

—Rog Barron, Nottingham, England

Full Metal Jacket

With the charts succumbing to Heavy Metal, Guns N' Roses revived the concept of a rock band that lived the hedonistic heavy rock lifestyle.

Heavy metal music was back in a big way in 1988. Van Halen continued to prosper without David Lee Roth on the album *OU812*, a chart-topper that was released in June, while British hard-rockers Def Leppard's *Hysteria* was still selling in huge quantities, hitting No. 1 after 49 weeks in the charts.

LA's Guns N' Roses offered a dirtier, more authentic take on the genre, calling it back to its 1970s roots and reacting against the poodle-haired image of glam-metal outfits like Mötley Crüe and Poison. The band also revived the decadent rock 'n' roll lifestyle that in post-Aids, post-Reagan America was in danger of extinction: Drink and hard drugs abounded as the band toured in support of its full-length debut album *Appetite for Destruction*, released at the end of 1987.

Their breakthrough came when the single "Sweet Child o' Mine" (written for singer Axl Rose's girlfriend Erin, daughter of Don Everly), became a smash in the summer of 1988 after heavy rotation on MTV. It was followed by a Top 10 placing for the reissue of "Welcome to the Jungle." A rereleased mini-album *GN'R Lies* nestled alongside *Appetite* in the charts, making them the first band to have two albums in the Top 5 in 15 years. Combined sales topped 10 million.

But the dark side emerged in August 1988 when two fans were killed in crowd congestion at a festival in England. The media unjustly blamed the band. In June 1991 Guns N' Roses sparked a riot in Riverport, Missouri, which left Axl Rose with an incitement charge hanging over his head for a year. The incident took place on a 26-month world tour to promote *Use Your Illusion 1* and *Use Your Illusion 2*. Both albums were released on the same day, debuting at Nos. 2 and 1, respectively, on the *Billboard* chart and creating their own piece of music history. The tour, however, proved the undoing of Guns N' Roses; the classic lineup of musicians has not performed together since, nor has the band released original material.

◄ Singer Axl Rose and lead guitarist "Slash" of Guns N' Roses.

JAMES BROWN JAILED

James Brown, the self-styled "Godfather of Soul," knew all about paying for misdemeanors: he had served three years when he was sixteen for his part in an armed robbery. This year saw him back behind bars, convicted of offenses including threatening pedestrians with a firearm, drug abuse, and failure to stop after an alleged high-speed car chase on the Interstate 120 in his native Georgia. Brown, who would serve half of his six-year sentence, had earlier in the year been charged with the attempted murder of wife Adrienne; he denied the charge, which was dropped. He clearly had substance abuse problems, having recently been arrested for the fifth time in ten months on drugs charges. Happily, he emerged from jail ready to restart his career.

James Brown, "the hardest working man in show business." ►

1989

STAND-OUT SINGLES

"Like a Prayer"—**Madonna**

"My Prerogative"—**Bobby Brown**

"Straight Up"—**Paula Abdul**

"Lost in Your Eyes"
—**Debbie Gibson**

"The Living Years"
—**Mike & the Mechanics**

"Eternal Flame"—**The Bangles**

"The Look"—**Roxette**

"She Drives Me Crazy"
—**Fine Young Cannibals**

"I'll Be There for You"—**Bon Jovi**

"Forever Your Girl"—**Paula Abdul**

"Wind Beneath My Wings"
—**Bette Midler**

"Satisfied"—**Richard Marx**

"Good Thing"
—**Fine Young Cannibals**

"If You Don't Know Me by Now"
—**Simply Red**

"Toy Soldiers"—**Martika**

"Batdance"—**Prince**

"Cold Hearted"—**Paula Abdul**

"Don't Wanna Lose You"
—**Gloria Estefan**

"Miss You Much"—**Janet Jackson**

▲ Madonna's "Blonde Ambition" look
was designed by Jean-Paul Gaultier.

Where were you when?

"I promised myself that I'd never actually admit to listening to New Kids on the Block."
—Alicia

"Joey McIntyre was the youngest in the band and my favorite. I would carefully cut him out of group posters and paste up this big montage of about 75 pictures on my bedroom wall that I called "100% Joey." My brother made himself public enemy No. 1 by adding graffiti."

— Linda Evans, Bris

New Kids on the Block

Any band that has "kids" in its name is destined to be shortlived, but New Kids on the Block's 15 minutes of fame burnt very bright while it lasted.

In 1989 New Kids on the Block reinvented the boy band, a concept that had its origins in the 1970s pop of the Osmonds and the Bay City Rollers. Behind them was Maurice Starr, a Boston-based songwriter, producer, and musician. Earlier in the decade, Starr had successfully masterminded New Edition, whose members included Bobby Brown, who later crossed over into the adult marketplace and married Whitney Houston.

Built around 15-year-old Donnie Wahlberg and also featuring Danny Wood, Joey McIntyre, and brothers Jon and Jordan Knight, New Kids on the Block was essentially a white version of New Edition. After their self-titled first album was released in 1986 and sank without trace, Starr spent almost two years fashioning the follow-up, *Hangin' Tough*. The single "Please Don't Go Girl" went to Top 10 at the end of 1988, and New Kids were poised to become the best-selling American act of 1989, shifting 7 million copies of an album that had four gold singles taken from it. Typically, their success upset so-called serious music lovers; readers of *Rolling Stone* magazine voted New Kids the Worst Band and "Hangin' Tough" the Worst Single of 1989.

Success continued into the new decade, with *Step By Step* becoming another huge seller—but boy bands tend to have a limited shelf life, no matter how large their initial fan base. Overexposure saw their popularity start to wane, and in 1992, in the wake of the Milli Vanilli lip-synching rumpus, they were hit by allegations that they did not sing on all of *Hangin' Tough*.

Although the accusations were unfounded, there was no denying that pop had moved on and that they had fallen out of fashion. No longer teenagers, they dismissed Starr and became officially known by the initials NKOTB. *Face The Music* in 1994 was an abortive attempt to create a harder-edged, more contemporary sound, and its failure hastened the demise of the band that June.

◄ New Kids from left to right, Danny Wood, Donnie Wahlberg, Jon Knight, Joey McIntyre and Jordan Knight.

PAULA ABDUL

Paula Abdul's rise from cheerleader for the Los Angeles Lakers basketball team, through choreographer to the stars, to superstar singer in her own right was relatively rapid. But her debut album *Forever Your Girl* took 62 weeks from release to heading the *Billboard* charts. Once there, a string of frothy pop-dance hits ensued, notably "Straight Up," "Forever Your Girl," and "Cold Hearted," all of which were chart-toppers in1989. A tempestuous marriage to actor Emilio Estevez and a rumored eating disorder would slow her progress, but she re-emerged in the 2000s as a judge on the influential television series *American Idol*.

Paula Abdul, now even more famous as the sympathetic panelist of *American Idol*. ►

1990-1999

STAND-OUT SINGLES

"Unbelievable"—**EMF**

"The Power"—**Snap**

"Hold On"—**En Vogue**

"It Must Have Been Love"
—**Roxette**

"Black Velvet"—**Alannah Myles**

"Hold On"—**Wilson Phillips**

"Free Fallin'"—**Tom Petty**

"Downtown Train"—**Rod Stewart**

"Pump Up the Jam"
—**Technotronic featuring Felly**

"Show Me Heaven"—**Maria McKee**

"Tom's Diner"—**DNA Featuring
Suzanne Vega**

"Groove Is in the Heart"
—**Deee-Lite**

"There She Goes"—**The LA's**

"Loaded"—**Primal Scream**

"Friends in Low Places"
—**Garth Brooks**

"Vogue"—**Madonna**

"Birdhouse in Your Soul"
—**They Might Be Giants**

"The Only One I Know"
—**The Charlatans**

▲ EMF were the first band from England's
rural Forest of Dean to score a *Billboard*
Hot 100 No. 1. The single was first
released in 1990.

Nothing Compares 2 U

Sinead O'Connor took a little-known Prince song and made it an international hit. But her unwillingness to compromise would seriously affect her career.

Dublin-born singer-songwriter Sinead O'Connor had released a handful of self-penned singles from first album *The Lion and the Cobra* when her manager Fachtna O'Ceallaigh suggested she record a Prince song. It proved a masterstroke as, promoted by a full-face video in which she appeared to cry real tears, the shaven-headed O'Connor's heartrending performance of "Nothing Compares 2 U" turned her into a worldwide star.

O'Connor subsequently met Prince but denounced him as having a "huge ego," claiming he was jealous she had enjoyed the hit with his song. "Nothing Compares 2 U" made No. 1 on both sides of the Atlantic, while the album *I Do Not Want What I Haven't Got* performed just as well. However, in the first of a series of impetuous and ultimately career-damaging decisions, O'Connor became the first person to refuse a Grammy when it was awarded to her for the Best Alternative Album. She believed that the award represented only commercialism.

BOOED OFF STAGE

The singer's subsequent career failed to sustain the emotional, creative, and commercial highs she reached in 1990, and she became more famous for actions like ripping up a photograph of the Pope on TV's *Saturday Night Live* in 1992 and being ordained a priest in the Latin Tridentine Church two years later. She was also booed off stage at a Bob Dylan tribute concert at Madison Square Garden.

Two more albums (*Am I Not Your Girl?* was a curious collection of other people's songs) made the Top 40 in 1992 and 1994, but by the time O'Connor announced her retirement from music in 2003 via her website, she had become a one-hit wonder to all but her most dedicated fans. A career that had promised much had fallen victim to her outspokenness and unwillingness to play the corporate game.

Sinead O'Connor's emotional re-working of a Prince song
yielded a simple but compelling video. ▶

Where were you when?

"I loved the original version by The Family. I remember being completely frustrated that O'Connor's version received so much more attention and airplay. It's good in its own way but to me doesn't compare to the original."

—T. Knox, Fort Lauderdale

"Sinead took a very average song from an overrated singer and made it into something special. It was pure class."

—Raj Singh, West London

"The first records I listened to were Aretha Franklin, but I was only affected by one band—the Smiths."

—Sinead O'Connor

MILLI VANILLI

In an unprecedented move, hit dance duo Milli Vanilli were asked to hand back their Grammy award for Best New Artist in November, nine months after beating Neneh Cherry, Soul II Soul, the Indigo Girls, and Tone Loc to the statuette. Their Svengali, disco producer Frank Farian, admitted during the year that Rob Pilatus and Fabrice Morvan, from Germany and France respectively, hadn't actually sung on their impressive run of five top singles that had included chart-toppers in "Baby Don't Forget My Number," "Girl I'm Gonna Miss You," and "Blame It on the Rain." More deserved wins were registered by veteran blues singer Bonnie Raitt and soul diva Anita Baker, both of whom were allowed to keep their awards.

1990

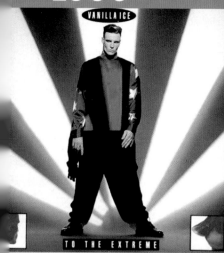

STAND-OUT ALBUMS

...But Seriously—**Phil Collins**

Nick of Time—**Bonnie Raitt**

I Do Not Want What I Haven't Got
—**Sinead O'Connor**

Please Hammer Don't Hurt 'Em
—**M. C. Hammer**

Step by Step—**New Kids on the Block**

To the Extreme—**Vanilla Ice**

Violator—**Depeche Mode**

Graffiti Bridge—**Prince**

Rhythm of the Saints
—**Paul Simon**

Affection—**Lisa Stansfield**

Wilson Phillips—**Wilson Phillips**

No Fences—**Garth Brooks**

Graffiti Bridge—**Prince**

Blue Sky Mining
—**Midnight Oil**

Blaze of Glory—**Bon Jovi**

Listen Without Prejudice Volume 1
—**George Michael**

Twin Peaks—**Angelo Badalamenti**

▲ Vanilla Ice's album *To the Extreme* remained at No. 1 for 16 weeks. Its stand-out single "Ice Ice Baby" (which sampled the bassline from "Under Pressure" by Queen and David Bowie) was the first rap single to reach No. 1 in the *Billboard* Hot 100 since Blondie's "Rapture" in 1981.

Where were you when?

"A special shout out to my man M. C. Hammer: a lot of people diss you, man, but they just jealous."

—Ice-T

"I was cleaning out my closet and I found 47 pairs of bright neon M. C. Hammer pants. They are absolutely the worst pants of all time. I can't remember being stupid enough to buy these, but I must have been."

—Jason Warnes, Austin

M. C. Hammer Time

M. C. Hammer raised rap music to a new level of popularity with his album *Please Hammer Don't Hurt 'Em,* which stuck at No. 1 for five months.

Born Stanley Kirk Burrell in 1962, M. C. Hammer took hip-hop to the top this year when his second album *Please Hammer Don't Hurt 'Em* became the first of the genre to exceed 10 million sales. It owed much of its appeal to the inclusion of the single "U Can't Touch This," which depended on a riff borrowed from Rick James's 1981 release "Super Freak." The single reached only No. 8 because it was released in 12-inch format, but it was followed up by "Have You Seen Her?" and the Prince-sampling "Pray," both of which made the Top 5.

"U Can't Touch This" vied for rap record of the year with "Ice Ice Baby" by Vanilla Ice, a former Hammer support act, who was also enjoying success. But Hammer (who dropped the M. C. prefix in 1991) was perceived as a gimmick with his ultrawide trousers and flamboyant dance moves.

Despite its multi-platinum certification and two Top 10 hit singles, in its title track and "Addams Groove," sales of Hammer's 1991 follow-up album, *Too Legit to Quit,* were one-third of those for the previous album. The record company considered it a commercial failure. A flamboyant tour ran overbudget and was canceled partway through, and (M. C.) Hammer was suddenly yesterday's man. He filed for bankruptcy in 1996; his record sales didn't sustain his lavish lifestyle, which included breeding thoroughbred racehorses.

He returned to the church where he had grown up and became an ordained minister, although—as with Little Richard—the lure of the stage and the charts would sometimes prove too great and he would pop up with a mini comeback.

Brief as his superstardom was, M. C. Hammer was a trailblazer in rap and hip-hop, who worked with Tupac Shakur before his death. Once regarded as a figure of fun, Hammer is now considered an influential artist. His dramatic rise and fall has left several legacies, including the use of rap stars in TV commercials and for promoting clothing lines.

◄ "U Can't Touch This:" M. C. Hammer became famous for his intense and electrifying performance style, which was often mimicked to comic effect.

"BLAZE OF GLORY"—BON JOVI

Bon Jovi had become America's leading band in the 1980s by combining hard-rock aggression with pop hooks to achieve universal appeal. Singles like "Livin' on a Prayer" and the multi-platinum *Slippery When Wet* album attested to their success. Yet the first hit of the 1990s to bear their name, the No. 1 single "Blaze of Glory," was actually a solo effort from singer Jon Bon Jovi. With the band on an extended hiatus, he wrote the song to head the soundtrack to the *Young Guns II* movie. With guitarist Richie Sambora also recording a solo album, rumors grew that the band had split up—but they would reassemble in 1992 to record their first album in four years, *Keep The Faith.* Enough fans had done just that to make it a Top 5 entry.

Jon Bon Jovi's "Blaze of Glory" won a Golden Globe Award for Best Original Song. ►

1991

THE SHOW MUST GO ON

Queen vocalist Freddie Mercury became the rock world's most high-profile casualty of AIDS. Rumors about Mercury's health had circulated for several years, and his gaunt, drawn appearance in the video for the single "I'm Going Slightly Mad," released in early 1991 to promote the album *Innuendo,* led to increased speculation. Mercury's death in November left the three remaining members of Queen a legacy—to raise public awareness and money to stamp out the blight of AIDS. They set the wheels in motion for A Concert for Life, held at Wembley Stadium on Easter Monday, 1992, and viewed by 1 billion worldwide, through which an estimated £10,000,000 ($20,000,000) was raised for the Terrence Higgins Trust. Four new songs were recorded by Queen for Nelson Mandela's campaign against AIDS. One of these, "46664—The Call," was released as a free download to publicize 2007 World Aids Day.

Where were you when?

"The film company wanted to have more period instruments to fit the film, and I said we don't want lutes or mandolins on this—this is a pop record. I think they're probably pleased with the way it turned out."

—Bryan Adams

"I think for fans, 'Summer of 69' is a much more important song. When Bryan sings that live it gets such a great reaction. 'Everything I Do' is shared by too many people."

—Wendy Milligan, Reading, England

(Everything I Do) I Do It For You

Bryan Adams dominated the charts worldwide with his record-breaking song from the film *Robin Hood Prince of Thieves.*

Canadian rock guitarist and singer Bryan Adams had been in the doldrums after accumulating 13 U.S. chart hits between 1982 and 1987, including the 1985 No. 1 "Heaven." One of his problems was sustaining the quality of his songwriting over the length of an album.

It was little surprise, then, that it was a single that proved his biggest success to date. He was assisted in its writing by film-score specialist Michael Kamen, whose original idea it had been, and producer Robert "Mutt" Lange. But the performance of "(Everything I Do) I Do It For You" was Adams' own work, and the rock-power ballad, played over the end credits of Kevin Costner's movie *Robin Hood Prince of Thieves*, was captivating.

Its position, "buried as far back in the film as possible," according to Adams, reflected a lack of confidence from the moviemakers. The song had been pitched by Michael Kamen to Kate Bush, Annie Lennox, Lisa Stansfield, and the duo Peter Cetera and Julia Fordham before Adams got involved.

It was a change of pace from Adams' customary rock fare, but America accorded it seven weeks at No. 1; in Britain the song created a record 16 consecutive weeks. And since Adams' album *Waking Up the Neighbors* was some four months distant, fans opted to buy the single rather than a mainly instrumental soundtrack album.

The singer developed a taste for film collaborations. He hit No. 1 again in 1994 with "All for Love," a three-way performance with Sting and Rod Stewart from the film *The Three Musketeers*. Adams scaled back his music work in the new millennium and established a career as a photographer.

◄ Bryan Adams performing at Shoreline Amphitheater in Mountain View, California.

APPLE BATTLE

After 116 days in the high court, ten at the court of appeal, and one at the European Commission, Apple computers and London-based Apple Corps—the Beatles' former record label—came to an amicable agreement about the former's use of the Apple trademark. The cost of the battle was estimated at $13.3 million, while Apple Computers, who settled the case for a reported $27 million, agreed not to enter the music business. The dispute would flare up again when Apple marketed its iTunes and iPod concepts, and legal action was rejoined in 2003. Four years later peace broke out again after Apple Inc. bought ownership of the name, agreeing to license some of those trademarks back to Apple Corps.

The Beatles' Apple boutique at 94 Baker Street, London. The store opened on December 5, 1968, but was closed within eight months due to financial losses. ►

1991

TOP-SELLING SINGLES

"(Everything I Do) I Do It for You"
—**Bryan Adams**

"Black or White"
—**Michael Jackson**

"Rush, Rush"—**Paula Abdul**

"It's So Hard"—**Boyz II Men**

"One More Try"—**Timmy T.**

"Gonna Make You Sweat
(Everybody Dance Now)"
—**C&C Music Factory featuring
Freedom Williams**

"I Wanna Sex You Up"
—**Color Me Badd**

"Justify My Love"—**Madonna**

"Emotions"—**Mariah Carey**

"Baby Baby"—**Amy Grant**

▲ "Black or White," taken from Michael
Jackson's *Dangerous* album, topped the
Billboard Top 100 for seven weeks. It also
reached No. 1 in the United Kingdom and
18 other countries.

Where were you when?

*"I went to the Hordern Pavilion in Sydney in 1991 to see Violent Femmes, Nirvana
and a few alternative bands. I was standing at a hot dog stand with a friend when he
suddenly introduced me to 'his friend' Kurt. I said hi and Kurt said 'Hi, great to
meet you,' and gave me a kiss on the cheek while my friend asked a random stranger
to take our photo. It hadn't occurred to me that my friend didn't know Kurt at all
and it wasn't until I was in the mosh pit of the headline act, Nirvana, singing
'Nevermind' and looked on stage that I realised who Kurt was. I still have
an accidental cigarette burn scar on my wrist from Kurt's cigarette."*

—Fiona Hannan, Sydney

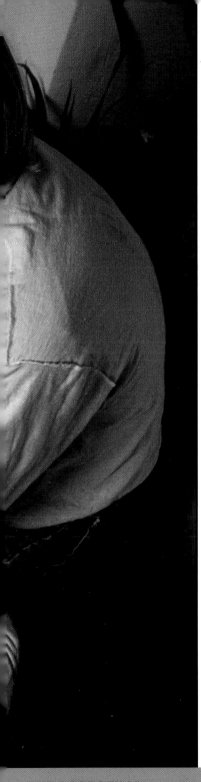

Nirvana

Nevermind and its lead single "Smells Like Teen Spirit" gave anthems to the "grunge" generation and brought alternative rock into the mainstream.

Having spent 1990 completing their definitive three-piece lineup with the recruitment of drummer Dave Grohl and exchanging the poverty of indie-band existence for a lucrative move to David Geffen's new label, DGC, Seattle trio Nirvana this year became even bigger than Geffen's last discoveries, Guns N' Roses.

With the release of its second album _Nevermind_ in September, Nirvana found itself the standard bearer of the "grunge" movement, a label applied to over-amplified music emanating from the west coast of the States. Other leading grunge acts included Pearl Jam, Soundgarden, Mudhoney, and Alice in Chains. Guitars were distorted, lyrics impenetrable, and vocals indistinct, while workshirts and other deliberately basic clothing added to the anti-image.

While it typified this musical collision of 1960s garage rock and punk attitude, _Nevermind_ intrigued even before it was heard: The cover picture of a naked baby in a swimming pool, about to make a grab for a dollar bill dangling on a fish hook, offered a memorable image of corrupted innocence.

Nevermind was a call to arms that contained as many of the ingredients of teen rebellion as the Sex Pistols' _Never Mind the Bollocks_ nearly one and a half decades earlier.

The opening track, "Smells Like Teen Spirit," was opening up the world's singles charts like a chain saw as the album was released. What the words delivered by leader/guitarist Kurt Cobain meant were anybody's guess. But the anthemic effect was undeniable. When _Nevermind_ leapfrogged over Guns N' Roses's _Use Your Illusion_, U2's _Achtung Baby_, and Michael Jackson's _Dangerous_ to top the American album chart, it was clear that in just a few short months Nirvana had made an indelible mark on popular music.

Unfortunately, the clock was already ticking for the seriously unbalanced Cobain, whose self-inflicted death in 1994 assured him immortality. Bassist Krist Novoselic later went on to become a political activist, while drummer Grohl strapped on a guitar to front the still popular Foo Fighters.

◄ Nirvana, photographed at the Warfield Theatre in San Francisco.
From left to right: Krist Novoselic, Kurt Cobain, and Dave Grohl.

THE DOORS FILM

The brightness and brevity of their spell in the spotlight in the late 1960s and early 1970s made the Doors an obvious target for Hollywood—not to mention the charismatic appeal and tragic demise of their lead singer, Jim Morrison. Val Kilmer was selected to play Morrison by director Oliver Stone, amid competition from John Travolta and Kyle MacLachlan, a longtime Doors fan, who settled for the role of Ray Manzarek. The Doors movie was in development for many years with different studios. Organist Ray Manzarek turned down Stone's requests to help in the movie and has since said that the movie is "a horrible account" of the history of the band. Critics agreed, however, that Kilmer's performance as the Lizard King was as extraordinary as the film was ordinary.

The original movie poster featuring Jim Morrison lookalike Val Kilmer. ▶

1992

STAND-OUT SINGLES

"Smells Like Teen Spirit"—**Nirvana**

"Mysterious Ways"—**U2**

"Under the Bridge"
  —**Red Hot Chili Peppers**

"Damn! I Wish I Was Your Lover"
  —**Sophie B. Hawkins**

"To Be With You"—**Mr. Big**

"Hazard"—**Richard Marx**

"November Rain"—**Guns N' Roses**

"Jump Around"—**House of Pain**

"End of The Road"—**Boyz II Men**

"Stay"—**Shakespears Sister**

"Creep"—**Radiohead**

"Killing in the Name"
  —**Rage Against the Machine**

"My Lovin'"—**En Vogue**

"The Drowners"—**Suede**

"Jump"—**Kriss Kross**

"Man on the Moon"—**R.E.M.**

"Cantaloop"—**US3**

"Connected"—**Stereo MC's**

"Erotica"—**Madonna**

"America: What Time Is Love"
  —**The KLF**

▲ Teenage rap duo Kris Kross remained at No. 1 on the *Billboard* Hot 100 for eight weeks with their catchy single "Jump."

Automatic for the People

Slow starters and pioneers of the alternative rock genre, R.E.M. released one of the most critically acclaimed albums of the 1990s.

Singer Michael Stipe and guitarist Peter Buck's chance meeting in the Wuxtry record store in Athens, Georgia, in 1978 led to the formation of America's leading "indie" band and, 14 years later, to a landmark album. Together with bass player Mike Mills and drummer Bill Berry, the singer and guitarist comprised R.E.M., college radio and critical favorites for their first recording decade. *Out of Time*, their second LP for multinational Warner Brothers, finally gave them a U.S. chart-topping album.

Although follow-up, *Automatic for the People*, stalled at No. 2 behind Garth Brooks on its October 1992 release, it was undoubtedly R.E.M.'s magnum opus. Its musical variety came from jams in studios across the United States, though an underlying downbeat feeling, according to guitarist Buck, reflected "that sense of turning thirty." The band received praise for dealing with dark themes like AIDS, suicide, and loss in a positive, mature way.

Automatic yielded an astonishing five hit singles, including "The Sidewinder Sleeps Tonight," "Nightswimming," "Everybody Hurts," "Drive," and a tribute to late lamented comedian Andy Kaufman, "Man on the Moon." The album went multi-platinum, selling about 10 million copies worldwide despite the band's not touring.

A return to touring on a grand scale in 1995 preceded many changes for the hitherto constant R.E.M., including parting with longtime manager Jefferson Holt and then after a health scare with drummer Bill Berry. The group's record sales dipped, and only with 2001's *Reveal* did they recapture the underlying spirit that had typified *Automatic for the People*.

Thirty years after their record-shop meeting, Stipe and Buck, with Mills, were still making music as R.E.M. They released their first live album in 2007, as well as being inducted into the Rock and Roll Hall of Fame. In a 1988 interview guitarist Buck had described typical R.E.M. songs as "Minor key, mid-tempo, enigmatic, semi-folk-rock-balladish things. That's what everyone thinks and to a certain degree, that's true." Some things, fortunately, did not change.

From left to right: Peter Buck, Michael Stipe, Mike Mills, and Bill Berry. ▶

Where were you when?

"'Everybody Hurts' was written for teenagers, basically saying don't kill yourself. My sister is a teacher and someone she knows who is 15 tried to kill himself…the idea was to write something that would appeal to someone who is having trouble."

—Michael Stipe

"I think Automatic for the People *would be just about the perfect album if only they'd replace 'New Orleans Instrumental No. 1.'"*

—Jim Cassidy, Dallas

MADONNA BECOMES MOGUL

Madonna did more than just confirm her status as the world's leading female singer when she signed a seven-year cross-media contract with Warner Brothers on behalf of her Maverick group of companies. This included record releases, music publishing, books, and television and motion picture projects and was reckoned to be worth over $60 million. She would remain with Warners until 2007, when she signed another, even bigger, all-enveloping contract with events company Live Nation, with whom she entered a 10-year global partnership said to be worth $120 million.

Erotica was Madonna's first album to be released through her Maverick record label. ▶

1992

STAND-OUT ALBUMS

Ropin' the Wind—**Garth Brooks**

Time, Love, and Tenderness
—**Michael Bolton**

Nevermind—**Nirvana**

Blood Sugar Sex Magik
—**Red Hot Chili Peppers**

Metallica—**Metallica**

Keep the Faith—**Bon Jovi**

Some Gave All—**Billy Ray Cyrus**

Us—**Peter Gabriel**

Adrenalize—**Def Leppard**

Stars—**Simply Red**

The Chronic—**Dr. Dre**

Rage Against the Machine
—**Rage Against the Machine**

Check Your Head—**Beastie Boys**

Little Earthquakes—**Tori Amos**

Copper Blue—**Sugar**

Ingénue—**k.d. Lang**

*3 Years, 5 Months and 2 Days
in the Life of…*
—**Arrested Development**

It's a Shame About Ray
—**The Lemonheads**

U.F. Orb—**The Orb**

Your Arsenal—**Morrissey**

▲ Red Hot Chili Peppers gained critical
acclaim and commercial success with
their fifth album, *Blood Sugar Sex Magik*.

Where were you when?

*"I kind of knew that it would have some potency to it, being Whitney Houston's
first acting role and in a film starring Kevin Costner. We knew it would be hot, but I
don't think we knew it would sell 25 million copies."*

—David Foster

*"I read on a trivia site that they originally planned the movie in 1976 with Steve
McQueen and Diana Ross. I think that would have been good, too."*

—Lois Feldtman, New York

I Will Always Love You

The unprecedented success of the single "I Will Always Love You" was matched by Houston's big-screen debut in hit movie of the year, *The Bodyguard*.

In 1992 soul diva Whitney Houston's recording of Dolly Parton's "I Will Always Love You," outsold U.S.A for Africa's "We Are the World," topping the U.S. charts for a record 14 weeks and sealing the success of her big-screen debut in *The Bodyguard*.

"I Will Always Love You" helped the movie's soundtrack, which featured five more Houston songs as well as contributions from Curtis Stigers, Joe Cocker, Lisa Stansfield and Kenny G, sell 17 million copies in North America alone. *The Bodyguard* soundtrack survived three different challenges to return to the top spot and rack up 20 weeks at the chart summit. It is still the best-selling movie soundtrack of all time.

The interracial aspect of the film was played down. *The New York Times* said her relationship with her costar lacked passion, but Houston laughed all the way to the bank as the film grossed more than $121 million in the United States and $410 million worldwide, thanks in large part to the success of the soundtrack.

"I Will Always Love You" had twice topped the country chart for its writer and was a standout of the filmed stage musical *The Best Little Whorehouse in Texas*. Houston's version took a chance in beginning totally acappella, an arrangement suggested by Kevin Costner. It proved a smash and created a record of longevity that would last until 1996.

Sadly, real life would not run as smoothly for her as the recording or the movie. Houston's career slumped amid stories of spousal and substance abuse.

Her 1998 album, *My Love Is Your Love*, would remain her sole commercial and creative highlight in the post-*Bodyguard* period—a disappointment for someone who had once registered seven consecutive U.S. No. 1 singles; "I Will Always Love You" was the tenth. After successful drug rehabilitation, she divorced bad-boy soul star Bobby Brown in 2006 and prepared to record her seventh album with Clive Davis, the record mogul who had discovered her.

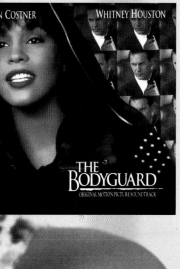

◄ Whitney Houston's contribution to *The Bodyguard* soundtrack helped it to sell over 44 million copies worldwide.

WAYNE'S WORLD

In a repeat of the Blues Brothers' success in crossing from TV show *Saturday Night Live* to the big screen, hit movie *Wayne's World* expanded on the geeky characters created by Mike Myers and Dana Carvey. Their public-access cable TV show in Aurora, Illinois proved an unlikely route to fame and fortune, not to mention rubbing shoulders with the likes of Alice Cooper and Meat Loaf. Wayne and Garth invented their own phrases and facial expressions—"schwing," "party on," and the use of "not" after a pause at the end of a sentence. Alice Cooper was delighted to "have kids running up to me at airports and places and going, "Hey, you're that guy from *Wayne's World*," while the use of "Bohemian Rhapsody" in a memorable headbanging sequence helped Queen score yet another hit.

Mike Myers as Wayne Campbell and Dana Carvey as Garth Algar. ▶

1993

NO. 1 SINGLES

"I Will Always Love You"
—**Whitney Houston**

"A Whole New World
(Aladdin's Theme)"
—**Peabo Bryson & Regina Belle**

"Informer"—**Snow**

"Freak Me"—**Silk**

"That's the Way Love Goes"
—**Janet Jackson**

"Weak"—**SWV (Sisters
With Voices)**

"(I Can't Help) Falling in Love
With You"—**UB40**

"Dreamlover"—**Mariah Carey**

"I'd Do Anything for Love (But
I Won't Do That)"—**Meat Loaf**

"Again"—**Janet Jackson**

"Hero"—**Mariah Carey**

▲ UB40's rerecording of Elvis's 1961 hit
"(I Can't Help) Falling in Love With You"
became the band's most successful song.

Garth Brooks— In Pieces

The success of Garth Brooks' album *In Pieces* made its mark on the pop charts and helped bring modern country music to a wider audience.

Country king Garth Brooks's annual album was a guaranteed revenue earner for any self-respecting record store. (Brooks is the top-selling solo artist of the 20th century, according to the Recording Industry Association of America.) He used the release of his *In Pieces* album to speak out against music stores who sold secondhand CDs, wanting them to be excluded from stocking his latest album. He believed it cheapened the value of CDs and cut into the profits made by new releases.

Brooks, a former Oklahoma State University advertising major who had sold millions of albums since his 1989 debut, asked his label, Liberty, not to supply retailers dealing in used CDs. This didn't happen, and a boycott of the release organized by small record shops failed to hurt the album's sales. *In Pieces* became his third album to sail in at the top of the U.S. pop and country chart with first-week sales of 405,000. It produced five hits: "Ain't Going Down ('Til the Sun Comes Up)," "American Honky Tonk Bar Association," "Standing Outside the Fire," "One Night a Day," and "Callin' Baton Rouge."

Brooks' rise to fame had been based on songs written by some of Nashville's best writers, cleverly mixing country with rock and 1970s singer-songwriter styles to create a brand of music that reached far beyond those who, like himself, wore a cowboy hat. He ventured away from this formula for 1992's brooding *The Chase* and suffered disappointing sales. He returned to pop country for *In Pieces* and created what *Rolling Stone* dismissively called "another solid collection of puffed-up anthems, emotional overkill, and cinematic C&W for the upwardly mobile."

In between times Brooks had also renegotiated what he considered the unreasonable contract he'd signed with Liberty when he was still a struggling hopeful. All was now set fair for the future, and *In Pieces* reflected that optimism. By 1998 its sales had reached 8 million.

Often photographed in his trademark Steston, Garth Brooks
has become a modern icon of country music. ▶

Where were you when?

"Part of the new deal was no deadlines. So In Pieces *was probably one of the most relaxed albums we ever made, and it reflects the live show more than any album we have done."*

—Garth Brooks

"Garth Brooks and his fine album In Pieces *got me started in country and it's a relationship that goes from strength to strength. For me 'Ain't Going Down (Till the Sun Comes Up)' is the best cut of all."*

—Ray Hall, Denver

PRINCE CHANGES HIS NAME TO SYMBOL

On his 35th birthday, Prince changed his name to a symbol in protest against his record label. This would last for five years, and was explained as follows: "The first step I have taken towards the ultimate goal of emancipation from the chains that bind me to Warner Bros. was to change my name from Prince to the Love Symbol. Prince is the name that my Mother gave me at birth. Warner Bros. took the name, trademarked it, and used it as the main marketing tool to promote all of the music that I wrote. The company owns the name Prince and all related music marketed under Prince. I became merely a pawn used to produce more money for Warner Bros. The only acceptable replacement for my name, and my identity, was the Love Symbol … it is who I am. It is my name."

Prince, wearing his insignia on his sleeve. ▶

1993

NIRVANA

IN UTERO

IN UTERO—NIRVANA

Having exploded onto the world's music scene with 1991's *Nevermind,* Nirvana had found it difficult to follow up with an album of new material—not only had they toured non-stop but mainman Kurt Cobain had become a father. When a new album, *In Utero,* eventually appeared, it contained not only the ultra-controversial "Rape Me" but a number of reflections on fame and fortune, notably the ironically titled "Radio Friendly Unit Shifter." *In Utero* quickly emulated its predecessor and proved the album of the year, its heavily confessional tone striking a chord in listeners and reviewers alike. A clue to Kurt Cobain's state of mind came with the album's previous two working titles: the bored-out-of-my-skull *Verse-Chorus-Verse* and the self-explanatory *I Hate Myself and I Want to Die.* It seemed he saw himself as having turned into something he despised, and the result was inevitably very personal: indeed, a copy lay beside his body when he was found dead in 1994.

Clapton is God (Again)

When Eric Clapton's acoustic set filmed for MTV's *Unplugged* series was released as an LP it earned three Grammy Awards, including Album of the Year.

The world was used to seeing Eric Clapton, former leader of 1960s supergroup Cream, with an electric guitar in his hand. So when an invitation came from music channel MTV to perform on their *Unplugged* acoustic showcase, it was not immediately accepted. "Eric was kind of reluctant," said producer Russ Titelman, who also explained that "if he intended it to be a record, he would have done things differently."

Yet the audio recording of a one-hour TV special would rejuvenate the career of a man whose world had collapsed when his son Conor fell to his death from a 53rd floor Manhattan apartment two years before. Ironically, it was the understated song that Conor Clapton's death inspired, "Tears in Heaven," that encouraged him to work acoustically.

Most of the other songs featured on *Unplugged* were written by blues legends of yesteryear, though Clapton devised a version of his rock standard "Layla" with second guitarist Andy Fairweather Low that completely removed it from its 1970 rock anthem status and made it sound like a J. J. Cale Cajun classic. His seven-piece backup band handled all the songs with similar restraint.

MTV's *Unplugged* strand had been launched in January 1990 and had attracted such big names as Don Henley, Elton John, and Paul McCartney, but Clapton's show garnered a record 1.3 million audience. This naturally led to calls for a commercial release, as had been the case with Paul McCartney. Russ Titelman, who had mixed the audio element of the show, was among the lobbyists and was vindicated when in March 1993, almost a year after the show had been aired, Clapton's *Unplugged* sat proudly atop the American charts.

Its rise to become Clapton's first U.S. No. 1 in nearly two decades had been fueled by six Grammy awards. As he collected his sixth—"Tears In Heaven" had been named Record of the Year—an emotional Eric thanked his late son for "the love he gave me and the song he gave me."

Unplugged was recorded on January 16, 1992, at Bray Film Studios in Windsor, England. ▶

Where were you when?

"I wasn't sure whether it should just be me solo or with another guitar and/or bass, but everyone had such a nice touch and they all managed to restrain themselves, so I ended using almost everyone on almost everything."

—Eric Clapton

"To hear Clapton's acoustic version of 'Layla' is to be impressed all over again with the man's songwriting skill. Unplugged *was a great vehicle for him because his style isn't frenetic like Townshend or Springsteen."*

—Josh Rowley, Perth, Australia

U2—THE ZOOROPA TOUR

After widescreen 1980s stadium-rock creations like *The Joshua Tree,* U2 had started incorporating elements of dance and electronica into their music with 1991's *Achtung Baby.* The next evidence of U2 reinventing themselves was the extravagantly staged Zoo TV world tour, which kicked off in New Jersey in August 1992 and reflected a theme of media overkill. By 1993, the tour had reached Europe, been rechristened Zooropa and would give birth to an album of the same name, recorded between legs of the tour and featuring a cameo performance by Johnny Cash. The two-year venture ended in December in Tokyo; three months later, when *Zooropa* won the Best Alternative Album award at the Grammies, singer Bono expressed his intention, "to continue to abuse our position and f*** up the mainstream."

U2, from left to right: Larry Mullen, The Edge, Bono, and Adam Clayton. ▶

1994

TOP-SELLING SINGLES

"The Sign"—**Ace of Base**

"I'll Make Love to You"
—**Boyz II Men**

"I Swear"—**All-4-One**

"On Bended Knee"—**Boyz II Men**

"Another Night"—**Real McCoy**

"Stay (I Missed You)"
—**Lisa Loeb & Nine Stories**

"The Power of Love"—**Céline Dion**

"Here Comes the Hotstepper"
—**Ini Kamoze**

"Bump N' Grind"—**R. Kelly**

"All For Love"—**Bryan Adams/
Rod Stewart/Sting**

▲ "The Sign" by Swedish band Ace of Base was the best-selling single of 1994 and remained at the top of the *Billboard* Hot 100 for six weeks.

Where were you when?

"The only way I could sell this idea to the Stones was to say to Mick Jagger and Keith Richards: 'Look, this is really cool, and it's never been done before. And if you don't do it, I'll do it with Aerosmith.'"

—Stephan Fitch, president of multimedia computer group Thinking Pictures

"The sound was very choppy. People say, 'Gee, that's all I get?' I say, 'Yes, and that's one of the limitations of the superinformation highway. Maybe now there can be discussion about expanding it.'"

—Olivier Pfeiffer, Thinking Pictures

It's Only Rock 'n' Scroll

The Rolling Stones lived up to their name when they became the first major band to broadcast their music in a live Internet concert.

Years before the power of the World Wide Web changed the way music was bought and marketed, it fell to the Rolling Stones to point the way. They arranged for a Dallas concert from their Voodoo Lounge tour to be broadcast over the still infant Internet on November 18.

The band not only performed for 50,000 people in Dallas's Cotton Bowl but also an (admittedly limited) audience gazing at computer monitors around the world. They used new technology called the Multicast Backbone, or M-Bone, which had first been used to simulcast an Internet Engineering conference in 1992 and, since then, had provided an opportunity for surgeons in other cities to observe and question a San Francisco surgeon performing a complex liver operation.

The Rolling Stones were prompted to take their Voodoo Lounge tour to the World Wide Web by the prospect of being beaten to the claim of being the first mainstream rock band to netcast. They already held the honor of being the first rock band to have a commercially sponsored tour, and they clearly wished to stay ahead of the competition.

A little-known band called Severe Tire Damage (whose band included members of the technical staff who developed the M-Bone concept) had already made the debut netcast in June of that year, leading the Stones to promote their webcast as "the first by a major band."

At this stage the technology was shaky. Even Mick Jagger commented during the Rolling Stones' broadcast that he hoped the Internet feed wouldn't be lost. Today's improved technology, coupled with increased bandwidth availability, means netcasting is a much-used medium of entertainment distribution. And the oldest rockers of them all can claim to have played a part in pioneering it.

◄ Mick Jagger and Keith Richards of the Rolling Stones perform at the 1994 MTV Video Music Awards at Radio City Music Hall, New York, on September 8.

KURT COBAIN SUICIDE

From Holly to Hendrix, Jim Morrison to John Lennon, the cult of the dead rock star has become a part of music mythology. Kurt Donald Cobain, who ended his own life with a firearm on (it is believed) the evening of April 5, had many demons to confront. The pressures success brought and the problems of living up to expectations, added to undiagnosed health problems, led him to look for a drug-assisted solution. Beyond that, there was what his wife Courtney Love called "the Cobains' curse": no fewer than three of his uncles had committed suicide. By 10:00 A.M. on April 8, Los Angeles radio stations and MTV had picked up on the news. For the youth of America, it was their own version of the Kennedy assassination and for the rock world, it was another idol frozen in time.

Fans gather in Seattle on 10 April, 1994. ►

STAND-OUT ALBUMS

The Division Bell—**Pink Floyd**

Ten Summoner's Tales—**Sting**

August & Everything After
  —**Counting Crows**

Music for the Jilted Generation
  —**Prodigy**

Monster—**R.E.M.**

Vitalogy—**Pearl Jam**

Dookie—**Green Day**

No Need to Argue—**Cranberries**

Music Box—**Mariah Carey**

Duets—**Frank Sinatra**

Dummy—**Portishead**

Grace—**Jeff Buckley**

The Downward Spiral
  —**Nine Inch Nails**

Superunknown—**Soundgarden**

Mellow Gold—**Beck**

MTV Unplugged in New York
  —**Nirvana**

Live Through This—**Hole**

CrazySexyCool—**TLC**

Protection—**Massive Attack**

The Holy Bible
  —**Manic Street Preachers**

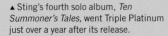

▲ Sting's fourth solo album, *Ten Summoner's Tales*, went Triple Platinum just over a year after its release.

Where were you when?

"One of the reasons for my voice is I have nodules on my vocal cords. My mother says I've had them since I was a kid. That's why I have the high register and the belting register and I can still be husky."

—Mariah Carey

"I always thought Mariah Carey was overrated and loved herself too much, until one day I decided to listen to the Music Box *album. The first song 'Dreamlover' was immaculate, her vocal range superb. She can do no wrong for me now."*

—Cy Jacobs, Vancouver

My Glittering Career

Blessed with a five-octave vocal range, Mariah Carey reached a personal high note with the release of her most successful album, *Music Box*.

Four years after her chart debut, it was clear that soul diva Mariah Carey was set to dominate the decade in the female vocal field. Detractors could claim that she enjoyed the advantage of having the president of Sony Music U.S. as a boyfriend (she met Tommy Mottola in 1988, married him in 1993 and divorced him five years later), but there was no doubt that her God-given talents demanded respect.

Carey's five-octave vocal abilities had brought her from the unpromising beginnings of a one-parent multi-ethnic family (her mother was Irish and absent father Afro-Venezuelan) in New York to the attention of Sony.

She would notch up 14 U.S. No. 1 singles (the first five consecutive) in the 1990s, making her the biggest star of the decade. But it was with *Music Box* that she came of age as an artist. Released in late 1993, it would sprinkle the following year with hit singles and enjoy three spells at the top of the charts. The album remains Carey's most successful to date, and by 2005 it had sold approximately 30 million copies worldwide.

She cannily continued recording her trademark ballads with Canadian writer producer Walter Afanasieff but seasoned the mix with dance tracks helmed by Babyface and C+C Music Factory, the teaming of Robert Clivelles and David Cole. The album became an international success, inspiring comparisons with Whitney Houston and confirmed Carey as a diva. Singles "Dreamlover" and "Hero" both made the U.S. No. 1 spot, while "Without You," a faithful cover of Harry Nilsson's 1972 chart-topper, was a late addition after Carey heard it on a jukebox while dining in Florida. The album's first two singles both received Grammy nominations, while "Without You" became a major worldwide success.

Carey, whose style and image has been emulated by the likes of Christina Aguilera and Jessica Simpson, had a disastrous beginning of the century. She suffered an apparent breakdown and a semi-autobiographic movie, *Glitter,* disappointed audiences. She then bought out an uncomfortable new contract with Virgin Records. She recovered some of her standing in 2005 with her tenth studio album, *The Emancipation of Mimi.*

◄ *Music Box* is Mariah Carey's most successful album to date. It was No. 1 for eight weeks and remained on the *Billboard* Top 200 for more that two years.

EAGLES—*HELL FREEZES OVER*

The seal was set this year on the Eagles reformation when *Hell Freezes Over* gave them their fifth U.S. chart-topping album; its predecessor, *The Long Run,* had been at No. 1 exactly 15 years earlier. The performance had been taped for MTV in April and was augmented by four brand new studio tracks, one of which, "Get Over It," was accorded a single release to coincide. The 50-date Hell Freezes Over Tour grossed more than $70 million, all but one of the shows selling out. The album's four bonus cuts would remain the sum total of the new music fans would hear from the post-reformation Eagles until a new album, *Long Road Out of Eden,* was released in 2007.

Glenn Frey, seen here performing on the Hell Freezes Over Tour, was one of the founding members of The Eagles. ►

SINGLE

1995

STAND-OUT SINGLES

"1979"—**Smashing Pumpkins**

"You Oughta Know"
—**Alanis Morissette**

"Wonderwall"—**Oasis**

"Earth Song"—**Michael Jackson**

"Kiss From a Rose"—**Seal**

"Gangsta's Paradise"
—**Coolio featuring LV**

"Free as a Bird"—**Beatles**

"A Girl Like You"—**Edwyn Collins**

"Lump"—**The Presidents of
the United States of America**

"Country House"—**Blur**

"Common People"—**Pulp**

"Born Slippy (NUXX)"—**Underworld**

"Stupid Girl"—**Garbage**

"Where the Wild Roses Grow"
—**Nick Cave and Kylie Minogue**

"High and Dry"—**Radiohead**

"Wake Up, Boo!"—**The Boo
Radleys**

"The Diamond Sea"—**Sonic Youth**

"Hyper-Ballad"—**Björk**

"Leave Home"
—**The Chemical Brothers**

"I'll Stick Around"—**Foo Fighters**

▲ The single "Gangsta's Paradise," which
appeared in the 1995 movie *Dangerous
Minds,* won Coolio a Grammy Award for
Best Rap Solo Performance.

Blur Versus Oasis

"The Battle of Britpop" commenced in August 1995 when Blur and Oasis went head-to-head in a race to secure the No. 1 spot on the U.K. singles chart.

When Oasis's sixth single, "Some Might Say," topped the U.K. charts in May 1995, the group struck the first blow in a music war, the Battle of Brit-Pop, that would occupy the British charts and headlines for most of that year. Londoners Blur were Manchester-based Oasis's bitter rivals, and for a few short publicity-fueled months the two groups' rivalry was something akin to the Beatles and the Stones in the 1960s.

Though Oasis's musical inspiration came squarely from the Beatles, the Gallagher brothers—outspoken vocalist Liam and guitarist Noel—were clearly more than comfortable inheriting Jagger and Richards' mantle as rock 'n' roll's kings of controversy.

Matters came to a head when, encouraged by music paper *NME*, Blur released a single, "Country House," in the same week as Oasis's "Roll With It." The likely winner was debated on the national news and Blur's success by 276,000 copies to 218,000 much trumpeted. To turn Noel Gallagher's insult on its head, the supposed middle-class wastrels had beaten the working-class heroes. But the press-fueled rivalry certainly helped sell records.

Oasis's 1995 album *(What's the Story) Morning Glory?* stayed for 145 weeks on the U.K. chart, and the band was still releasing British chart-toppers a decade later while four years separated Blur albums *13* (1999) and *Think Tank* (2003).

Oasis enjoyed a brief run of U.S. success, beginning in 1995 with the Top 40 single "Live Forever" and peaking the following year with the No. 8 "Wonderwall." While Blur made little Stateside impact beyond college radio, their frontman Damon Albarn was more successful in the current millennium with Gorillaz, an MTV-friendly band whose musicians let cartoon alter egos promote their records via animated videos.

Blur, from left to right: Dave Rowntree, Damon Albarn, Alex James, and Graham Coxon. ▶

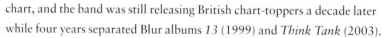

Where were you when?

"We lost the battle, won the war. I always said we would. It's not a quick sprint. We know how good we are, we don't have to prove ourselves to anyone—least of all journalists."

—Noel Gallagher, Oasis

"I'm glad that Blur beat Oasis. If it had been the other way round you would never have heard the end of it. Typical Man City fans. Oasis are just a Beatles tribute band with an argumentative singer and a gobby lead guitarist."

—Nigel Easter, Edinburgh

BYE BYE RAMONES

Legendary New York punks the Ramones this year hung up their leather jackets and ripped jeans for the final time with a farewell tour, three decades after they had burst out of the Bowery with their 20-minute sets of two-minute songs, each counted in with a rapid "One-two-free-four." The band's irreverent attitude saw them acclaimed as America's Godfathers of Punk, but by the time they were inducted into the Rock and Roll Hall of Fame in 2002 Joey Ramone had died of cancer and Dee Dee from a heroin overdose. Guitarist Johnny would succumb to cancer in 2004, leaving drummer Tommy the sole surviving founder.

Although the band members were not related they all used Ramone as a stage name. From left to right: Johnny, Joey, Marky, and Dee Dee. ▶

1995

▲ With *Me Against the World*, 2Pac
became the first artist to have an album
debut at No. 1 while incarcerated.

Jagged Little Pill

Alanis Morissette's angst-ridden lyrics and untamed vocals were the winning combination that made *Jagged Little Pill* the best-selling debut album of all time.

Exploding seemingly from nowhere, Canadian rock singer-songwriter Morissette (born 1974) captured attention with her lyrically explicit, diary-like album *Jagged Little Pill*, which won her four Grammies and spawned seven major U.K./U.S. hits. It remains the best-selling debut album by a female artist in the United States (more than 14 million copies) and the highest-selling debut album worldwide in music history, with sales of 30 million.

The former teen pop star had grabbed the reins of her career and turned in an emotionally charged manifesto (released on Madonna's Maverick record label) that had the pop savvy to succeed where the likes of Liz Phair and Courtney Love had failed. "You Oughta Know," a savage warcry from a spurned lover, and "Ironic" were the picks of the bunch.

The album took two months to record at the California home of collaborator-producer Glen Ballard, who'd worked with Michael Jackson and Paula Abdul. "It was compatibility at first sight," said Morissette, who used musicians from the Red Hot Chili Peppers, among others, to help put musical muscle behind her angst-ridden lyrics. She was classed alongside Garbage, a female-fronted band with equally forthright lyrical concerns, as the commercially acceptable progeny of the "riot grrl" movement that grew up on the United States West Coast via hardcore bands such as Bikini Kill and L7.

Such overnight success would prove hard to follow. Fans had a three-year wait for a second album, *Supposed Former Infatuation Junkie*, in which she turned her formula on its head and deliberately subverted traditional song structures at the expense of radio-friendliness. (Despite this, the single "Thank U" reached No. 2 in late 1998.)

To commemorate the tenth anniversary of *Jagged Little Pill*, Morissette released an acoustic version in June 2005 through Starbucks coffee shops. By 2006 she had morphed into a TV star, appearing on *Nip/Tuck*; the musical inspiration that hit the chart with hurricane force in 1995 had apparently blown out.

Morissette's scathing lyrics and energetic performance style are
often credited for inspiring a new generation of uncompromising
female artists such as Avril Lavigne and Pink. ▶

Where were you when?

"*During the writing of this album I felt I was being very self-indulgent with the lyrics and the music. I was writing what I wanted and it was from a very personal place. The fact that it was received so well on the outside I found sort of ironic.*"

—Alanis Morissette

"Alanis Morissette's Jagged Little Pill *was my Elvis moment. I heard it and I wanted to be a rock star and went out and bought an acoustic guitar and learnt three of her numbers, plus three of Joni's. She and Sarah McLachlan are my inspiration.*"

—Kirsten Morris, Toronto

SEAL—"KISS FROM A ROSE"

While British soul vocalist Seal (born Sealhenry Samuel) made an impression in the United Kingdom—by providing lyrics and vocals for Adamski's "Killer," a chart-topper in 1990—and registered a U.S. Top 10 hit with "Crazy," it wasn't until 1995 that his fame went truly global when "Kiss From a Rose" was featured on the soundtrack to the movie *Batman Forever.* The No. 1 pop single would become a career peak and, despite further success, the singer is as well known now for being half of a celebrity couple with supermodel wife, Heidi Klum, whom he married in 2005, as for his musical exploits.

"Kiss From a Rose," which was written by Seal, won him two Grammy Awards, for Song of the Year and Record of the Year. ▶

1996

BECK! ODELAY

STAND-OUT ALBUMS

From the Muddy Banks of the Wishkah—**Nirvana**

Odelay—**Beck**

Pre-Millennium Tension—**Tricky**

New Adventures in Hi-Fi—**R.E.M.**

Unchained—**Johnny Cash**

Being There—**Wilco**

The Score—**The Fugees**

Load—**Metallica**

It Was Written—**Nas**

Everything Must Go—**Manic Street Preachers**

All Eyez on Me—**2Pac**

Roots—**Sepultura**

Beautiful Freak—**Eels**

Antichrist Superstar—**Marilyn Manson**

In Sides—**Orbital**

1977—**Ash**

Reasonable Doubt—**Jay-Z**

Coming Up—**Suede**

▲ *Odelay* by Beck received a Grammy for Best Alternative Album and was named Album of the Year by *Rolling Stone* and *NME*. The album cover is a photograph of a Hungarian Komondor dog jumping over a hurdle.

Where were you when?

"My mama always used to tell me: 'If you can't find somethin' to live for, you best find somethin' to die for.'"

—Tupac Shakur

"I still find it hard to conceive how so much adulation can be channeled toward a man who served a prison sentence for sexual abuse and was prone to casual violence. It's depressing that a certain part of the music business is keen to treat women in such a negative and disparaging way."

—Helen Day, Glasgow

Gangsta Killing

Released while Tupac was behind bars, *Me Against the World* was hailed as one of the most influential rap albums of all time.

Rap music has had more than its share of bad boys—but Tupac Shakur, the former roadie and backing dancer of the Digital Underground who was gunned down this year, victim of an east coast versus west coast hip-hop feud, was undoubtedly the biggest and baddest. His first album *2Pacalypse Now* was denounced by former U.S. vice president Dan Quayle for its images of violence, though he also had a surprisingly sentimental side, as shown by the Top 10 hit "Dear Mama."

2Pac (as he was styled on his recordings) earned a place in history by becoming the first artist to celebrate a No. 1 album while behind bars, as he did in 1995 when *Me Against the World* knocked Bruce Springsteen off the top. It wasn't his first spell in jail, having served time in 1993 and 1994 for assaults. *Me Against the World* took shape while he was on trial on sexual assault charges. Found guilty, he served 11 months until released on appeal after the intervention of Death Row Records. In return for $1.4 million bail, Tupac released the first rap double album, *All Eyez on Me*, as his commitment to Death Row. The album included hits like the chart-topping "How Do You Want It" and Top 10 entry "California Love," but it also attacked his enemies and spoke of his early death as inevitable.

On September 7, after watching a Mike Tyson boxing match, he was the victim of a drive-by shooting in Las Vegas. Shot four times, he died a week later. Fellow rapper Biggie Smalls (aka Notorious BIG), who was suggested as being behind the attack, was to be gunned down six months later in what many thought was an act of revenge. On one of Tupac's recent hits, "Hit Em Up," he claimed to have slept with Small's wife, Faith Evans.

Despite his death, the Tupac legend continued to grow as, like Elvis and Hendrix, his catalog was swelled by a slew of posthumous releases. He is now the world's best-selling rap artist, with an estimated 75 million albums sold, while reissues and remixes of his music have continued to chart, notably "Ghetto Gospel" featuring Elton John. In 2001 a posthumous collection *Until the End of Time* debuted at No. 1, underlining the fact that Tupac had secured rap's place in the musical mainstream.

◄ Tupac in the film *Poetic Justice*, which also starred Janet Jackson.

THE RISE OF MARILYN MANSON

By combining the Christian name of icon Marilyn Monroe with the surname of serial killer Charles Manson in 1989, Brian Warner revealed his intention to create an all-American monster. And 1996 was the year the gender-bending shock-rocker had not only his homeland but also the rock world dancing to his tune. Second album *Antichrist Superstar* entered the chart at its No. 3 peak in September but told only part of the story—it was Manson's bizarre, asexual visual impact and views on religion, sex, drugs, and politics that affronted Middle America. Cynics could cite Alice Cooper, Jim Morrison, Bowie, Johnny Rotten and others whose attitudes Manson had liberally borrowed. Yet every generation needs a shaman and, as a new millennium loomed, Marilyn Manson had claimed his place as America's Most Wanted.

Manson performing at The Joint, Las Vegas, in December 1996. ►

1996

MADONNA'S MOVIE CAREER REVIVED

The film of Tim Rice and Andrew Lloyd-Webber's hit musical *Evita* finally reached the big screen at the end of 1996. Though Antonio Banderas had been an easy choice to play Argentinian dictator Juan Peron, the choice of who would play Eva Peron was more tortuous. Lloyd Webber made it known he wanted a Spanish-speaking actress for the part, but Madonna went about persuading him otherwise. Her tenacity in securing the role ahead of Michelle Pfeiffer and others paid off in her best film performance since her debut in *Desperately Seeking Susan*. Some critics thought that the English composer's initial reluctance was through trying to erase memories of *Who's That Girl?* and *Shanghai Surprise*— Madonna had picked up three Razzie awards for Worst Actress up until that point. Despite some objections, Madonna turned in a highly rated performance in the film and picked up a Golden Globe for Best Actress in 1997.

Where were you when?

"At 11 years old, the Spice Girls exploded into my life with their kick-butt, no-fuss, can-do, you-go-girl attitude. The first time 'Wannabe' aired on radio was the most exciting moment of my life (on par with the day I discovered body glitter). With Baby Spice as my muse, I was transformed into an overnight feminist—albeit one who wore ankle-twisting heels and pigtails painstakingly straightened with mum's iron. Sky-high platforms soon infiltrated the family shoe rack. Photos serve as an enduring reminder of my inspired Spice Girl get-ups, pairing plaid with fluoro spandex tops and pink platforms. Love truly is blind."

—Beatrix Hon, Montreal

Spice Girls

The Spice Girls proved they had "Girl Power" with their feisty debut "Wannabe"—the biggest-selling single ever by an all-female group.

The worldwide success of the Spice Girls made 1996 the year of Girl Power. Their single "Wannabe" was the hit of the summer, and even though it took six months to top the U.S. chart the musical message of Scary, Sporty, Baby, Ginger, and Posh was all but inescapable.

The three studio albums and ten singles the quintet released in their short lifetime sold in excess of 55 million worldwide, but the message of Girl Power inspired a generation—as was proved in 2007 when they re-formed for a massively oversubscribed world tour.

The British vocal group originated from an ad in *The Stage* magazine placed by father-and-son management team Chris and Bob Herbert. Originally christened Touch, they showed surprising ruthlessness when they hijacked their demo recordings and signed with high-powered Simon Fuller's 19 Management, having delayed inking contracts with the Herberts.

Victoria Adams, Melanie Brown, Emma Bunton, Geri Halliwell, and Melanie Chisholm each had her own identity, making them in one commentator's view "the most widely recognized group of individuals since John, Paul, George and Ringo." Girls wanted to be them, boys wanted to be with them, and although their music was churned out by faceless writing teams, the demand for the end product was insatiable.

"Wannabe" debuted on the Hot 100 Chart at No. 11, then the highest-ever debut by a British (or non-American) act in the United States, beating the previous record held by the Beatles for "I Want To Hold Your Hand." It reached No. 1 four weeks later. Follow-ups "Say You'll be There" and "2 Become 1" also made the Top 5.

While *Spiceworld: The Movie,* their version of *A Hard Day's Night,* was critically panned, it proved to be a box-office hit, generating more than 100 million dollars including DVD sales. The girls split after 2000's poorly received third album, *Forever.*

All the girls have since enjoyed solo careers. Adams would go on to marry David Beckham, then captain of the England soccer team, which ensured her even greater fame.

◄ The Spice Girls strike familiar poses in Tokyo, September 1996.

"MACARENA" BY LOS DEL RIO IS A GLOBAL HIT

Middle-aged Spanish male duo Los del Rio (Antonio Romero Monge and Rafael Ruíz), an attraction in their home city of Madrid but hardly much further, found unlikely world acclaim this year with "Macarena," a multi-platinum dance hit that sold over four million in the United States alone and accorded Los del Rio the title of all-time biggest one-hit wonders. It spent a record 14 weeks at No. 1, making it the longest-running debut chart-topping single in American music history. Furthermore, the song is destined to be played at every future wedding party as drunken uncles struggle with the dance moves demonstrated in the video.

The year's most unlikely chart toppers: Antonio Romero Monge and Rafael Ruíz. ►

STAND-OUT SINGLES

"I'll Be Missing You"—**Puff Daddy and Faith Evans**

"Bitter Sweet Symphony" —**The Verve**

"MMMBop"—**Hanson**

"How Do I Live"—**LeAnn Rimes**

"Tubthumping"—**Chumbawamba**

"The Rain (Supa Dupa Fly)" —**Missy Misdemeanor Elliott**

"Criminal"—**Fiona Apple**

"Song 2"—**Blur**

"Paranoid Android"—**Radiohead**

"Un-Break My Heart" —**Toni Braxton**

"Mo Money Mo Problems" —**Notorious BIG**

"Around the World"—**Daft Punk**

"On and On"—**Erykah Badu**

"Monkey Wrench"—**Foo Fighters**

"Risingson"—**Massive Attack**

"Got 'Til It's Gone"—**Janet Jackson**

"Kowalski"—**Primal Scream**

"Never Ever"—**All Saints**

"Staring at the Sun"—**U2**

"Brimful of Asha"—**Cornershop**

▲ All Saints won two Brit Awards for their single "Never Ever," whose tune was in part based on the hymn "Amazing Grace."

Where were you when?

"When the coffin came into Westminster Abbey, I cried, and when it went out, I cried, but the only time I came close to it during the song was at the beginning of the third verse. I just had to grit my teeth. It was an honor to be able to sing that song. I don't think anything will ever match it for me."

—Elton John

"Given that he was such a close friend of Diana, I'm astonished at Elton's performance at the funeral ceremony. There was no one else but him who would have been right for the occasion and carried it off."

—D. Harrison, Arbroath, Scotland

Goodbye England's Rose

Elton John's poignant rendition of "Candle in the Wind" at Princess Diana's funeral was watched by the world and became the biggest-selling song of all time.

When singer-songwriter Elton John and lyricist Bernie Taupin collaborated in 1973 on an elegy to movie star Marilyn Monroe, it seemed inconceivable the song, "Candle in the Wind," would top charts worldwide nearly a quarter of a century later. The death of the Princess of Wales in a Paris car crash in August 1997 inspired this unexpected occurrence.

Elton, a friend of the princess, wanted to re-record the song in her honor, especially as they had been reconciled after a disagreement at the funeral of fashion designer Gianni Versace earlier in the year.

Taupin faxed through amended lyrics within an hour of being commissioned ("Goodbye Norma Jean" becoming "Goodbye England's Rose"), while Beatles producer George Martin devised a string arrangement as his last job before retiring.

On September 6, at Diana's funeral, Elton John performed the song for mourners in Westminster Abbey and a world TV audience of two billion. Live coverage of the day ended with a reprise of the performance, and when the disc went on sale a few days later, lines formed outside record shops worldwide for a keepsake of the People's Princess.

"Candle in the Wind 97" topped the U.K. chart exactly three weeks after Diana's death while in the United States where it made the top on advance orders alone, it stayed at No. 1 for 14 weeks. Worldwide sales of 33 million made the single the all-time best seller. Two other new songs appeared on the disc. One, "Something About the Way You Look Tonight," was unrelated to the princess though the sentiment was not inappropriate.

The reprised "Candle in the Wind" won Elton John the Grammy Award for Best Male Pop Vocal Performance, an achievement he has yet to repeat.

In 2007, ten years later, John would open the Concert for Diana at London's Wembley stadium, organized by her sons William and Harry.

◀ Elton John's emotional performance of "Candle in the Wind" was televised live throughout the world.

BUENA VISTA SOCIAL CLUB

Legendary guitarist and world music pioneer Ry Cooder joined forces with a group of elderly Cuban musicians to produce an unlikely best-seller. His 1997 release *Buena Vista Social Club,* recorded in just six days, was met with extraordinary critical acclaim and went on to win a Grammy. It was named after a club in Havana where people would meet and play music together. In 1999 Wim Wenders released a documentary film of the same name, in which he profiled the musicians involved and recorded their experiences as they performed in Cuba and abroad, eventually appearing at New York's Carnegie Hall. The film helped immortalize both the music and its now-famous practitioners, most of them veterans of the club's 1940s heyday, who had been living in near poverty, all but forgotten in their own country.

Buena Vista Social Club inspired new interest in Latin American music. ▶

1997

MICHAEL HUTCHENCE KILLS HIMSELF

Michael Hutchence, wildman lead singer of Australian rock group INXS, was found dead in a Sydney hotel room on November 22. Hutchence hanged himself with his belt and the buckle broke away, leaving his naked body kneeling on the floor of the hotel room. The death was declared a suicide, though there was the suggestion the singer died as a result of an act of auto-eroticism. The coroner said Hutchence had consumed vodka, beer, and champagne the night before and had cocaine, the anti-depressant Prozac, and other prescription drugs in his blood. He had reportedly been in a "severe depressed state" due to his relationship with girlfriend Paula Yates and her custody dispute with her former husband Sir Bob Geldof. INXS ceased operations but would reconvene in the new millennium.

Radiohead

Radiohead's third album *OK Computer* was greeted with a combination of critical praise and commercial success that guaranteed the band's worldwide popularity.

Having seen their first LP *Pablo Honey* saved from obscurity by a sleeper single "Creep," and having overcome the difficult second album syndrome with the stylish *The Bends*, Radiohead, five ordinary males from the English university town of Oxford, were ready in 1997 to unleash their magnum opus. And *OK Computer* did not disappoint.

PARANOID ANDROID

In spite of its technological-sounding title and sci-fi themes, the music on *OK Computer* was firmly grounded in rock tradition. All the vocals were first takes because the theme of the album was about being "in the moment." The lyrics reflected vocalist Thom Yorke's belief that in this computerized age, people were being reduced to pixels on a screen, serving a higher power which manipulated them. Its highlight was "Paranoid Android," a dramatic six-minute-plus epic with alternating time signatures and wild dynamic shifts. *Rolling Stone* magazine rated it "one of the best rock records of the year in large part because it is the most inscrutable. *OK Computer* vigorously defies fast analysis, flip judgment and easy interpretation."

CRITICS' CHOICE

A chart-topper at home, *OK Computer* made No. 21 in the States, though the 1998 Grammy for Best Alternative Music Performance paved the way for a chart-topping follow-up in 2000's *Kid A*. *OK Computer* was also voted second greatest British album ever behind the Beatles' *Revolver* in a survey of rock critics at the turn of the millennium. Since then, Radiohead's musicians have shown the music business they intended to participate on their own terms, a fact underlined by such ventures as a tour in a marquee tent and the Internet release of their 2008 album, *In Rainbows*, that could be downloaded for whatever price the consumer wished to pay—if any.

Radiohead, from left to right: guitarist Jonny Greenwood, singer Thom Yorke, drummer Phil Selway, bassist Colin Greenwood, and guitarist Ed O'Brien. ▶

Where were you when?

"Glastonbury in 1997 was all about Radiohead. They were the Saturday night headline act, just six days after OK Computer *came out, and the result was one of those performances that top those 100 Best Gigs of All Time polls. They opened with 'Lucky,' which was a huge gamble—the biggest gig of their lives and they start with a slow song—but it was an unforgettable moment. The gig itself wasn't without its hitches, Thom Yorke had to change guitar during 'Paranoid Android,' he was so hacked off with how 'Talk Show Host' was going, he stopped it half way through, but even so, it was amazing to watch the moment the band came of age."*

—Tom Bromley, Salisbury

PUFF DADDY DOMINATES THE CHARTS

This was the year of Sean Combs, better known as rapper Puff Daddy. After starting the year with "Can't Nobody Hold Me Down," a hit collaboration with Mase, a solo album was eagerly anticipated. But the violent death in March of his friend Notorious BIG (aka Biggie Smalls) caused a change of plan. "Puffy" recorded a track entitled "I'll Be Missing You" that sampled the Police's 1984 chart-topper "Every Breath You Take" in memory of his best pal. This track topped charts worldwide. His solo album, *No Way Out,* went platinum and featured hits such as "It's All About the Benjamins" and "Been Around The World." Meanwhile he was working with such artists as Busta Rhymes, Lil' Kim, Boyz II Men, and Mariah Carey, underlining his position as No. 1 in rap.

No Way Out debuted at No. 1 on the *Billboard* album chart. ▶

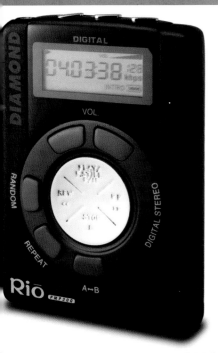

My Heart Will Go On

The theme song from blockbuster film *Titanic* gave Celine Dion her ultimate power ballad, as well as a No. 1 single throughout the world.

Born in 1968, the fourteenth child of her family in the small town of Charlemagne in Canada's Laurentian Mountains, Celine Dion's long and winding road to worldwide superstardom took her via Switzerland (on whose behalf she won the Eurovision Song Contest in 1988) and a cinematic passage on the ill-fated RMS *Titanic*.

The choice of "My Heart Will Go On" as theme for the blockbuster movie *Titanic* starring Kate Winslet and Leonardo DiCaprio that created world records with takings of over $600 million confirmed that Celine had finally arrived at the very top of her chosen profession.

Written by James Horner and Will Jennings, "My Heart Will Go On" was the ultimate power ballad in a series of Dion recordings that included the likes of "Think Twice" and "Falling Into You," and achieved a U.S. radio record of 116 million plays in a single week. It went to No. 1 all over the world, including the United States, United Kingdom, and Australia, and is the second most successful song released by a solo female musician behind Whitney Houston's "I Will Always Love You."

THE POWER OF LOVE

Celine had overcome the handicap of not speaking English to record her first non-French album in 1990, a year after learning the language. Her first chart-topper, *The Power Of Love*, was released three years later. Dion had a very personal reason for gravitating toward love ballads. She met future husband, René Angelil, at age 12 when he became her manager and, despite an eyebrow-raising two-and-a-half-decade age difference, they were able to marry in 1994. She retired from showbiz for two years at the end of the decade to spend time with her husband, then suffering from cancer, and produce a family of their own. The birth of a son in 2001 led to her decision in 2003 to sign up for a three-year, 600-show engagement at a new 4,000-seater theater at Caesar's Palace, Las Vegas. Celine Dion's voyage was very much back on course.

"My Heart Will Go On" won several awards, including the Academy Award for Best Original Song and Grammy Awards for the Record of the Year, Song of the Year, and Best Female Pop Vocal Performance. ▶

FIRST MP3 PORTABLE PLAYER ON SALE

The patent for the first digital music files or MP3s was awarded to German Karlheinz Brandenburg in 1989; he had been working on the concept since 1977. The first player was developed in 1997 by Tomislav Uzelac of Advanced Multimedia Products, and the first commercial examples, including the Diamond Rio PMP300 (pictured), were made available to the public this year. The AMP MP3 Playback engine was ported to Windows by two university students, Justin Frankel and Dmitry Boldreyev, creating Winamp, which was the means by which, for better or worse, file sharing over the Internet began.

▲ The Diamond Rio PMP300 ("the player that puts Internet music into the palm of your hand"), was released in 1998 and went on sale for $250. It was powered by one AA battery.

Where were you when?

"I will perform 'My Heart Will Go On' for the rest of my life and it will always remain a very emotional experience for me."

—Celine Dion

"It's impossible to listen to Celine singing that song and not think of Leonardo DiCaprio and Kate Winslet in wonderful Titanic. *I fully expect to be dancing to it at my daughter's wedding in twenty years time and most likely my granddaughter's too. That song will go on and on."*

—Emily Gable, San Diego

NATALIE IMBRUGLIA—"TORN"

Doe-eyed Australian Natalie Imbruglia followed the Kylie Minogue route to pop fame and fortune by graduating from a TV soap opera. Two years after leaving *Neighbours,* where she starred as Beth Brennan, Imbruglia launched a highly successful singing career with the international hit, "Torn" and debut album *Left of the Middle,* which sold 7 million copies worldwide. "Torn" was No. 1 radio single in the United States from March to July 1998 and won her an MTV Award for Best New Artist in 1998 plus Grammy Awards nominations. But the success of the single and album would prove impossible to emulate with future releases.

"Torn" was a rerecording of a song from Ednaswap's self-titled debut album released in 1995. ▶

1998

TOP-SELLING SINGLES

"Too Close"—**Next**

"The Boy Is Mine"
—**Brandy & Monica**

"You're Still the One"
—**Shania Twain**

"The First Night"—**Monica**

"Truly Madly Deeply"
—**Savage Garden**

"Nobody's Supposed to Be Here"
—**Deborah Cox**

"Together Again"—**Janet Jackson**

"Nice & Slow"—**Usher**

"Lately"—**Divine**

"I'm Your Angel"
—**R. Kelly & Celine Dion**

▲ "Truly Madly Deeply" by Savage Garden
is the only one-sided single ever to spend
a full year in the Top 30 of the U.S.
Billboard Hot 100.

Where were you when?

*"I refuse to play down the way I look in order to be taken seriously as an artist, I
mean if I had an office job, I wouldn't show up for work baring my midriff. But
this is entertainment. I don't want to be 50 years old and thinking I should have
enjoyed it while I had it."*

—Shania Twain

"With shows like Pop Idol *churning out instantly fabricated stars it's good to know
there are people like Shania who have suffered to get where they are. That's a true
country star for you. She's paid her dues in full."*

—Loella Lawson, Arkansas

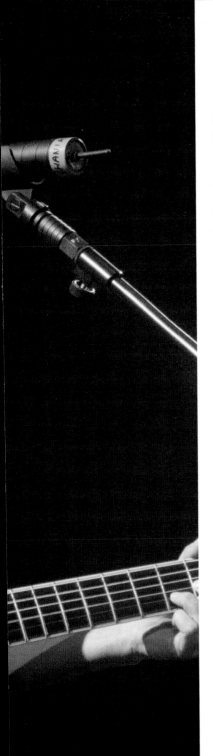

Shania Twain

Country singer Shania Twain found worldwide success with the release of her third LP *Come on Over*—the biggest selling album of all time by a female artist.

The 90s was the decade that female vocalists like LeAnn Rimes and Faith Hill emerged from country music roots to become bona fide pop stars. But no one succeeded as definitively as Shania Twain. Born Eilleen Regina Edwards in Canada in 1965, she began her rise by tapping into the rock knowledge of producer Robert "Mutt" Lange (whom she married in 1994) to create a multi-layered, made-for-radio sound.

Her second album, *The Woman in Me*, was her first collaboration with Lange, singles like "Any Man of Mine" and "Love Gets Me Every Time" crossing over into the U.S. pop charts after topping the country listings. But it was *Come on Over* that broke the mold, with smashes like "That Don't Impress Me Much" and "Man! I Feel Like a Woman" heading straight for the world's Top 10. By the time the album was certified six times platinum in November, no fewer than nine U.S. or U.K. hit singles had resulted, and it would be acclaimed as the biggest-selling album of all time by a female artist.

A MULTI-PLATINUM FUTURE

Twain was keen not to lose her country following and would even mix her recordings in different versions for the roots and mainstream markets. But it was soon clear her multi-platinum future lay in the latter direction. Twain boosted sales by employing her long-limbed good looks in promotional videos: the clip for "Man! I Feel Like a Woman," which effectively parodied Robert Palmer's glamorous "Addicted To Love" clip, was much remarked upon.

Twain's fourth album *Up!* entered the U.S. charts at No. 1 on its 2002 release, selling 874,000 in the first week alone. It charted at the top for five weeks. And though her output slowed as she approached 40, concentrating on family life and motherhood in Switzerland and New Zealand (a *Greatest Hits* was released in 2004) there was little doubt Twain would return to resume her meteoric career at a time of her choosing.

◄ The commercial success of *Come on Over* fully established Shania Twain as a crossover artist. She gained substantial chart successes but still managed to win Grammy Awards for Best Country Song and Best Female Country Performance (both for "You're Still the One").

BACKSTREET BOYS FINALLY EMERGE AS POP IDOLS

The latest example of that profitable pop staple, the boy band, the Backstreet Boys made their triumphant homecoming this year after conquering Europe and the Far East. America had seemed immune to the charms of Nick Carter, Howie Dorough, Brian Littrell, A. J. McLean, and Kevin Richardson, but by combining the best songs from their first two albums for U.S. release they stormed the Top 5. Their landmark year was not without problems: they sued their creator Louis Pearlman in an attempt to win greater control of their finances while Littrell was hospitalised for heart surgery in mid-tour. Despite these problems the group was still performing in the 2000s, though without Richardson who left in 2006.

As a testament to their growing popularity in the United States, *Rolling Stone* readers voted Backstreet Boys the Best New Band of 1998. ▶

1999

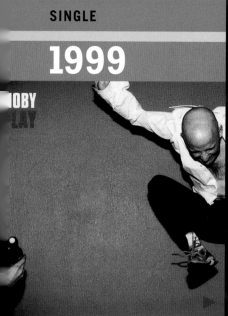

STAND-OUT ALBUMS

Play—**Moby**

Midnite Vultures—**Beck**

Significant Other—**Limp Bizkit**

The Slim Shady LP—**Eminem**

The Fragile—**Nine Inch Nails**

Bad Love—**Randy Newman**

Mary—**Mary J. Blige**

When the Pawn—**Fiona Apple**

The Battle of Los Angeles
    —**Rage Against the Machine**

Supernatural—**Santana**

Summer Teeth—**Wilco**

Black on Both Sides—**Mos Def**

Us and Us Only—**Charlatans**

Californication
    —**Red Hot Chili Peppers**

Surrender—**The Chemical Brothers**

On How Life Is—**Macy Gray**

The Mountain—**Steve Earle**

Performance and Cocktails
    —**Stereophonics**

Beaucoup Fish—**Underworld**

▲ Moby combined gospel influences with his dance music sensibility for his sixth album *Play*. Many of the songs on the album were licensed for use in film, television, and commercial advertising.

Where were you when?

"That's why I'm here right now, because I dreamed of these moments. Kids need that. If they don't dream, they have what? That's what makes you feel spiritual, connected with God. But don't take it too literally. Just watch the performance, be drawn in. And if you don't like it, change the channel."

—Britney Spears, *Newsweek* magazine

"The video of Britney Spears performing in school uniform was far more powerful than any R&B bump and grind video. She drove the new internet teen geeks crazy."

—Stefan Lorrus, Fort Wayne, Indiana

Britney Spears

With its famous video, featuring the 18-year-old singer in a schoolgirl uniform, Britney Spears's debut single hit No. 1 in every chart throughout the world.

Blonde bombshell Britney Spears's impact on pop culture was immediate and immense. The Louisiana-born teen arrived at the top of the charts in 1999 via TV's *Mickey Mouse Club* (whose Justin Timberlake and Christina Aguilera would follow in her wake) and Sweden where her debut hit "…Baby One More Time" was fashioned by writer/producer Max Martin.

The other vital ingredient was a video that saw her cavorting in a school dressed in tie, blouse, gymslip and knee-high socks, pouting seductively to the camera. The concept, Spears's idea, was designed to appeal to girls her age (seventeen), but ended up captivating a rather larger audience.

The insanely catchy song, whose title line ("Hit me baby…") if taken literally was somewhat provocative, hit the top of the U.S. and U.K. charts, and inspired cover versions from artists as diverse as Weezer, Dweezil Zappa, and Barenaked Ladies.

OOPS!…I DID IT AGAIN

"…Baby One More Time" would prove the first of a string of successful singles for Spears, whose follow-ups included "Oops!…I Did It Again," "Toxic" (which won her first Grammy), and "Stronger." Prince and Madonna collaborated with her, the former writing "I'm a Slave 4 U" and the later featuring on a 2003 single "Me Against the Music." When 2003's *In the Zone* reached No. 1 in the charts during its debut week, selling over 609,000 copies, it made Spears the only female in music history to have her first four studio albums to debut at the top. She is currently eighth best-selling female artist in American music history with over 80 million records sold.

But it took less than a decade for Britney's personal life to unravel. Having at one point been Justin Timberlake's girlfriend, she married twice in quick succession, bore two children by her second husband, rapper Kevin Federline, then split from him before suffering a series of breakdowns in the full glare of the media spotlight.

◄ A relaxed Britney Spears in a publicity shot for her debut album *…Baby One More Time.*

GIRLS ON TOP

Sisters were doing it for themselves this year as female artists dominated the charts. The Top 5 U.S. singles of 1999 were all registered by female singers. Veteran Cher weighed in at No. 1 with the dancey "Believe," closely followed by trio TLC with the ballsy "No Scrubs." In third place came Monica with "Angel of Mine;" in fourth place, Whitney Houston/Faith Evans/Kelly Price with "Heartbreak Hotel;" and in fifth place, the former Mickey Mouse Club TV star Britney Spears, with "…Baby One More Time." Add Destiny's Child, Jennifer Lopez, and Mariah Carey and the picture is complete.

At the age of 53, "Believe" gave Cher the best-selling single of her career. It is also the third most successful song released by a solo female artist after Whitney Houston's "I Will Always Love You" and Celine Dion's "My Heart Will Go On." ▶

1999

nnifer lopez | if you had my love

NO. 1 SINGLES

"Have You Ever"—**Brandy**

"...Baby One More Time"
—**Britney Spears**

"Angel of Mine"—**Monica**

"Believe"—**Cher**

"No Scrubs"—**TLC**

"Livin' La Vida Loca"
—**Ricky Martin**

"If You Had My Love"
—**Jennifer Lopez**

"Bills, Bills, Bills"—**Destiny's Child**

"Wild Wild West"
—**Will Smith featuring Dru Hill
and Kool Moe Dee**

"Genie in a Bottle"
—**Christina Aguilera**

"Bailamos"—**Enrique Iglesias**

"Unpretty"—**TLC**

"Heartbreaker"—**Mariah Carey
featuring Jay-Z**

"Smooth"—**Santana
featuring Rob Thomas**

▲ Jennifer Lopez's "If I Had Your Love"
was one of the biggest dance-pop singles
of the summer. It reached No. 1 in the
Billboard Hot 100 on June 12 and stayed
there for five weeks.

Where were you when?

*"The homosexual community wants me to be gay. The heterosexual community
wants me to be straight. Every writer thinks, I'm the journalist who's going to make
him talk. I pray that they get a life and stop living mine!"*

—Ricky Martin

*"His success was no surprise to me as I'd followed his career right from the start,
ever since he was in Menudo. I'd prefer him to lose the beard he has now, though,
because with a few extra pounds he starts to look like Carlos from* Desperate
Housewives. *He should keep his 90s look."*

—L. Martinez, Miami

Livin' La Vida Loca

The Puerto Rican pop star from San Juan took the charts by storm and became an international star overnight with his Latin-influenced No. 1 single.

Puerto Rico-born Ricky Martin led the Latin-pop wave that brought names such as Jennifer Lopez and Enrique Iglesias to the charts this year. His swarthy good looks and all-action stage style gained him overnight acclaim, though the singer (born Enrique Martin Morales in 1971) had in fact graduated gently to solo star status via a five-year stint with Puerto Rican boy band Menudo and a series of Spanish-language albums, as well as a part as bartender Miguel Morez on TV's *General Hospital.*

A short spell on Broadway in *Les Miserables* broadened his experience still further, while he was accorded the 1998 official soccer World Cup song "The Cup Of Life/La Copa De La Vida," that reached No. 1 in the charts of 60 countries. But it was after an appearance with Madonna at the 1999 Grammy Awards ceremony that his career crossed over.

The song that did the trick was "Livin' La Vida Loca," penned by Robi Rosa and Desmond Child. The latter had written hits for Cher, Bon Jovi, and Michael Bolton, and had no problem furnishing the ideal pop-dance anthem for Ricky to deliver with ass-shaking aplomb. The self-titled English-language debut album on which it appeared became one of the top-sellers of 1999, and was certified seven times platinum, selling over 17 million copies worldwide.

Martin's Top 40 hits would continue through 2001 with "She's All I Ever Had," "She Bangs," "Shake Your Bon Bon" and (with Christina Aguilera) "Nobody Wants to Be Lonely" but he would never lose touch with his Hispanic roots and recorded another Spanish-language album in 2003. Martin has also donated royalties to educating disabled children in his home country, though playing President Bush's inaugural ball caused a rift between him and songwriter Robi Rosa.

Ricky's sexuality has long been a subject of debate, but while his fans flocked from both genders he was happy to entertain them all.

◄ While "Livin' La Vida Loca" (or "Living the Crazy Life," as it translates) was voted one of the 20 Most Annoying Songs in a *Rolling Stone* magazine poll, it didn't stop Martin enjoying a worldwide No. 1 smash hit.

CHRISTINA AGUILERA

Born in New York to Ecuadorian-Irish parents, diminutive blonde Christina Aguilera became the latest graduate of Disney's *Mickey Mouse Club* TV show to follow Justin Timberlake and Britney Spears to stardom. Her self-titled debut album sold more than 14 million copies worldwide, topping the *Billboard* chart on the back of the mega-selling single "Genie in a Bottle," and set the stage for a new mini-diva. Aguilera would continue her upward progress, revamping her "little girl" image as raunchy ("Dirrty," 2002) and retro (*Back To Basics,* 2006) while displaying remarkable savvy as she steered her own career.

Following the success of "Genie in a Bottle" Aguilera won a Grammy Award for Best New Artist. ►

2000-2008

EMINEM—"STAN"

The two best-selling British solo artists to emerge this year were David Gray and Dido. Manchester-born Gray had released three flop solo albums of acoustic folk-pop before hitting big, initially in Ireland, with the sequenced percussion-based "Babylon," while former Faithless backing singer Florian Cloud de Bounevialle Armstrong, better known as Dido, scored a worldwide hit with debut album *No Angel*—with a little help from an unlikely friend. Rapper Eminem sampled her "Thank You" on his hit "Stan," and the rest was history. "Stan" was the third single from *The Marshall Mathers LP*, Eminem's fastest selling album. In response to his own increasing fame, Eminem based the fictional character of Stan on an obsessive fan. In the song Stan writes to Eminem but receives no response. When Eminem's reply arrives, it is too late—Stan kills himself and his pregnant wife. Due to its complex song structure and multiple narratives "Stan" has become one of Eminem's most critically acclaimed songs.

Metallica take on Napster

Metallica became the first musicians to sue an Internet file-sharing network in a groundbreaking case against illegal music downloads.

Metal giants Metallica became the first band to legally oppose Napster, the filesharing company who had made their music freely available on the Internet. It was the brainchild of student Shawn Fanning from Boston who, using his knowledge of programming, created a decentralized, easily distributed program that would allow users to share music and other files over the Internet without paying royalties to the copyright holder.

When Metallica discovered that a demo of their song "I Disappear" had been circulating across the Napster network before it had even been released, drummer and bandleader Lars Ulrich went to war, his intention to put Napster out of business. He was at pains to stress the issue was not money—"I'm taken care of for 10 f***ing lifetimes"—but the effect on new artists trying to break through if people obtain songs from the Internet and don't buy their record.

Ulrich used the MTV video awards to demonstrate his point, forcibly "borrowing" the belongings and clothing of a Napster user played by show host Marlon Wayans. His band came in for much flak for taking a stand, particularly as they appeared to be targeting fans—three universities were cited in the lawsuit for allowing students access to Napster through their campus networks. But an unrepentant Ulrich insisted "If the requirement of being a Metallica fan is that I give you music for free, I don't want you as a fan. Go away, leave us alone."

Having peaked with 26.4 million users worldwide in February 2001, Napster was liquidated in 2002. In the meanwhile the company agreed with Metallica not to distribute their music illegally. (The name Napster was later revived for a legitimate download service.)

Filesharing became an issue on the wider musical agenda thanks to Metallica, if at some cost to their own popularity.

Lars Ulrich doesn't regret his stand against illegal downloads, despite being named one of the "biggest wusses in rock" for his "anti-Napster crusade" by *Blender* magazine. ▶

Where were you when?

"Why is it only people who've computers have the right to free music? Should all music not be free then? Can we just throw the doors open at Tower Records and do away with the cash registers? It doesn't make sense."

—Lars Ulrich

"Metallica got voted by Blender *mag as one of the 'Biggest Wusses in Rock' for their lawsuit against Napster. Ultimately that's what people will remember them for, not their music. They've cemented their place in music history as rock's complainers."*

—Dean Savage, Leicester, England

METALLICA

SANTANA MAKES A COMEBACK

Mexican-born guitarist and bandleader Carlos Santana had been a much-loved part of the musical landscape since 1969, when he was a star of the Woodstock festival, and 1970 when his debut album hit the Top 10. But even his most avid fans could hardly have predicted a comeback that would see him hit the top of the singles and album charts as one century ended and another began. "Smooth," a single with vocals from Matchbox 20's Rob Thomas, was the last singles chart-topper of 1999 and the first of 2000, to be followed by "Maria Maria" (featuring the Product G&B and Wyclef Jean), while parent album *Supernatural* was equally successful. Santana continued this "guest vocal" tactic over two more albums, *Shaman* and *All That I Am*.

The album *Supernatural* earned Santana nine Grammy Awards. ▶

2000

TOP-SELLING SINGLES

"Independent Women Part I"
—**Destiny's Child**

"Maria Maria"—**Santana**
featuring Wyclef Jean and
The Product G&B

"Breathe"—**Faith Hill**

"Music"—**Madonna**

"With Arms Wide Open"—**Creed**

"I Knew I Loved You"
—**Savage Garden**

"Bent"—**Matchbox Twenty**

"Amazed"—**Lonestar**

"Try Again"—**Aaliyah**

"Smooth"—**Santana/Rob Thomas**

"I Wanna Know"—**Joe**

"Everything You Want"
—**Vertical Horizon**

"Oops!...I Did It Again"
—**Britney Spears**

"Shape of My Heart"
—**Backstreet Boys**

"Say My Name"—**Destiny's Child**

Destiny's Child's single "Independent
Women Part 1" (from the *Charlie's Angels*
movie soundtrack) stayed at No. 1 on the
Billboard Hot 100 for 11 consecutive
weeks. It was Destiny's Child's first U.K.
No. 1 single. ▼

Where were you when?

"I saw the band play on the day 'Yellow' entered the charts. Round the back of the
venue just before the gig the band were playing football using garages for goals—
and my friend and I joined in! The band members were still unknown even if the
song wasn't. I remember saying to Chris Martin 'It must be so weird to be in the
charts' and he just couldn't stop smiling. That night they played 'Yellow' twice."

—Malcolm Croft, London

She Was So Yellow

The release of Coldplay's acclaimed debut album *Parachutes* set them on the road to becoming one of the biggest-selling bands of the new millennium.

In four short years, Coldplay transformed themselves from a quartet of London students to the first superband of the new millennium, thanks largely to the songs of non-specific yearning penned by vocalist Chris Martin. The contributions of Jonny Buckland (guitar), Will Champion (drums) and Guy Berryman (bass) behind Martin's plaintive vocal on the singles "Yellow" and "Trouble" helped Coldplay's debut album *Parachutes* become a transatlantic hit. And they were well rewarded. After initial disagreements, the band decided each member should receive one quarter of their income—which, with 40 million albums sold by the middle of the decade, was considerable.

Coldplay were likened to Pink Floyd in being virtually anonymous—four regular guys it would be easy to walk past on the street. But Martin's profile soared due to a relationship with movie star Gwyneth Paltrow, whom he married in 2003, and this publicity did no harm to the sales of follow-ups *A Rush of Blood to the Head* (2002) and *X&Y* (2005). In commercial terms they eclipsed labelmates and rivals Radiohead, even though their music was somewhat less complex.

Record company Parlophone's 40,000 sales estimate was quickly exceeded; by Christmas 2000, 1.6 million copies of *Parachutes* had been sold in their home country alone. It would prove a slower haul in the States, where appearances on the top-rated talk shows helped the album achieve double-platinum status. But it was only in 2002, when it picked up a Grammy Award for Best Alternative Music Album, that the album—and Coldplay—could be said to have arrived. Its U.S. peak chart position of 51 was misleading, as its successors would hit Nos. 5 and 1 respectively.

Coldplay and Chris Martin would use their fame to make political points about the environment and the unfair distribution of wealth: Martin also aligned himself with John Kerry's unsuccessful U.S. presidential campaign. This increased comparisons to U2, but Coldplay were laughing all the way to the bank.

◄ Coldplay, from left to right: Guy Berryman, Will Champion, Jonny Buckland, and Chris Martin.

O BROTHER, WHERE ART THOU?

The soundtrack to *O Brother, Where Art Thou?*, a comedy movie made by the Coen Brothers and set in Mississippi during the Great Depression, became the year's unexpected hit soundtrack album. The film chronicles the exploits of a trio of escaped convicts headed by George Clooney, and along with a blues musician they meet along the way they perform country, folk, and bluegrass tunes as the Soggy Bottom Boys. This unlikely concept caught the public imagination and, after the film's release, the fictional band became so popular that some of the actual talents (who were dubbed into the movie), which included Ralph Stanley, John Hartford, Alison Krauss, Emmylou Harris, Gillian Welch, and Dan Tyminski, performed music from *O Brother, Where Art Thou?* in a Down from the Mountain concert tour.

MUSIC FROM THE MOTION PICTURE
O BROTHER, WHERE ART THOU?

2001

GEORGE HARRISON

Beatles lead guitarist George Harrison became the second of the Fab Four to check out when he died of cancer on November 29 in Los Angeles. He was 58. Wife Olivia and son Dhani were at his bedside. The most private of the Beatles, his body was to be cremated in a cardboard coffin and his ashes scattered on the River Tamuna in India, in accordance with his religious beliefs. His family's statement read: "He left this world as he lived in it, conscious of God, fearless of death, and at peace…" Harrison's life and musical legacy would be celebrated by all-star concerts in Liverpool (in February 2002, Sir Paul McCartney guesting) and at London's Albert Hall on the first anniversary of his death. The latter, featuring McCartney and Ringo Starr, was later released on CD and DVD.

America: A Tribute to Heroes

Following the terrorist outrage of 9/11, actor George Clooney put together a star-studded concert to raise money for the families of those who died.

The demolition of the twin towers by terrorist action on 9/11 gave the United States a bloody nose. But proof that the nation remained proud and unbowed came in the shape of a televised benefit concert screened ten days after the atrocity by all four major television networks.

Actor George Clooney was the man who pulled the show together, and the acts appearing, 21 in number over two hours, ranged from Neil Young singing John Lennon's "Imagine" through soul superstar Stevie Wonder to nu metal chart-toppers Limp Bizkit, who lyrically modified Pink Floyd's "Wish You Were Here" for the occasion. Faith Hill represented country, while Sting and Celine Dion became honorary Americans for one night. All the songs chosen had relevance, and were performed on a stage illuminated only by candles. Bruce Springsteen's "My City of Ruins," written about his home neighborhood of Asbury Park, took on a new relevance, while Tom Petty spat defiance in every syllable of "I Won't Back Down," originally aimed at his record company as bankruptcy proceedings loomed but now a challenge to Al Quaida.

In between the musical offerings, actors and non-musical celebrities ranging from Muhammad Ali and Will Smith to Clint Eastwood and Tom Cruise spoke messages of defiance and hope, while many more were seen manning the telephones to record pledges from the public.

A total of $30 million was raised by the concert, a total that would be added to by CD and DVD sales. *Rolling Stone* magazine would later nominate America: A Tribute to Heroes, as one of 50 moments that changed rock 'n' roll. It was bracketed with The Concert for New York City that was staged at Madison Square Garden on October 20, hosted by Paul McCartney. This included performances by the Who, Mick Jagger, Elton John, David Bowie and other mainly non-American musicians.

◄ Bruce Springsteen, whose song "My City of Ruins" was given an unexpected poignancy by the events of 9/11.

Where were you when?

"It was a moving experience to watch and there were both highs and lows. Eddie Vedder's voice and barely controlled emotion were haunting. Sheryl Crow and Faith Hill displayed facets I had never seen before. Celine Dion's version of 'God Bless America' was brilliantly understated. Mariah Carey was patronizing. Limp Bizkit needed a lot more backing and I wish they'd found someone other than Willie Nelson for 'America the Beautiful.'"

—Seb Kortowski, Boston

2001

STAND-OUT SINGLES

"Butterfly"—**Crazy Town**

"Get Ur Freak On"—**Missy Elliott**

"Clint Eastwood"—**Gorillaz**

"Stuck in a Moment You Can't Get Out Of"—**U2**

"Fat Lip"—**Sum 41**

"Survivor"—**Destiny's Child**

"Let Me Blow Ya Mind"
    —**Eve featuring Gwen Stefani**

"Fallin'"—**Alicia Keys**

"Rollin'"—**Limp Bizkit**

"Whatever Whenever"—**Shakira**

"Fell in Love with a Girl"
    —**The White Stripes**

"Get the Party Started"—**Pink**

"Juxtaposed with You"
    —**Super Furry Animals**

"Plug-in Baby"—**Muse**

"We Need a Resolution"—**Aaliyah**

"Island in the Sun"—**Weezer**

"Lapdance"—**N.E.R.D.**

"Hash Pipe"—**Weezer**

"The Middle"—**Jimmy Eat World**

"New York, New York"
    —**Ryan Adams**

▲ Shakira Isabel Mebarak Ripoll, more commonly known as plain Shakira.

Elt 'n' Eminem

Rap artist Eminem had come under fire for his homophobic lyrics. So to help appease his critics, he agreed to perform with Elton John at the Grammies.

The pairing of Elton John and rapper Eminem, 25 years his junior, at the Grammy Awards was clearly contrived by the organizers with headlines in mind. And they got them!

The white 28-year-old who had emerged from a Chicago trailer park to become the biggest name in rap had attracted much critical flak for his outspoken dislike of homosexuality. Indeed his last CD, *The Marshall Mathers LP*, which was nominated in three rap categories, contained "hatred and hostility [that] has a real effect on real people's lives [and] creates even more bias and intolerance toward an entire community," said the Gay and Lesbian Alliance Against Defamation. But openly gay singer-songwriter John was unfazed by the threatened picketing and agreed to appear.

Eminem ended the joint performance of his recent hit "Stan" by embracing Elton, then raising his two middle fingers to the crowd. "If I didn't make a statement with Elton John tonight, I don't know what else to do," Eminem told MTV News following the ceremony, bizarrely claiming he hadn't been aware his performing partner was gay. "I didn't know anything about his personal life. I didn't really care."

HAVE GUN WILL TRAVEL

Eminem's third full-length album, *The Eminem Show*, released in summer 2002, topped the charts and sold well over a million copies in its first week of release. The tone of his lyrics was noticeably more personal and less offensive, while a 2005 greatest hits compilation signalled a two-year period of silence as he re-evaluated his career. His personal life continued to ferment, however, as he remarried and then divorced his wife, Kim, the mother of his daughter Hailie and the target of many offensive lyrics over the years.

How the world's most controversial rap star intends to continue his career remains to be seen. He starred in the semi-autobiographical film *8 Mile* in 2002 and played a bounty hunter in *Have Gun Will Travel* in 2008. Early in 2008 he called in to New York radio station Hot 97 and said he was busy working on his fifth studio album.

Eminem 'n' Elton share an awkward embrace at the Grammies. ▶

Where were you when?

"I'm a big fan of Eminem's music, and I said I would be delighted to (sing). I know I'm going to get a lot of flak from various people who are going to picket the show."

—Elton John

"We view this moment not only as musically significant, but also as an opportunity to help tear down some of the unfortunate walls of division that Eminem's lyrics have built."

—National Academy of Recording Arts and Sciences CEO Michael Greene

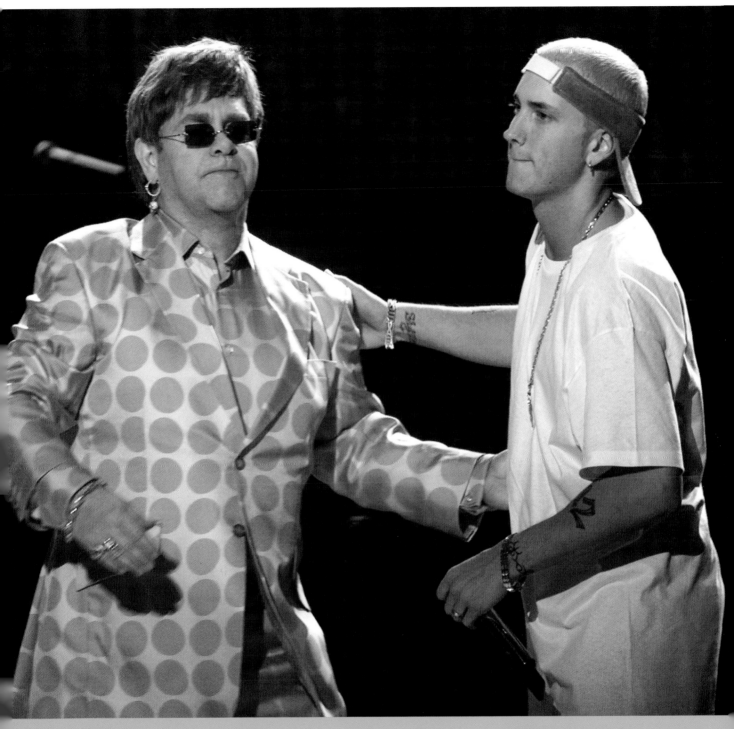

NICKELBACK

Canadian rockers Nickelback made an unexpected play for global stardom this year with an outstanding single, "How You Remind Me" from third album *Silver Side Up*. Their original lineup consisted of brothers Chad and Mike Kroeger on guitars/vocals and bass, their drummer cousin Brandon Kroeger, and lead guitarist Ryan Peake. Their name came from Mike's spell in a coffeehouse where prices dictated that he give customers a nickel back with every cup. While it seemed "How You Remind Me" would remain their one worldwide hit of note, they surprised everyone in 2008 by coming up with another singalong rock anthem in "Rockstar."

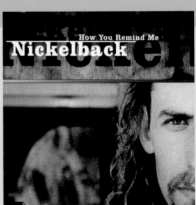

2002

STAND-OUT SINGLES

"A Moment Like This"
—**Kelly Clarkson**

"Hot in Herre"—**Nelly**

"Complicated"—**Avril Lavigne**

"Girlfriend"—**N Sync & Nelly**

"Sk8er Boi"—**Avril Lavigne**

"Can't Fight the Moonlight"
—**LeAnn Rimes**

"Dirrty"—**Christina Aguilera**

"A Thousand Miles"
—**Vanessa Carlton**

"Heaven"—**DJ Sammy**

"Gimme the Light"—**Sean Paul**

"The World's Greatest"—**R Kelly**

"Jenny From the Block"
—**Jennifer Lopez Featuring
Jadakiss & Styles**

"Courtesy of the Red, White and
Blue (The Angry American)"
—**Toby Keith**

"Goodbye to You"
—**Michelle Branch**

"Can't Get You Out of My Head"
—**Kylie Minogue**

"The Game of Love"—**Santana
Featuring Michelle Branch**

"Young'n (Holla Back)"—**Fabolous**

▲ Avril Lavigne's "Sk8er Boi" describes
the relationship between a skater boy and
his preppy ballet-dancing girlfriend.

Where were you when?

"*Directly after the show people might have
responded better to it, but who really knows. It
did what it did and while it seems like a failure
to most but it was a success for me and has
given me so many opportunities.*"

—Justin Guarini (Losing finalist)

"*It's weird how everyone
saw it as a big competition,
because all of us didn't see
it as that. I mean, nobody's
taught to fail, you don't
want second, but we all
just wanted exposure....*"

—Kelly Clarkson

American Idol's First Star

It was a talent contest that gripped America. Kelly Clarkson won the first *American Idol* competition, establishing a winning formula for herself and the program.

The concept of the *American Idol* TV show was very much in the American tradition. Just as anyone, however humble his or her origin, could theoretically attain the presidency, so could each hopeful performer auditioning for the televised talent contest have an equal chance of ending with a recording contract in hand.

The format showed the ever-decreasing numbers of contestants enjoying master classes with established stars, as they submitted themselves weekly to a public vote in a modernized version of the Christians and lions of ancient Rome. A panel of opinionated music business judges, including Randy Jackson, Paula Abdul, and Simon Cowell, gave their opinions, but the ultimate decision came via the phone lines.

The show's first-ever winner was Kelly Clarkson, a 20-year-old cocktail waitress from Texas with no formal training, whose consistently strong performances of songs like "Respect," "Natural Woman," "Stuff Like That," and "Without You" earned enough audience votes to claim one of the contest's two finalist positions. On beating Justin Guarini, she immediately soared to No. 1 in Canada and the United States with "A Moment Like This," a song specially written for the winner of the program to perform.

Over a million copies had been preordered before the winner was known, but Clarkson capitalized on her break with a No. 1 album *Thankful*, released in April 2003. By 2007 she had made two more albums and had won two Grammies. She then, however, decided to split with her management to take greater control of her own career.

Clarkson wasn't the only beneficiary of *American Idol:* Acid-tongued judge Simon Cowell with his sharp opinions was a big hit with viewers, and he would end the year voted one of America's Top 5 entertainers.

◄ September 4, 2002, Kelly Clarkson is congratulated by her fellow contestants, Tamyra Gray, Justin Guarini, Christina Christian, Nikki McKibbin, and Ejay Day at the Kodak Theatre in Hollywood.

COME AWAY WITH ME—NORAH JONES

Singer-songwriter-pianist Norah Jones appeared from seemingly out of nowhere to sweep all before her with her debut album *Come Away With Me*. It transpired, however, that stardom was in the genes as she was the daughter of revered Indian musician Ravi Shankar. The album took off, selling over 20 million and winning eight Grammies, while its follow-up, *Feels Like Home,* sold a respectable 10 million. Her understated jazzy style owed something to boyfriend/bassist Lee Alexander, who produced a third album, *Not Too Late*, in 2007. Back in 2002 the five-foot-tall bundle of talent was still wide-eyed and amazed at the success of her album, a (Carole King) *Tapestry* for the times.

Norah Jones's debut album *Come Away With Me.* ▶

2002

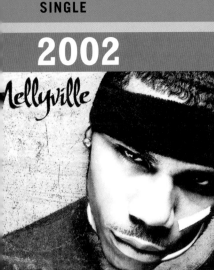

STAND-OUT ALBUMS

The Rising—**Bruce Springsteen**

The Eminem Show—**Eminem**

Yankee Hotel Foxtrot—**Wilco**

A Rush of Blood to the Head—**Coldplay**

By the Way—**Red Hot Chili Peppers**

Maladroit—**Weezer**

Rock Steady—**No Doubt**

Songs for the Deaf—**Queens of the Stone Age**

Yoshimi Battles the Pink Robots—**The Flaming Lips**

Up the Bracket—**The Libertines**

American IV: The Man Comes Around—**Johnny Cash**

O—**Damien Rice**

When I Was Cruel—**Elvis Costello**

Have You Fed the Fish?—**Badly Drawn Boy**

Home—**Dixie Chicks**

One by One—**Foo Fighters**

Nellyville—**Nelly**

▲ *Nellyville* was the second album from rapper Nelly, featuring the singles "Hot in Herre," "Dilemma," "Roc the Mic," and "Work It." It reached No. 1 on the *Billboard* album charts, selling over 700,000 in its first week.

Where were you when?

"'Can't Get You Out of My Head' is the perfect marriage of fantastic song and great video. Even though Kylie trades on her sexuality, she has an enormous number of loyal female fans. At Kylie gigs it's almost as interesting to see who's there and what they're wearing."

—Cheryl Palmer, Bristol, England

"I've been accustomed to being famous and having a certain level of attention for 14 years, but in the last few months, it's changed. It's like on the arcade game, I've gone up to the next level."

—Kylie Minogue

Can't Get You Out of My Head

Kylie Minogue's first shot at pop stardom was a massive success, but by the late1990s her career had stalled badly. Then came a killer single and video.

Having first come to public attention as a teenage actress on the Australian TV soap opera *Neighbours* and having enjoyed pop fame in the late 1980s, Kylie Minogue emerged from a 14-year exile from the American charts to hit the Top 20 with the infuriatingly catchy "Can't Get You out of My Head."

Born in 1968, Minogue had enjoyed her first singing success in the late 1980s with a cover of Little Eva's "The Loco-Motion" which gave her a No. 3 hit in late 1988. London-based dance songwriter/producers Stock Aitken and Waterman took her in hand and wrote her a series of worldwide pop successes, but only "I Should Be So Lucky" and "It's No Secret" added to her U.S. hits. Attempts to take control of her own career, encouraged by her some-time lover Michael Hutchence of INXS, had narrowed her appeal, resulting in a spell on an indie label in the 1990s where she was accorded credibility by the pop press but could not sell records.

As the new millennium arrived, Minogue placed her career in the hands of outside writers and producers once more, this time on her own terms, and the compromise paid off. "Spinning Around," written by 1980s star Paula Abdul, regained popularity in 2000, promoted by a video in which her gold hotpants made her as famous for her backside as her vocal ability.

Returning to the U.S. charts early in 2002, Kylie souped up her image still further to create SexKylie—a far cry from the doe-eyed doll figure of old. The popular press caught on, and she began to dominate the radio airwaves and dance floors. A huge gay following was a bonus.

Three years later, a diagnosis of breast cancer took Kylie out of the public eye. She returned a year later, rejuvenated, and, as her 40th birthday approached, determined to continue her upward trajectory.

◄ Few stars are known by just their first names, but Kylie belongs in that select group, along with Shakira and Beyoncé.

THE OSBOURNES

A reality television series, *The Osbournes,* in which the family house in Los Angeles was opened to the cameras of MTV, made an unlikely star of former Black Sabbath hell-raiser Ozzy—not to mention his wife Sharon, daughter Kelly, son Jack, and a wide-ranging menagerie. *The Osbournes* drew record ratings on both sides of the Atlantic and ran to two further 20-week series. The second gained unexpected poignancy when Sharon, also Ozzy's manager and the undisputed ruler of the household, was diagnosed with colon cancer—father and son were already separately battling alcohol and substance abuse. Happily, both men successfully fought their demons and Sharon recovered enough to regain the reins of a household in which, though all four characters clashed constantly, a genuine affection ruled.

Sharon, Ozzy, Jack, and Kelly. ►

2003

ARISE, SIR MICK

Mick Jagger was awarded a knighthood in this year's Queen's Birthday Honors, joining Paul McCartney, Elton John, George Martin, and Cliff Richard as British knights of the realm. Rolling Stones guitar buddy Keith Richards announced that he would not be according his friend any special deference. "I don't want to step out onstage with someone wearing a coronet and sporting the old ermine," Richards told British music magazine *Uncut*. "I told Mick it's a paltry honor. It's not what the Stones is about, is it?" *Sgt. Pepper* cover designer Peter Blake was also knighted.

▲ Sir Michael Phillip Jagger as he was presented to the Queen on December 12, 2003. Jagger was given the award for services to music. Unlike Sir Elton John and Sir Paul McCartney, Jagger has no high-profile charitable work to his credit.

Dangerously in Love

Destiny's Child was the most successful girl trio since The Supremes, and like Diana Ross, it was the catapult for solo success for singer Beyoncé Knowles.

With the help of her manager-father Mathew, soul diva Beyoncé Knowles graduated from the ranks of soul vocal group Destiny's Child to attain stardom in an almost identical fashion to that achieved by Diana Ross some three decades earlier.

Born in Texas in 1981, Beyoncé had formed Destiny's Child as Girl's Tyme with childhood friends LaTavia Roberson and Kelly Rowland, along with LeToya Luckett. When they showed promise at local talent competitions, her father quit his job with Xerox to guide their careers. Roberson and Luckett left after their initial 1998 hit "No No No" and were replaced by Michelle Williams. Many more hits followed, notably pop chart-toppers "Bills Bills Bills," "Say My Name," and "Independent Woman."

Knowles was well placed to prosper when it came to launching a solo career. She collaborated with boyfriend/rapper Jay-Z on the infectious 2003 hit "Crazy in Love," while the album *Dangerously in Love* spawned a second No. 1 single in "Baby Boy," which sold over 12 million copies worldwide. When single and album simultaneously topped their respective listings in both the United States and the United Kingdom in July 2003, Beyoncé became the first act to achieve this feat since Men at Work 20 years earlier.

Her racy image ran counter to a professed religious upbringing, but more positive was Knowles's defense of her voluptuous figure, refusing to conform to size zero strictures—a philosophy contained in the chart-topping "Bootylicious."

Destiny's Child was put on hold in 2005, exiting with a bang after being crowned the World's Best-Selling Female Group of all time at the World Music Awards. A second solo album *B'Day* was released the following year, earning Knowles her seventh solo Grammy award (she has won 10 in total).

As with Diana Ross, Hollywood beckoned, and the 2006 musical film *Dreamgirls* won Beyoncé two Golden Globe Award nominations. The sky was clearly the limit for the bootylicious Beyoncé.

Beyoncé strikes a pose in front of the MGM Grand Hotel in Las Vegas, December 10, 2003. ▶

Where were you when?

"I wrote 'Bootylicious' because, at the time, I'd gained some weight and the pressure that people put you under to be thin is unbelievable. I was just 18 and you should be thinking about building up your character and having fun."

—Beyoncé

"It was slightly ironic seeing Beyoncé play 'the Diana Ross role' in Dreamgirls. *Destiny's Child surpassed The Supremes in chart sales, but imagine how many more records The Supremes would have sold if they could have marketed their records with slick and sexy videos like Destiny's Child?"*

—Iris Jackson, Chicago

BILLBOARD INTRODUCES A DOWNLOADS CHART

For the first time this year, *Billboard* recognized the growing importance of Internet music purchases by giving downloads their own chart. Digital downloads of individual songs were not only reported on the Tracks chart, topped for the first time by Beyoncé Knowles's "Crazy in Love," but downloads of full albums and packaged singles were added to existing album and single chart data. CD sales in 2002 had fallen 8.7 percent, and while downloaded tracks accounted for a fraction of total sales—the new chart's Top 10 totaled just over 7,000 units compared to just over 207,000 for the Top 10 singles sold in stores and 1.14 million for the Top 10 albums—but a boom was anticipated.

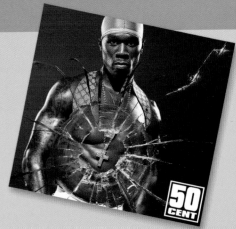

Artists like 50 Cent benefited from the move to include official downloads. ▶

2003

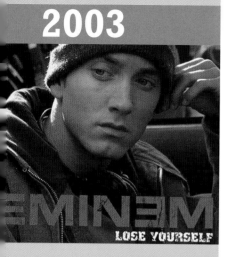

EMINƎM
LOSE YOURSELF

NO. 1 SINGLES

"Lose Yourself"—**Eminem**

"Bump, Bump, Bump"
—**B2K featuring P. Diddy**

"All I Have"—**Jennifer Lopez
featuring L.L. Cool J**

"In Da Club"—**50 Cent**

"Get Busy"—**Sean Paul**

"21 Questions"—**50 Cent
featuring Nate Dogg**

"This Is the Night"—**Clay Aiken**

"Crazy in Love"—**Beyoncé
featuring Jay-Z**

"Shake Ya Tailfeather"
—**Nelly/P. Diddy/Murphy Lee**

"Baby Boy"
—**Beyoncé featuring Sean Paul**

"Stand Up"—**Ludacris
featuring Shawnna**

"Hey Ya!"—**OutKast**

▲ "Lose Yourself" has been Eminem's most successful single, spending 12 weeks on top of the *Billboard* Hot 100, a record stay for a rap artist and also scoring No. 1s in Canada, Australia, and the United Kingdom. It was written during a break in filming for the movie *8 Mile*.

Justin Timberlake

He broke hearts as a member of teen pop band N Sync, but the former Disney Mousketeer had eyes on a more adult career and audience.

Justin Timberlake made the tricky transition from boy band member to solo white-soul sensation by delivering an album, *Justified*, that ticked as many boxes as (and sounded suspiciously similar to) Michael Jackson's breakthrough albums two decades earlier.

Timberlake, born in Memphis in 1981, was groomed for stardom by his mother and became a TV star when he joined the Mickey Mouse Club at age 12. His first experience of making headlines came with his status as boyfriend to pop queen (and fellow Mickey Mouse Club star) Britney Spears. But the end of the relationship in March 2002 appeared to fuel his muse.

His spell with boy band N Sync started with their formation in 1995. The band took a break in 2001, after three best-selling albums and innumerable tours. While the band were apart, Timberlake contacted Timbaland and the Neptunes production team with a view to launching his solo project. *Justified* didn't sell as well as N Sync albums at the beginning, but sales started to build throughout 2003 with the release of singles "Like I Love You," "Rock Your Body," and "Senorita."

The album would go on to sell more than 3 million copies in the United States and over 7 million worldwide, while even outtake "I'm Lovin' It" earned millions when used for a hamburger commercial. His career would burgeon, the only false step a performance at Superbowl XL in 2004 with Janet Jackson, during which he exposed her breast in the famous "wardrobe malfunction" incident. He made a public apology weeks later as he picked up two Grammies: Best Pop Vocal Album for *Justified* and Best Male Pop Vocal Performance for "Cry Me a River."

While his follow-up album *FutureSex/LoveSounds* was long delayed, its late-2006 appearance, four years after *Justified*, consolidated Timberlake's position as a major teen heartthrob with adult crossover appeal. The single "Sexyback" gave him his first U.S. chart-topper, while he was voted sexiest man by *Teen People* and *Cosmopolitan* magazines —consolation for a broken romance with film star Cameron Diaz.

Justin Timberlake's debut album was a slow-burning hit. ▶

Where were you when?

"I spent an afternoon photographing Justin Timberlake and the rest of N Sync around London before they made it big. Lance, JC , and Joey were really sweet; they were obsessed with feeding the pigeons in Trafalgar Square. Chris was trying hard to be cool, but Justin acted like he was above it all. I can remember thinking, 'What a poser.' I'm not surprised that he's the one who's been successful."

—Frank Hopkinson, Esher, Surrey

"In Tennessee you either play football or you don't do anything at all, so I was a bit of a loner. Being interested in music, I was not cool. I was a bit of an outcast."

—Justin Timberlake

ELEPHANT—WHITE STRIPES

The relationship between guitarist/vocalist Jack White and drummer Meg White of rock duo White Stripes was just one of the enigmatic garage band's attractions. Were they a married couple or, as they claimed, siblings? One thing was for sure: their fourth album *Elephant* was one of the year's musical landmarks. It was recorded in two weeks during 2002 in London on deliberately antiquated equipment, including an eight-track tape machine and pre-1960s recording gear, for the requisite period charm, while six different covers for U.S./U.K. issues offered much for the collector. Musically, *Rolling Stone* called it "a work of pulverizing perfection." The album reached No. 6 on the *Billboard* chart, winning Grammies for Best Alternative Album and Best Rock Song for "Seven Nation Army."

One of six alternative covers for *Elephant*. ▶

2004

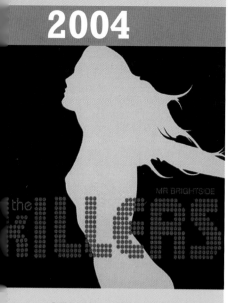

STAND-OUT SINGLES

"Vertigo"—**U2**

"American Idiot"—**Green Day**

"Take Your Mama"
—**Scissor Sisters**

"Take Me Out"—**Franz Ferdinand**

"Bedshaped"—**Keane**

"Yeah!"—**Usher featuring Ludacris**

"Drop It Like It's Hot"
—**Snoop Dogg featuring Pharrell**

"Dry Your Eyes"—**The Streets**

"Mr Brightside"—**The Killers**

"Jesus Walks"—**Kanye West**

"Since U Been Gone"
—**Kelly Clarkson**

"First of the Gang to Die"
—**Morrissey**

"I Predict a Riot"—**Kaiser Chiefs**

"Hollaback Girl"—**Gwen Stefani**

"Can't Stand Me Now"
—**The Libertines**

"Hounds of Love"
—**The Futureheads**

"Portland, Oregon"
—**Loretta Lynn featuring Jack White**

▲ "Mr Brightside" by The Killers reached No. 10 in the United Kingdom and the United States.

Avril Lavigne

Straight-talking teen Avril Lavigne had produced a stunning debut album at the age of 17. Following it up, though, would not be easy....

Following up a smash debut album has been the undoing of many a new star, but Avril Lavigne made it look remarkably easy as she eclipsed 2002's six times platinum *Let Go* (16 million copies sold worldwide) with an album celebrating her imminent arrival in her 20s.

Lavigne, was born in Belleville, Ontario, in 1984, and arrived at pop via country and gospel. Once signed to the Arista label, she pitched herself as a rebellious, straight-talking teen. Discarding her necktie-over-T-shirt garb for something darker, both fashionwise and musically, she made *Under My Skin* and proved she was no one-album wonder.

The material was cowritten with a variety of writers and producers, and not the production team Matrix, who had fueled her early success. *Rolling Stone* claimed it was her nature as a "blank canvas" that made her best songs so irresistible. "Whether it's a fit of faux punk or a maudlin ballad, she sings it all absolutely straight: You can hear whatever you want to hear."

GROWING UP IN PUBLIC

Under My Skin lacked the smashes like "Complicated," "I'm With You," and "Sk8er Boi" —only "My Happy Ending" emulating their U.S. Top 10 status—but reflected her roller-coaster ride of the past two years. This time fans skipped the singles and went straight for the album; *Under My Skin* debuted at No. 1 in the United States, United Kingdom, Germany, Japan, Australia, and Canada and sold more than 380,000 copies in the United States alone in its first week.

But life was soon to change even further for the one-time teen queen who began dating fellow Canadian Deryck Whibley, singer with pop-punk band Sum 41. They would marry in 2006 in California, confirming Lavigne had indeed grown up in public. Whibley helped produce Lavigne's third album *Best Damn Thing*, giving it a punk-pop edge, and it gave her a first *Billboard* No. 1 single in "Girlfriend." She had already achieved that feat in Canada with her debut single "Complicated," way back in 2002.

Avril Lavigne plays on the Carson Daly New Year's Eve television special, broadcast from Rockefeller Plaza, December 31, 2004. ▶

Where were you when?

"*Whenever I write a song, I know exactly how I want it to be. And if that means I have to take it to a second producer if the first one doesn't get it right, then I will.*"

—Avril Lavigne

"*All rock stars grow old and boring, but I hope Avril's star continues to shine brightly and she can carry her vision forward. Whatever she does next, to have created two breathtaking albums by the age of 20 has the pedigree of Lennon and McCartney.*"

—Colby Cornwall, Ontario

AMERICAN IDIOT—GREEN DAY

Many assumed Californian trio Green Day—Billie Joe Armstrong (vocals/guitar), Tre Cool (drums), and Mike Dirnt (bass)—had shot their commercial and creative bolt after their unexpected 1993 success with major label debut *Dookie*. Instead, a Greatest Hits compilation in 2001 was followed three years later by the controversial *American Idiot*. A punk rock concept album built around elaborate melodies, odd tempo changes, and a collection of songs that referenced the Beatles and Pink Floyd, it was the first Green Day album to reach No. 1 in both the United States and the United Kingdom and won them one Grammy Award from five nominations. The title song has been described by the band as "a public statement in reaction to the confusing and warped scene that is American pop culture since 9/11."

STAND-OUT ALBUMS

Confessions—**Usher**

Speakerboxxx/The Love Below —**OutKast**

Closer—**Josh Groban**

The Diary of Alicia Keys —**Alicia Keys**

Feels Like Home—**Norah Jones**

Franz Ferdinand—**Franz Ferdinand**

Funeral—**Arcade Fire**

A Grand Don't Come Free —**The Streets**

College Dropout—**Kanye West**

How to Dismantle the Atomic Bomb —**U2**

Scissor Sisters—**Scissor Sisters**

Hot Fuss—**Killers**

▲ Outkast, *Speakerboxxx/The Love Below.*

Alicia Keys, *The Diary of Alica Keyes.* ▼

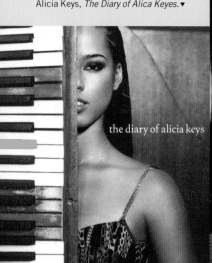

Material Girl

Madonna had always set high standards with her stage shows, but the aptly named Re-Invention Tour earned a lot of money as well as critical acclaim.

Madonna celebrated two decades at the top in 2004 in spectacular fashion with her aptly titled The Re-Invention Tour, the most successful series of concerts of the year with a gross of $124.5 million. It took in a total of 20 cities in seven countries, selling out all but one of its 56 shows and attracting more than 900,000 fans.

The tour kicked off at Los Angeles's Forum on May 24 and moved across the United States to Miami by early August. From there it traveled to the United Kingdom, Ireland, France, the Netherlands, and Portugal, ending at Lisbon's Pavilhão Atlântico in mid September.

The presentation was divided into five acts with many costume changes: An opening French Revolution sequence was followed by an army act in which Madonna played guitar to uniformed dancers. A jazzy cabaret sequence was followed by an acoustic mini-set, including the only cover, John Lennon's "Imagine." The finale consisted of crowd-pleasing greatest hits such as "Into the Groove," "Holiday," and "Music."

Madonna decided to make every Friday a rest day on the tour, obeying the teaching of the Kabbalah religious sect that she and her husband, Guy Ritchie, joined in the late 1990s. Kabbalah is based on fifth- and twelfth-century Jewish mystical texts from Spain and the Middle East.

There was, however, an unwelcome coda weeks later when Sir Elton John accused her of charging high ticket prices and miming at her concerts. He told an audience at Q music magazine's annual awards that anyone who charged such an amount "should be shot" and that Madonna, being nominated for Best Live Act was a "****ing joke." Madonna quickly issued a statement saying she did not lip-synch.

The pop stars feuded for three years before they met up at a GQ magazine awards ceremony in 2007, where Elton announced: "I have written a groveling apology and offered to join the Kabbalah!"

◄ Madonna's Re-Invention Tour hits New York, June 2004.

BRIAN WILSON—*SMILE*

The Beach Boys' *Smile* album, conceived in 1966 by Brian Wilson as a follow-up to the legendary *Pet Sounds,* had become the Holy Grail to fans primarily because it never entered the public arena. Indeed, it was never completed due to Wilson's drug-induced breakdown. The concept was watered down the following year into the relatively lightweight *Smiley Smile*, bulked up with the addition of singles "Good Vibrations" and "Heroes and Villains," Wilson's first collaboration with songwriter Van Dyke Parks. Thirty-eight years later he decided to complete the original with Parks' help and re-record it with his own solo band. (None of the original recordings were used due to problems between Wilson and some of his former band mates.) The live premiere of the fabled *Smile* took place in 2004 at London's Royal Festival Hall.

2005

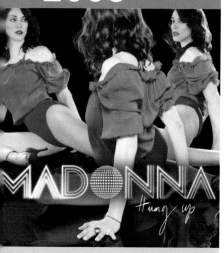

MADONNA AND ELVIS

When Madonna's single "Hung Up" jumped seven places to No. 7 on the *Billboard* Hot 100 singles chart, the pop icon had matched Elvis Presley's tally for Top 10 hits—36, the most for any artist in the rock era. She racked up her tally in just over 21 years, starting with 1984's "Borderline." By contrast, Presley scored his 36 Top 10 hits half a decade quicker, in just over 16 years, from 1956's "Heartbreak Hotel" until 1972 with "Burning Love." Her reported reaction was: "Me and Elvis? Are you kidding? I'm gonna tell my dad. Maybe that will impress him!" "Hung Up" was the first single to be taken off Madonna's tenth studio album, *Confessions on a Dance Floor.* One of the major attractions of the song was the heavy sample of Abba's hit single "Gimme Gimme Gimme (a Man After Midnight)." Madonna was so worried that writers Benny and Bjorn might turn her down she sent a friend to Stockholm with a begging letter.

▲ Madonna's single, "Hung Up."

Gwen Stefani

The former No Doubt lead singer captured a whole new audience and set digital download records with her single "Hollaback Girl."

Born in 1969, svelte Californian Gwen Stefani broke through to solo stardom this year, having used her first band No Doubt as a springboard to fame. No Doubt's biggest hit was the ballad "Don't Speak," a No. 1 in 1997, a far cry from their usual ska-punk fare. Using Madonna as her role model, Stefani developed a multifaceted yet always danceable style. Her collaboration with dance and hip-hop producers, such as Dr. Dre and the Neptunes, hit pay dirt in the form of her debut album *Love Angel Music Baby*.

Stefani had tested the waters with a 2001 hit duet with Eve, "Let Me Blow Ya Mind." But despite the three-year gap, *Love Angel Music Baby* outsold any No Doubt album, spawning five singles including the U.S. No. 1 single "Hollaback Girl." This song, which hit the top in May, was the first U.S. digital download to sell more than 1 million copies legally, while record sales for 2005 made Stafani one of the top-selling female artists in the world.

THE SWEET ESCAPE

Like Madonna, Stefani juggled motherhood with music, having given birth to a son, Kingston, in 2006 with husband Gavin Rossdale of Bush. A clothing line and a fragrance were among the lifestyle accessories offered to the many Stefani wannabes. A movie career also beckoned: Stefani played Jean Harlow in Martin Scorsese's *The Aviator* in 2004.

Stefani's second solo album, *The Sweet Escape*, was released in December 2006. It included writing and production collaborations with No Doubt's Tony Kanal, Linda Perry, and the Neptunes, and with Akon and Tim Rice-Oxley from British rock band Keane. The album was more dance-oriented than its predecessor, but singles success, except for the *Sound Of Music*–sampling "Wind It Up," was relatively slim. Stefani was a mentor on the sixth season of TV's *American Idol* in an effort to promote the album, which was reviewed as a less energetic reprise of her all-conquering debut. There was no doubt, however, that she remained a role model to many.

Gwen Stefani performing at the Hard Rock Casino, Las Vegas, on May 30, 2005. ▶

Where were you when?

"*Someone one time called me a cheerleader, negatively, and I've never been a cheerleader. So I was, like, 'You want me to be a cheerleader? Well, I will be one then. And I'll rule the whole world, just you watch me.'*"

—Gwen Stefani

"*It's such a confusing video! Gwen is supposedly the captain of the cheerleader squad; she is the girl who 'hollas' the chants, not one of the girls who 'hollas' them back. Given that the squad is preparing to mash somebody up on Gwen's behalf, she obviously rules her squad with an NFL-like discipline.*"

—Todd Doyle, Akron

LIVE 8

The 20th anniversary of Live Aid was celebrated on July 2 with a series of concerts aimed at raising awareness, rather than money. These shows were aimed to pressure leaders of the so-called G8 countries to drop the debt of the world's poorest nations, increase and improve aid, and negotiate fair trade rules in the interest of poorer countries. Organized by Bob Geldof and Bono, they took place in the G8 countries—Japan, France, Italy, the United Kingdom, Canada, Russia, Germany and the United States—and South Africa and were timed to precede a policy-making summit to be held in Scotland. Several of the Live Aid acts reprised their earlier performances, notably U2, Paul McCartney, Elton John, and Madonna, while newer acts included Coldplay and Robbie Williams.

Mariah Carey with Bob Geldof and Paul McCartney. ▶

2006

GEORGE MARTIN REMIXES BEATLES

The Beatles had been notoriously reluctant to allow anyone access to their music. But this year saw surviving members McCartney and Starr, together with Yoko Ono and Olivia Harrison, give producer George Martin the go-ahead to remix their music and create an album that would be the soundtrack to a stage show by Cirque du Soleil in Las Vegas. *Love* was created by Martin, 80, with the help of son Giles, 37, and was a soundscape of familiar Beatles' songs. Some tracks like *Help!* were used in almost their original form, whereas others were ambitiously remixed. In all, elements from 130 individual recordings were used, and the result, which peaked at No. 4 on the chart with sales of over 1.5 million, was considered worthy of Grammies for Best Compilation Soundtrack Album and Best Surround Sound Album.

▲ Paul McCartney responded positively to *Love:* "This album puts The Beatles back together again, because suddenly there's John and George with me and Ringo."

High School Musical

Disney's high-energy musical was never going to win awards for most original plot, but as a piece of teen entertainment, it was in a class of its own.

Every generation needs a feel-good musical to let its youngsters dance their cares away, and the Disney-sponsored *High School Musical* laid down the benchmark for the new millennium when it hit the world's television screens in January. There were inevitable echoes of *Grease, West Side Story*, and even *Romeo and Juliet* in the paper-thin plot that found Troy Bolton (played by Zac Efron) and Gabriella Montez (Vanessa Hudgens) auditioning for lead parts in their high school's musical production.

Troy's peers disapprove of his acting ambitions, fearing they could affect the championship aspirations of the East High Wildcats basketball team that he captains. Gabriella's nemesis is Sharpay Evans (Ashley Tisdale), who covets the lead roles for herself and brother Ryan, and who also has designs on Troy.

The unlikely pairing of a basketball-playing jock and a shy, studious science student, who not only find love on screen but in real life—undoubtedly to the delight of the Disney corporation whose most successful made-for-TV movie it rapidly became—suspends belief.

An impressive 7.7 million U.S. viewers tuned into *High School Musical*'s premiere broadcast, inspiring both a 2007 made-for-TV sequel and a bigger-budget, big-screen spinoff. Meanwhile, the soundtrack took just three weeks to reach the Top 10; more than 3 million copies had been sold by August 2006, when it was certified quadruple platinum by the RIAA, and it enjoyed two separate weeks at No. 1. Last but far from least, a DVD release was accompanied by a Special Edition of the album featuring a bonus karaoke disc.

The year of *High School Musical* ended with a concert tour kicking off in San Diego, California, in November. This featured all of the original cast members except for Zac Efron, who had movie commitments, while Vanessa Hudgens, Ashley Tisdale, and Corbin Bleu (who played Chad Danforth), all of whom now had budding solo careers, were permitted to showcase their own material.

From left to right, Vanessa Hudgens, Zac Efron, Monique Coleman, and Ashley Tisdale. ▶

Where were you when?

"It was high concept/low concept: a movie musical and just a group of kids in school. You put that together and you pray, and it came out beyond our expectations."

—Rich Ross, president of Disney Channel Worldwide

"In sixth grade my basketball team made it to the league championships. In double overtime, with three seconds left, I rebounded the ball and passed it—to the wrong team! They scored at the buzzer and we lost the game. To this day, I still have nightmares."

—Zac Efron

ARCTIC MONKEYS

Sheffield guitar band Arctic Monkeys, who played their first U.S. tour in March of this year, achieved the fastest-selling debut album in British chart history with *Whatever People Say I Am, That's What I'm Not,* which sold 360,000 copies in its first week. It has since gone quadruple platinum in the United Kingdom. The album included both tracks from the band's original EP, *Five Minutes with Arctic Monkeys,* as well as their first two singles and U.K. chart-toppers, "I Bet You Look Good on the Dancefloor" and "When the Sun Goes Down." The Monkeys' success was due to clever use of the Internet to market their music to potential fans and inspired a rash of MySpace bands and artists, the likes of Lily Allen, Kate Nash, and Sandie Thom, among those cited as following in their footsteps.

Debuting on the Internet, the Arctic Monkeys. ▶

2006

STAND-OUT ALBUMS

Back to Bedlam—**James Blunt**

The Breakthrough—**Mary J. Blige**

Modern Times—**Bob Dylan**

Stadium Arcadium
   —**Red Hot Chili Peppers**

*One Day It Will Please Us
   to Remember Even This*
   —**New York Dolls**

Taking the Long Way Home
   —**Dixie Chicks**

The Black Parade
   —**My Chemical Romance**

FutureSex/LoveSounds
   —**Justin Timberlake**

Broken Boy Soldiers
   —**The Raconteurs**

The Greatest—**Cat Power**

*Orphans: Brawlers, Bawlers,
   and Bastards*—**Tom Waits**

Rather Ripped—**Sonic Youth**

The Life Pursuit
   —**Belle and Sebastian**

The Drift—**Scott Walker**

Alright, Still—**Lily Allen**

Begin to Hope—**Regina Spektor**

The River in Reverse—**Elvis
   Costello & Allen Toussaint**

Surprise—**Paul Simon**

▲ Mary J. Blige, *The Breakthrough*.

Where were you when?

"I think there are reasons why I get criticized in Britain. It comes from my being from a privileged background, being from a privileged school. I was there at that school because my father was in the army. The army doesn't pay well but they do fund one's schooling. So I am not a working-class hero like John Lennon. I think some of the media found that difficult to deal with. I had amazing and ridiculous levels of early success—unexpected to everyone, including myself. I think people found that threatening in a way."

—James Blunt

James Blunt

Elvis Presley had been made to join the army, but James Blunt emerged from a voluntary spell in the armed forces to create one of pop's classic singles.

Former British army officer James Blunt returned to civilian life with a guitar, not a gun, in his hand and stormed the world's charts with some very old-fashioned musical virtues. With no discernible image, he let his music speak for him and was rewarded when his track, "You're Beautiful," became the first British single to top the U.S. *Billboard* Hot 100 chart since Elton John in 1997. (Interestingly, Elton had identified a kindred spirit and invited Blunt to tour with him in 2004.)

Born James Hillier Blount (with an "o") in 1974 to a military family, Blunt served four years in the Lifeguards, a unit of the Household Cavalry. To repay the British Army, who had sponsored his university education, Blunt went to Kosovo with the NATO peacekeeping force in 1999. He rose to the rank of captain, but left in 2002 and recorded his first album, *Back To Bedlam*, the following year after signing to Pink star maker Linda Perry's record label.

It was his third single, "You're Beautiful," that catapulted Blunt to unexpected fame; a transatlantic No. 1, it took the album to the top in his home country. While Blunt insisted that "it's probably one of the least meaningful songs on the album and by no means people's favorite," it nevertheless received three Grammy nominations.

ALL THE LOST SOULS

Blunt's first album was the best-selling LP in the United Kingdom in 2005 and in the world in 2006, so the follow-up was awaited with interest (a ragbag CD/DVD compilation, *The Bedlam Sessions*, having been issued to fill the gap). Half the material on his second studio effort, *All The Lost Souls*, released in September 2007, had been road-tested during his most recent tours. The retro-styled first single, "1973," topped the charts in Britain but flopped in the United States. So far there has been no reprise of "You're Beautiful."

◄ James Blunt's scruffy appearance is in stark contrast to his "posh" accent, which was initially seen as a barrier to signing a record deal. Blunt attended Harrow, Winston Churchill's school.

GNARLS BARKLEY—"CRAZY"

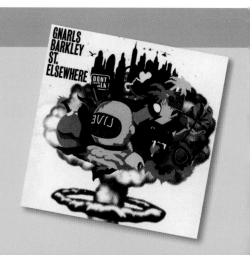

In April, "Crazy" by Gnarls Barkley—the duo consisting of U.S. producer Danger Mouse (real name Brian Burton) and hip-hop artist Cee-Lo—became the first song to top the charts in the United Kingdom on music download sales alone. Until this point, downloads could only count toward a chart position if the song could also be bought in stores. But new rules meant that downloads counted as long as physical copies went on sale the following week. The song had been downloaded more than 31,000 times from legitimate Internet sites—peanuts compared with the single's heyday 30 years earlier, but enough to create history. "Crazy" topped the charts in Canada and the United Kingdom where it stayed for nine weeks.

2007

BRITNEY BREAKDOWN

The trials of Britney Spears since her pop breakthrough in 1999 had come close to outweighing the triumphs, but 2007 was the year the world came crashing down on the twice-divorced mother of two. As her 16-year-old sister Jamie Lynn got pregnant, she dealt with the death of a beloved aunt Sandra by shaving her head, checked in and out of rehab, was charged with driving offenses and attacked a paparazzo's car with an umbrella. Her parenting skills were questioned, and she fought to regain custody of her own children after custody was granted to their father, Kevin Federline, in October. She was ordered to undergo random drug and alcohol testing as her behavior became more unpredictable. Amid all the media attention, a new single "Gimme More" emerged and her performance of it (pictured above) was described as, "one of the worst (ever) to grace the MTV Awards." It was clear that the Britney Spears story was no longer about the music but the price an individual must pay for fame.

Police Reunited

After an acrimonious split in the 1980s and Sting's continuing solo success, it looked unlikely that the Police would ever work together again.

Having disbanded bitterly at the height of their fame in 1984 after five best-selling albums, five Grammys, and six U.S. Top 10 singles, new wave supergroup the Police — Andy Summers, Sting, and Stewart Copeland—laid aside their differences to tour the world this year. A one-time reunion when they were inducted into the Rock and Roll Hall of Fame in 2003 had seemed likely to remain just that, but a mini-set at the 2007 Grammies had been followed by the announcement fans had long despaired of ever hearing.

Relations among the members had been notoriously difficult, and Sting's solo fame made it unlikely he would turn back the clock and revisit the band with which he first made his name. But just as with Eric Clapton and Cream two years earlier, he relented and let his less-celebrated colleagues enjoy one last hurrah. Critics claimed it was a boost to their pension fund: Andy Summers, at a well-preserved 64, was close to retirement age.

CAN'T STAND LOSING YOU

After a musically rocky start in Vancouver on May 28 in front of 22,000 fans, the Police Reunion Tour progressed through New Zealand, Australia, Singapore, Japan, the United States, France, Germany, Norway, Denmark, United Kingdom, Poland, and Brazil, where they played for 75,000 people. The reunion trek was the top-grossing and top ticket-selling tour of 2007 in North America with earnings of $131.9 million. The trio's ticket sales were almost double those of its nearest rival, country star Kenny Chesney, who finished the year with $71.1 million.

The Police reunion extended into 2008 to fulfill gigs canceled due to illness, and headlining festival appearances were added to the schedule. The year marked the 30th anniversary of the release of "Can't Stand Losing You," the single that scored their first-ever chart success. Sting insisted that no new music would be added to their catalog—but fans kept their fingers crossed.

Sting ably demonstrates that The Police are far from a spent force. Andy Summers plays lead guitar with Stewart Copeland, as ever, on drums. ▶

Where were you when?

"The Police re-forming was one of those gigs you never quite expected to see. I saw them play at London's Twickenham Stadium, and it felt like being transported back to 1983 when they were the biggest band in the world. They played a set of greatest hits, together with a few clunkers—why they dusted down 'Walking in Your Footsteps' with its rhyme about 'Mr Brontosaurus' having a 'message for us,' God only knows. Highlights for me included the whole crowd singing along to 'Regatta de Blanc,' and the cheery policeman on horseback holding us back at the train station afterwards, telling everyone, 'Don't stand so close to me.' "

—Tom Bromley, Salisbury

LED ZEPPELIN ATTRACT 20 MILLION

When Led Zeppelin announced their dissolution in 1980, following the demise of drummer John Bonham, they honored their late colleague's memory by refusing calls to re-form—excluding one-off reunions for Live Aid (in 1985) and Atlantic Records' 40th Anniversary (1988) with guest drummers Phil Collins and John's son Jason. The death of Atlantic's long-time Svengali Ahmet Ertegun gave them a third excuse, and their sole gig at London's O2 Arena in December, with Jason Bonham in the drum seat, set records as the most over-subscribed show in the history of rock 'n' roll; 20 million fans registered their interest on-line for the 20,000 tickets. In the end, the show was delayed by days when guitarist Jimmy Page broke his hand, but eventually went ahead to ecstatic reviews.

Robert Plant holds center stage at the O2 Arena. ▶

2008

BACK TO BLACK

The life and career of 24-year-old Londoner Amy Winehouse, possessor of the finest white soul voice since the late Dusty Springfield, was played out in the world's press. Her tattoos, unkempt beehive hairdo, and aquiline features were an all too familiar sight on front pages as performances were cancelled and her self-destructive behavior chronicled. Winehouse's album *Back to Black* caught the public's imagination, but the singer's off-stage problems ended up diverting attention from her work. And the album's lead single, "Rehab," with its defiant "I won't go" message, proved all too ironic, as Winehouse was in and out of rehab on a semi-regular basis. Marriage to boyfriend Blake Fielder-Civil in 2007 only seemed to pour fuel on the flames. Five Grammy awards for *Back to Black* only preceded rumors of yet more drug problems. Meanwhile, as she was quoted as being worth $20 million on the latest rich list, Amy Winehouse was finding out that money can't buy you happiness.

Where were you when?

"When Simon (Cowell) stops all this stupid hype about her, that's when we'll see if she can deliver. Like every artist Simon has, she'll fade into obscurity eventually. Leona is a poor man's Mariah Carey."

—R&B star Jamelia (talking after *The X Factor* final)

"It was amazing, I got to meet my all-time musical heroine Whitney Houston. I don't think I managed to say much though, I was overwhelmed! I was told afterwards that when I performed she had said, 'My God, she's a baby me!' Wow, what a huge compliment!"

—Leona Lewis

Leona Lewis

Previous winners of *The X Factor* had scored instant success, then sunk without a trace. Simon Cowell's protegé Leona Lewis certainly bucked the trend.

The success of Leona Lewis, who topped the U.K. charts after winning TV talent show *The X Factor*, was not unpredicted. Yet the fact that her debut album came straight in at the top of *Billboard*'s listing a year and a half later suggested a bigger talent than that production line had hitherto disgorged.

Lewis, born in 1985, had studied at stage school but had no luck in breaking into the music business until her boyfriend persuaded her to audition for *The X Factor*—Simon Cowell's British version of *American Idol*. Her exotic looks and vaulting vocal range combined to win her the series in December 2006, which brought with it a $2 million recording contract with judge Simon Cowell's Syco record label.

Ironically her first single, released immediately after the final, was a cover of *American Idol* winner Kelly Clarkson's "A Moment Like This." It created a world record in December 2006 when it was officially downloaded 50,000 times in 30 minutes. A million copies were pre-ordered by stores guaranteeing her the coveted Christmas No. 1 spot in the United Kingdom.

BLEEDING LOVE

There then followed a year's silence as debut album *Spirit* was created with the help of Whitney Houston Svengali Clive Davis, who paid $9.7 million to secure her signature for the United States. The wait proved worthwhile when it became a transatlantic chart-topper in April 2008, the first British artist to post a debut album at No. 1. A single from the album, "Bleeding Love" followed suit on the *Billboard* Hot 100, the first time a U.K. female had achieved that feat since Kim Wilde in 1987. She joins a list of six that includes Petula Clark, Lulu, Sheena Easton, Wilde, and Bonnie Tyler. Her predecessor on top of the album charts was Sade.

◄ Leona Lewis's single "Bleeding Love" achieved the rare feat of reaching No. 1 on the *Billboard* chart, dropping to No. 2, and then returning to the No. 1 position.

SCORSESE'S *SHINE A LIGHT*

The Rolling Stones' live act, honed over four and a half decades, made it to the big screen in 2008, when Martin Scorsese took two performances from the Stones' A Bigger Bang tour and merged them with archive footage from the band's career to make *Shine a Light*, his personal tribute to a band that had helped shape his career. "I really wanted to do a concert film because their performance is what makes them still so special," he said, noting that he had often used Rolling Stones' music in his scripted movies. Highlights included guest duets by Christina Aguilera, Buddy Guy, and the White Stripes' Jack White. The movie's world premiere was at the 58th Berlin International Film Festival in February.

Shine a Light's accompanying album. ►

Index

Acknowledgments

I would like to thank the record companies on both sides of the Atlantic who have contributed pictures and the odd quote to include in this book. Without their generous assistance it would not have been possible. I would also like to thank Hayley Johnson for her assistance in composing charts from four different markets and the ever-patient David Salmo who diligently sub-edited the book. Thanks also to Richard Havers for his total recall of all things Rolling Stones and Bill Wyman for agreeing to write the foreword.

Picture Credits

Anova Books is committed to respecting the intellectual property and rights of others. We have therefore taken all reasonable efforts to ensure that the reproduction of all content on these pages is done with the full consent of copyright owners. If you are aware of any unintentional omissions please contact the company directly so that any necessary corrections may be made for future editions.

R=Right L=Left M=Middle C=Center T=Top B=Bottom

Back cover: L Anova Image Library, T Anova Image Library, RM Anova Image Library, RB Anova Image Library.
Front cover: TL Brendan McDermid/epa/Corbis, TM Pierre Fournier/Sygma/Corbis, TR Jacques M. Chenet/Corbis, ML Bettmann/Corbis, MR Pierre Ducharme/Reuters/Corbis, BL Courtesy of Record Company, BM Dave Kaup/Reuters/Corbis, BR Hulton-Deutsch Collection/Corbis, CT Anova Image Library, CB Getty Images.
Spine: Courtesy of Record Company.

Anova Image Library
9, 12L, 12R, 13B, 14B, 16R, 17T, 20-21, 22L, 23R, 23B, 24L, 25B, 26LT, 26LB, 27B, 28L, 30L, 32, 34L, 35B, 38, 39T, 43B, 44L, 46L, 47B, 48L, 49B, 52L, 53B, 54T, 54B, 56L, 59B, 63B, 67RT, 71B, 74L, 75 (inset), 75B, 77B, 79RT, 79RB, 80L, 81B, 83T, 89B, 91B, 93B, 96L, 100LB, 102LT, 104L, 108L, 110, 112, 113B, 143RT, 148T, 157RB, 160, 171B, 183RT, 185B, 193B.

Corbis
Alan Pappe/Corbis: 127.
Bettmann/Corbis: 16L, 28R, 31B, 40R, 55B, 85B, 121T, 125T, 224R.
Bryce Duffy/Corbis: 222R.

Bueno Santiago/Corbis Sygma: 187T.
Bureau L.A. Collection/Corbis: 202R.
Deborah Feingold/Corbis: 150R, 155T, 164R.
Denis O'Regan/Corbis: 126.
E.J. Camp/Corbis: 191T.
Henry Diltz/Corbis: 6R, 82-83C, 91T, 96R, 99B, 162R, 180R.
Jeff Albertson/Corbis: 111T.
Joe Giron/Corbis: 7LB, 172R, 184R.
John Van Hasselt/Corbis Sygma: 195B.
Lynn Goldsmith/Corbis: 130R, 138R, 142R.
Mario Anzuoni/Reuters/Corbis: 3RB, 218-219.
Matthew Fearn/Pool/Reuters/Corbis: 232.
Michael Levin/Corbis: 6LT, 31T.
Natacha Connan/Kipa/Corbis: 212R.
Neal Preston/Corbis: 2RB, 3RT, 4-5, 86-87, 103, 106R, 108R, 109R, 116R, 132R, 159T, 167T, 174R, 176-177, 182L, 197B, 201T, 213B.
Nick Vaccaro/Corbis: 196R.
Reuters/Corbis: 228R.
S.I.N./Corbis: 204R, 221B.
Stephen Stickler/Corbis: 209T.
Ted Streshinsky/Corbis: 72R.
Trapper Frank/Corbis Sygma: 189B.
TWPhoto/Corbis: 231B.

Courtesy of Daily Mirror
88 (inset).

Courtesy of Dollywood
167B.

Courtesy of EMI Records
199T.

Courtesy of Epic Records
149, 184L.

Courtesy of Grundig
30R, 53TR, 61B.

Courtesy of Mirrorpix
70T.

Courtesy of Philips
145B.

Courtesy of Record Company
17B, 18RB, 24R, 33B, 40L, 42L, 45B, 48R, 50L, 51TR, 58LT, 58LB, 60, 62, 64L, 66L, 69R, 70B, 72L, 73B, 76, 78L, 82L, 84L, 88LT, 88LB, 89RT, 90L, 94LT, 94LB, 100LT, 100 (inset), 102LB, 102R, 106LT, 106LB, 115B, 116L, 117RT, 118L, 119B, 120, 121B, 123 (inset), 123B, 124LT, 124R, 125B, 128L, 129RT, 130L, 132L, 133TR, 138L, 139B, 142L, 143RB, 144, 146, 147B, 148B, 151B, 153B, 154, 155B, 157RT, 163B, 170L, 175B, 179B, 180L, 187B, 188L, 188R, 189 (inset), 192L, 194L, 198L, 198R, 200, 202L, 204L, 207B, 209B, 211B, 214L, 215B, 216L, 217 (inset), 220, 221 (inset), 223B, 227B, 228L, 229B, 230L, 233B, 234, 235B, 236, 237B, 238LT, 238LB, 240, 242, 243B, 244L, 245B, 249B.

Courtesy of Sony Records
131B, 170R.

Getty Images
13T, 15B, 25T, 33T, 34R, 41B, 42RT, 46R, 50R, 55T, 65B, 66R, 67RB, 80R, 84R, 88R, 98LT, 115T, 118R, 122R, 179T, 182R, 191B, 206R, 222L, 224L, 227T, 233T, 241B, 244R, 246, 247T, 248R.
AFP/Getty Images: 201B, 216R.
Bob Thomas/Getty Images: 2RT, 36-37.
Exclusive by Getty Images: 247B.
FilmMagic: 7R, 194R, 241T.
Getty Images for MTV: 221T.
Michael Ochs Archives/Getty Images: 7LT, 14T, 15T, 18T, 19B, 39B, 42B, 44R, 49T, 51B, 57R, 61T, 63T, 64R, 77T, 78R, 90R, 98RT, 98B, 101B, 105B, 111B, 113T, 128R, 140R, 152R
Popperfoto/Getty Images: 2LB, 52R, 56R, 58R, 134-135.
Sony Music Archive/Getty Images: 211T.

Courtesy of Philips
145B.

Time & Life Pictures/Getty Images: 2LT, 6LB, 10-11, 22T, 26R, 68, 74R, 83B, 94R, 137T, 217B.
WireImage: 100R, 124LB, 173B, 214R, 226.

Library of Congress Prints and Photographs
18LB.

Perfectly Formed Publishing Limited
92, 93T, 95B, 104R, 114, 117RB, 122L, 129RB, 133BR, 136, 137B, 140L, 141B, 147T, 150L, 152L, 156L, 158, 159B, 161T, 161B, 162LT, 162LB, 164L, 165B, 166, 168, 169B, 172L, 174L, 178, 181B, 186, 190L, 196L, 199B, 206L, 212L.

Rex Features
156R, 203B, 210, 230R, 238R.
Albert Ferreira/Rex Features: 237T.
Bill Zygmant/Rex Features: 183RB.
Brian Rasic/Rex Features: 193T
Eugene Adebari/Rex Features: 145T.
Everett Collection/Rex Features: 71T.
Fotex/Rex Features: 205B.
Jason Mitchell/Rex Features: 235T.
Newspix/Rex Features: 208, 243T.
Peter Brooker/Rex Features: 169T.
Richard Young/Rex Features: 248L.